"In this important book Carolyn Jackson-Brown addresses the immense role played by television in the representation of disability. She presents a fascinating account of how public perceptions of disabled sportspeople can be shifted from a discourse of strangeness and embarrassment to admiration and inclusion. Many books about television tell us about failures of representation; this one presents a story of bold risk-taking."

Stephen Coleman, Professor of Political
Communication, University of Leeds, UK

"It is now clear that Channel 4's broadcasting and promotion of the 2012 Paralympics was a turning point for disability and parasport broadcasting, which changed the conversation about disability in the UK and had lasting reverberations for broadcasters across the world. This unique book provides the definitive inside story of Channel 4's Paralympic broadcasting strategy towards 2012 and beyond. Filled with rich insights and engagingly written throughout, this book is the most in-depth study of Paralympic broadcasting strategy to date."

Dan Jackson, Associate Professor of Media
and Communication, Faculty of Media and
Communication, Bournemouth University, UK

Disability, the Media and the Paralympic Games

This book focuses on the ground-breaking coverage of the London 2012 Paralympic Games by the UK's publicly owned but commercially funded Channel 4 network, coverage which seemed to deliver a transformational shift in attitudes towards people with disabilities.

It sheds important new light on our understanding of media production and its complex interactions with sport and wider society. Drawing on political economy and cultural studies, the book explores why and how a marginalised group was brought into the mainstream by the media, and the key influencing factors and decision-making processes. Featuring interviews with key people involved in the television and digital production structures, as well as organisational archives, it helps us to understand the interplay between creativity and commerce, between editorial and marketing workflows, and about the making of meaning. The book also looks at coverage of the Rio Paralympics, and ahead to the Tokyo Games, and at changing global perceptions of disability through sport.

This is fascinating reading for any advanced students, researchers, or sport management or media professionals looking to better understand the media production process or the significance of sport and disability in wider society.

Carolyn Jackson-Brown is Senior Lecturer in Journalism & Sports Journalism at Leeds Trinity University, UK. Her research focuses on media production and representations of difference.

Routledge Research in Sport, Culture and Society

For more informati on about this series, please visit: www.routledge.com/sport/series/RRSCS

Disability, the Media and the Paralympic Games

Carolyn Jackson-Brown

Routledge
Taylor & Francis Group

LONDON AND NEW YORK

First published 2020
by Routledge
2 Park Square, Milton Park, Abingdon, Oxon OX14 4RN

and by Routledge
52 Vanderbilt Avenue, New York, NY 10017

Routledge is an imprint of the Taylor & Francis Group, an informa business

British Library Cataloguing-in-Publication Data
A catalogue record for this book is available from the British Library

Library of Congress Cataloging-in-Publication Data
A catalog record has been requested for this book

ISBN: 978-0-367-43445-8 (hbk)
ISBN: 978-1-003-00321-2 (ebk)

Typeset in Sabon
by Wearset Ltd, Boldon, Tyne and Wear

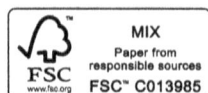

MIX
Paper from
responsible sources
FSC
www.fsc.org   FSC™ C013985

Printed in the United Kingdom
by Henry Ling Limited

Dedication

This book is dedicated to my late grandfather, Christopher Pascoe Hill, who wrote a book about an important topic when I was a child. I wondered what it would be like to do that. I also dedicate this work to my late mother, Jacomin, who took a thalidomide tablet before I was born, and gave me something to write about.

Contents

Acknowledgements

Thank you to all the producers, executives, and technicians who spared me their time and contributed such valuable frank accounts of their roles in the London 2012 Paralympics media coverage. I appreciate very much your openness and your willingness to take part in this research.

Special thanks to Alison Walsh, for fact-checking some of the sections, to James Walker for spotting other inaccuracies, and to Natalia Dannenberg-Spreier for explaining to me the complexities of the Paralympic global broadcasting system. I must also thank Sara Cohen and the library team at Leeds Trinity University for locating and supplying an eCopy of the very latest Paralympic scholarship in less than three hours, when I needed it rather urgently towards the end of the write-up. If this wasn't a Paralympic world record time, it surely was a personal best.

This book would not have materialised had it not been for the patience and insight of my two doctoral supervisors, Professor Bethany Klein and Dr. Nancy Thumim. I would like to thank them wholeheartedly for their support and their ability to keep me on track. The research culture in the University of Leeds Media and Communication department helped shape my thinking too, and I am so grateful to all the colleagues and staff there for their support.

Some material in Chapter 6 was previously published in Jackson-Brown, C. (2020). 'Borrowing Brands to Create a Brand: The Commercial Mediation of Paralympic Athletes'. *Communication & Sport*. https://doi.org/10.1177/2167479519896542

Abbreviations

AMC	Arthrogryposis Multiple Congenita
BBC	British Broadcasting Corporation
BPA	British Paralympic Association
C4	Channel Four
C4TVC	Channel Four Television Corporation
CDS	Critical Disability Studies
IMG	IMG Sports Media
IPC	International Paralympic Committee
LOCOG	London Organising Committee of the Olympic and Paralympic Games

Chapter 1

Introduction

In the late summer of 2012, a dramatic shift in media representations propelled a minority group of relatively unknown athletes unexpectedly into the mainstream. The International Paralympic Committee (IPC) considered it a turning point for their movement saying:

> London was the real game-changer for the Paralympics. For the first time ever both TV and sponsors covered the Games in a totally different way. Instead of focusing on disability, it was much more about the sport, and athletes were portrayed in a more gritty, hard-hitting way, compared to previous Games where it was all about the sob story. Videos about Paralympians went viral and the Paralympics was the top sporting event on Twitter in the UK – even ahead of the Olympics.
>
> (IPC Digital Marketing Manager, *Interview*, 2015)

It has since been established that the host nation media coverage of the London 2012 Paralympic Games affected not only the viewing habits of television and digital platform sports viewers and the profiles of previously marginalised parasport athletes, but also, as other research has shown, perceptions about disability were changed (see Jackson et al., 2015) for very many of the general public as well.

This book explores what happened, why the producers of the media coverage decided to change the game, and what decisions they took to get them there.

Paralympic scholars Schantz and Gilbert (2012) have urged that it is now time to investigate producer perspectives regarding the way the Paralympics is delivered through the media. Because televised sport is a mediated process there needs to be a focus, again, they say, on the encoding stage of the representation process, to counter-balance the more prolific literature focusing on texts and audiences. With this in mind, they conclude their important collection of media and Paralympic sport scholarship, *Heroes or Zeros*, by saying:

> There is a lack of understanding of thoughts and ideas of the Olympic and Paralympic television [...] producers' perspectives, regarding the

many ways in which the Paralympics are delivered to the public. It would be of great interest to interview these powerful people and try to understand their ideas regarding the delivery of Paralympic sports to the public.

(Schantz and Gilbert, 2012, p. 237)

My research is based on interviews with some of those 'powerful people', from the Head of Television to the Video Editor in a cutting room, providing an in-depth media production case-study of London's pivotal televisual moment. With reference to more recent events, and the continuing conversation around media, disability, and Paralympic sport, this empirical study establishes producer intentions, and contributes to understandings about how meanings are made.

Throughout the book I expose external and internal influences on the production of meaning, from inside the workforce, acknowledging also that these same influences might affect media representations and consequent cultural understandings relating to other groups of minorities as well. What makes the framing of meanings about disability a pertinent focus within the Paralympics setting is that mediated sport, and the Olympic Games in particular, is a cultural product that has an implicit reliance on bodily perfection. The portrayal of physically impaired parasports athletes, therefore, offers a new perspective on that key tenet, making the dilemmas and decisions that media producers face anyway in other settings, more visible.

The change in media portrayals of disability, particularly the reframing of the athletes for the UK's coverage of the London 2012 Paralympic Games, has been both welcomed and contested by scholars in the fields of disability, media, and sport and this book seeks to contribute further to those debates. The study focuses on those who created the media coverage, investigating why the marginalised group was brought into the mainstream, finding out who decided to 'normalise' disability, and establishing what influenced those decision-makers to make that onscreen content. Because media representations of disability have predominantly been negative, across every genre of programming since cameras were first invented (see Chapter 2), presenting international parasports as mainstream entertainment raises questions that clearly need to be explored.

It was the Toronto Paralympic Games that was first fully televised and shown daily to the Southern Ontario audience in 1976. Media reach has grown dramatically since then, yet it was not until 2012 that televisual meanings about disability were recognisably redefined. The creative producers collectively decided to 'remove disability from their thinking' (see Chapter 3) and this changed the camera angles, the tone of voice, and the flavour of their social media output. Since it is changes in meaning, not just changes in representation, that bring the invisible or the derided in from the margins, my study examines all of these aspects in order to make sense of the media trigger for social change in this case.

Audience research has shown that it was the UK's domestic media coverage of the 2012 Games, with its ground-breaking reframing and normalisation of para-athletes, that affected not only the mainstream sports audience, but also changed attitudes towards disability for 1 in 3 of the population – roughly 20 million of the UK's citizens (IPC, 2019). Globally, London 2012 was the first truly social and online Games, with 82.1 million views of the International Paralympic Committee's Facebook pages and over 1.3 million tweets mentioning 'Paralympic' during the course of the Games (ibid.). Beyond the media footage supplied by the Olympic Broadcast Service (OBS), available to all participating countries, the UK rights holders (Channel 4) did much more through their associated media production houses, reaching over 69 per cent of the British population. They made their domestic coverage look and feel like the Olympics, elevated the competition to elite sports mega-event within their schedules, and applied the biggest marketing budget in their history to attract digital consumers to the Games.

The Paralympic Movement has a social change mission, and it was claimed by the organisers that there had been a 'seismic shift' in perceptions during London 2012, although this was felt to be temporary by some media scholars and disputed by critical disability theorists. However, the Office of National Statistics released figures in December 2018 revealing nearly one million more people with disabilities were now in employment in Great Britain compared to 2013, the year after the Games (Spence, 2018). Further research could perhaps investigate this potentially indirect element to the Paralympic social-shaping influence; whether the saturation in media coverage affects perceptions for future host nation employers as well as those wondering whether to risk applying for a job in the 'normal' world.

The following Sochi 2014 Winter Paralympics were broadcast to nearly 2.1 billion people in more than 55 countries and, crucially, NBC showcased the Paralympics for the first time that year in the USA (IPC, 2014). Compared to 1980 when the old USSR 'declined the opportunity to stage the Paralympics because they said the country had nobody with an impairment' (ibid.), the 2014 Winter Games impacted both government and society providing an infrastructure within Sochi that was designed to be barrier-free. Now, 200 other Russian cities are also using that blueprint to make their cities and transport systems accessible to all (ibid.), and the organising committee for the Olympics in the USA, recognising the tourism and legacy potential for their city, is already prioritising the Paralympics for the Los Angeles 2028 Games, according to the IPC's Head of Brand and Engagement (*Interview*, 2020).

Whilst the Tokyo 2020 Paralympic documentary '*Harder than You Think*' (working title) was in production, the Executive Producer, who was also the Director of Brand, Marketing, and Culture for the London

Olympics and Paralympics, explained the opportunities for disseminating his message across YouTube, Amazon, and Netflix, saying:

> It's much harder in future to see the Paralympics as a small thing. It's a big thing. And I think in that sense, if you couple that with this next decade, Tokyo, China, Paris, Italy, America, it's like this is the decade where, if all of our attitudes changed, that would be an amazing place to be.
>
> (Executive Producer, *Interview*, 2019)

The success of hosting a sports mega-event in any city, however, whether in the Global North or South, is symbiotically linked to the quality and quantity of the media coverage that goes with it (Roche, 2000; Horne, 2012), which makes that coverage an important area for continued and detailed scrutiny. Especially, perhaps, a continued focus on the executives and producers who construct the meanings within that media, from cultural, political economic, and sociological perspectives.

There has been much discussion by other scholars about the results of what happened in 2012 (e.g. Jackson et al., 2015), including whether the Paralympics media coverage has served the wider disabled community or commodified a marginality (Beacom et al., 2016). As commercial pressures drive the need for media producers to reach mainstream audiences with new content, previously marginalised groups are inevitably being identified as a target for these new initiatives. However, it is becoming increasingly apparent, particularly after the success of the 2019 FIFA Women's World Cup media coverage, that there is now some appetite amongst digital sports media consumers, too, for previously marginalised athletes to be brought into the mainstream.

In order to explore the meaning-making process, the specific contexts of the cultural conditions that year need first to be understood. The unprecedented popularity of the London 2012 Paralympic Games amongst the home audience may have been, in part, due to the tide of national euphoria widely reported in the press following on from the Queen's Diamond Jubilee that same summer and the London Olympics, for which many potential spectators were unable to obtain tickets. Prior to the event, Channel 4 also ran poster and street furniture marketing campaigns and raised the profile of disability sports, placing 'disability', and certain individuals, firmly under the media spotlight. The media coverage was designed and prepared in anticipation of, but long before, the scale of this Home Games enthusiasm and sense of collective belonging could have been accurately predicted. Therefore there must have been other contributing factors illuminating why this moment happened, with such far-reaching consequences, and my research in this book explores these factors.

I should also perhaps say that there was a noticeable cultural shift in the acceptance of disability, particularly in public places, during the UK's Home

Games that had not been there before. As a publicly performing café pianist myself, with a visibly deformed hand on view, I personally found that, from the onset of that 2012 televised coverage, people started to treat me differently. I was approached and asked about my disability, and jokes were made that signified a cultural taboo had been broken. It was from personal experience too, then, that I understood meanings about disability to have been changed, as the UK's Channel 4 media coverage of an international sporting event produced something beyond just showing us the Paralympics.

Research objectives

The objectives of the research were to discover what the influencing factors on media producers had been, in order to illuminate how and why new meanings about disability had emerged. I wanted to establish what changes, if any, had happened inside the media organisation, asking who had decided to do it, why in this transformative way, and what other reasons there may be behind what Channel 4 had done. The opportunity arose, given the nature of these questions, to explicitly engage with theoretical discussions around the representation of 'others', and also to contribute insight into the reasons for the manipulation and/or dismantling of media tropes and stereotypes that are normally used to reinforce the stigma and meaning of 'difference'.

The organisational circumstances in which the creative portrayals were formed also contribute a significant part of this study on representation. This is because Channel 4 sits uniquely within the industry as a publisher-broadcaster with a public service remit that is also supported by a commercially funded, but publicly owned, business model. In order to explore how the particular depictions of disability came about in 2012, ones that were markedly different from the representations presented in previous BBC highlights packages for Sydney 2000, Athens 2004, and Beijing 2008, I considered organisational and institutional structures, and their bearing, or not, on individual creative agency. There was clearly more coverage that year because it was a Home Games, but the style and tone, and positioning of the athletes, was also quite different.

Creative independence has been a hallmark of Channel 4's output throughout the history of the channel (see Darlow, 2004; Hobson, 2008). However, commercial pressures, too, inevitably impinge on creativity, and these would be particularly visible in this instance, given that Channel 4's unique funding model relies on advertisement revenue in order to fund its public service programme content. For the first time a positive advertising campaign for a marginalised group ran on an unprecedented 78 television channels simultaneously. The media coverage, and marketing of it, was an intrinsically important televisual moment that was intended to change perceptions in society (C4TVC, 2009; C4TVC, 2013a). Using the London

2012 Paralympics as a case-study, then, a focus on the media producers provides rich empirical material to contribute to existing theoretical debates about the production of culture within the political economic environment surrounding it.

Additionally, understandings about what currently happens inside the complex and fragmented media production process are in need of constant revision, in order to keep abreast of important changes to the media landscape (see Blumler and Gurevitch, 1995; Hesmondhalgh, 2013). Channel 4, as a hybrid model of publisher-broadcaster, provides an opportunity for detailed research into this area of complexity and critical political economists of communication continue to assert the need to integrate this type of detailed production research into their own analyses. Murdock and Golding (2016) have stressed the need for studies showing 'how shifting webs of pressure and opportunity impinge on the everyday business of crafting cultural goods in particular settings' (p. 763). My study explores those pressures and opportunities in relation to Channel 4's new and unprecedented depictions of disability sport in 2012.

The parliamentary remit, unique business model, and funding mechanism were some of the organisational and structural factors that impinged on creativity. Other influences and influencers too, from the marketing team to outside stakeholders, affected the decisions made by editors and producers of these specific meanings that caused the shift in audience perceptions. As such, creative agency and editorial judgement were exercised on many levels across the media organisation and its subsidiaries. Many production scholars (see, for example, Klein, 2009; Zoellner, 2009a; Hesmondhalgh, 2013) have stressed the need to escape the binary separation of political economy and cultural production studies, in order to better explore the broad range and extent of influencing factors. By looking at representations determined during production, some of the cross-disciplinary complexities can be untangled.

The intersection of representation and production can be best understood at the encoding stage of the process (Hall, 1973; 1980), using the seminal conceptualisation of a 'circuit of culture' (Du Gay et al., 1997) as a tool for the analysis of meanings. The circuit broadly emphasises five particular 'moments' in cultural production where meanings can be significantly created or changed. These points are articulated as 'regulation', 'consumption', 'identity', 'representation', and 'production'. Whilst all these moments overlap to some degree, it is primarily the last two with which this study is concerned in order to locate and investigate the pockets of editorial and creative power. Throughout this research I investigated the construction of meaning, through the practice of making onscreen representations, taking into account the full range of overlapping 'moments' in their production.

Hall (1997) has identified representation as one of the 'central practices which produce culture' (p. 1) so any changes to that practice ought to be examined. By studying representation at the point of production, it is possible to contribute to the cultural understanding of meaning-making whilst adding definition to recent work being debated by critical theorists of political economy, for example, around creative labourers as agents of change (see, for example, Hesmondhalgh, 2006). In addition, scholars have argued there is also always a need to update knowledge in the field of media production studies because of continual shifts (Paterson et al., 2016) and changing complexities with audience fragmentation, changes to commissioning, and other commercial pressures (see Prendergast, 2000; Klein, 2009; Webb, 2009; Zoellner, 2009a). Born (2004) in her production study of the BBC refers to access and workforce issues as relating directly to programme content (p. 16), and my study provides a useful comparison by looking similarly at the work environment within Channel 4. In this context, a better understanding of the working realities for cultural producers can be derived by investigating their creative and commercial pursuit of suitable disability representations for London 2012.

One of the key findings, arising from my production research which explores the influencing factors affecting the decision-makers, is that, irrespective of perception changes within the audience, a fundamental change has happened within the media organisation. Directly correlated with this is another legacy, of reframed and newly acceptable onscreen disability representations, potentially now influencing other programme genres too. Close-up portrayals of visible difference were normalised in the sporting context and directly displayed onscreen in an inclusive way. Whether this moment in television history has had any lasting effect on society only time will tell. It has certainly had an impact on media producers' creative choices, however, and the potential effects of these are being much anticipated for Los Angeles 2028, who will be hosting, for their first time, the Paralympics in the same city as the Olympics.

Conclusions drawn from my study suggest that some of the change, at least in terms of what types of representations are seen on television and across digital media output, will be permanent. This is partly because, as this book will show, the producers changed audience/digital consumer perceptions whilst also changing their own attitudes and practices. Following their insightful research of both London 2012 and Rio 2016, Pullen et al. (2019) suggest there is now a greater need to explore production philosophies, practices, and decisions, and call for other external factors on parasport coverage to be examined. The upcoming chapters reveal details of both internal and external factors affecting the producers on a variety of levels during the preparation and production of London 2012's UK media coverage. This study reveals how, whilst attempting to effect a change in the audience, the agents additionally affected some of the structures that constrained or enabled them. The consequences of these changes may well affect representations of other diversities in due course.

Most of the producers that I encountered also experienced a change in perceptions and attitude towards disability themselves. I will show how some of the structures were purposefully dismantled, others were dented through the sheer effort of their achievements, and others were changed through necessity at the time and are now permanently remodelled with new parameters. Channel 4, by seeking to remove stigma, were creative with the programme formats, and after following their parliamentary remit on accessible employment, subsequently also wrote their own *Diversity Charter* (C4TVC, 2013b) to retain the advantages for minorities within the workforce they had created, extending the proportion of disabled producers and talent employed for their coverage of Rio 2016 and beyond (C4TVC, 2017). I will demonstrate how each of these sets of actions affected meaning-making and ultimately contributed towards the framing of disability for future onscreen representations.

Theoretical framework

The theoretical starting point for this study is based around the encoding of media representations of 'otherness' (Hall, 1997), and the framing of meanings currently understood by scholars in the fields of disability (Oliver, 1990; Barnes, 1992a; Thomson, 1996; 1997; Shakespeare, 2013) and mega-event sport (Whannel, 1992; Dayan and Katz, 1994; Roche, 2000; Horne and Whannel, 2012). Meanings are encoded within televisual representations, and are particularly shaped by the programme genre in which they are embedded. They are also defined by the time of day in the schedule that they are delivered, whether during mainstream hours or the marginalised late or early diversity 'graveyard' slots.

Questions around meaning-making continue to be at the heart of studies of representation (e.g. Van Zoonen, 1994; Prendergast, 2000; Gill, 2007; Webb, 2009; Parry, 2010; Orgad, 2012; Frosh, 2015; Thumim, 2015; Aiello and Parry, 2019). It is also foundational for those who teach in this field (e.g. Kidd, 2015). Seeking to understand social change and cultural shifts, my analytical paradigm is based on Hall's (1997) theory of representation, in particular notions of 'the spectacle of the other' (pp. 223–277). His earlier identification of the 'encoding' process (Hall, 1973; 1980), with producers shaping meanings for intended audiences, suggests production as the obvious starting point for an exploration of how meanings are made, and by whom.

Representation, as a field of study, has been thought by some scholars (e.g. Prendergast, 2000; Webb, 2009; Kidd, 2015) to have limitations for advancing theory in interpretive contexts. This is partly due to the subjectivity of 'preferred meanings' and individual readings of those that are 'decoded' by the receiver (see Hall, 1997). Nevertheless, others, including Perkins (2002) and Frosh (2015), have asserted that, even with a post-structural perspective, representation is fundamentally political. The influencing factors present at the construction of meanings during the production stage are important indicators of creative freedom and constraints, and of mediated power (Thumim, 2015) which continues to be of interest within the media and communications literature.

There is direct value in focusing on representations specifically for this purpose, as Kidd (2015) has observed, they are 'ensnared in complex and infinite entanglements' (p. 2) relating to identity, production, and the other elements of the 'circuit of culture' (Du Gay et al., 1997). I will not be looking at the stability of those meanings when unpacked, or decoded, by the reader, consumer, or audience. There is already considerable textual and audience research being generated around the Paralympic Games as it travels around the globe. My investigation is into the process of meaning-making at its constructed source, with the executives, holders of the purse-strings, stakeholders, and vocational creatives. As Kidd (2015) has articulated:

> When people create representations of the world there are agendas at play, and particular sets of ideas, values, attitudes and identities assumed and normalised. There are thus issues of power, ownership, authenticity and meaning at stake.
>
> (p. 3)

Building on the work of early cultural theorists (e.g. Hoggart, 1957; Thompson, 1963), Hall understood cultural shifts as better prioritised by agency than what he called 'reductive economism' and 'organisational determinism' (Hall, 1980, p. 58). It is this cultural construction paradigm that is so applicable to my study. Du Gay (1997), alongside Hall (1997), built on this embryonic form of cultural studies and included the study of representation, in particular as a key focus for understanding better some of the socially constructed aspects of 'reality'.

Like many other studies my study of representation has attempted to strike a balance between what political economy and cultural studies offer. Micro and macro perspectives were held by my participants and through a study of both, particular themes emerged. Other theorists have considered this break from the economic and organisational schools of thought helpful and kept the ideas separate in different academic disciplines. Production studies have tended to rely heavily on Marxist paradigms of economic superstructures and power, without necessarily regarding individual human agency within these same studies.

At the other end of the spectrum, the cultural studies approach has been considered to be too interpretive and subjective. As a consequence production studies have tended to contribute to the body of knowledge using analysis based mainly on political economic and/or organisational perspectives. With their respective epistemologies and methodologies either one of these binary positions would not and could not answer my particular enquiry by themselves and other scholars also take account of a broader range of perspectives. For example, Curran and Gurevitch (2005) argue that the production process is more nuanced, and Hesmondhalgh (2013) has more recently argued that the division between political economy and cultural studies should be reconsidered and the gap closed between them.

As Zoellner (2009b) points out, whilst there have been studies situated on a scale between the two, fundamentally macro observations say little about the micro realities, at the point of production. It is these micro sites that often play such a significant role in influencing media texts (ibid., p. 220). The London 2012 Paralympic Games coverage is a case in point. Looking at the influencing factors, within the cutting rooms and corridors of the creative workforce, provides complimentary insights to add to the broader overview that regulatory and hierarchical structure research provides. Along with Zoellner, I agree that these detailed micro studies are of great value, and this study is designed around that approach. Banks (2009) also suggests that 'embedded industrial theorisations of production and culture must be harvested from practitioners and analysed by scholars at every point in the production process' (p. 96). This is because the production of meaning is so deeply embedded in the actual practice of representation, particularly of 'others'.

The intentions of producers, as affected by institutional and cultural structures, may well have prevailed over the representations of disability developed through the London 2012 media coverage. Certainly, at the UK awards ceremonies those producers and broadcasters took the credit for their work and their decisions. The story of the economic pressures, external stakeholder interests, and internal wrangling affecting those decisions is the backdrop to this study. Limits were set, and pressures exerted, whilst a level of autonomy was continually maintained. Struggles of this kind have been identified in the fields of both media studies and cultural studies and my research has been designed to contribute theory and empirical evidence to both bodies of work.

I will establish how onscreen representations were affected by working conditions and hierarchies, alongside, in the case of Channel 4, a passive kind of state intervention, through the terms of the parliamentary *Communications Act* (2003), updated by the *Digital Economy Act* (2010). The conditions of Channel 4's broadcast remit, and perceptions of it by its own producers, influenced the shaping of representations as they appeared on our screens. In addition, the cultural ideologies of mainstream TV and international sport also impinged on and informed the way the production process was carried out. It was on ideological levels, as well as operational ones, that the agency of the executive, editorial, and creative teams was performed.

To satisfy the objective of understanding how and why disabled elite athletes were thrown into the limelight, this research seeks to understand how the act of representation, and decisions made around those representations, contributed to the onscreen content. Theoretical considerations include whether the representations reflect and therefore mimic existing social realities, or whether they are constructed to create new realities. This book explores the case of the London 2012 Paralympic Games media coverage to establish further these dynamics of reflection and construction, within the microcosm of the UK's niche public service provider, with their media production process as its focus.

Whilst the study of representation through textual analysis answers other questions about, for example, meaning-making by the audience, there is a strong case for interrogating the creators of onscreen representations to learn more about media production and industrial contexts. So, rather than looking directly at content, I investigate the decision-making that shapes content within the production process, to reveal the political, social, cultural, and ethical layers of influence that occur there. Mayer et al. (2009, p. 1) note that 'we frequently come to know about media producers and their work ironically through the representations they make', and this study joins the many others that have sought to connect production practices with onscreen representations (e.g. D'Acci, 1994; Born, 2004; Saha, 2012; Lieb, 2016). Finding out who decides what, and under what conditions, provides insights, not just about the meanings that are made onscreen but how these depictions are produced.

Who decides?

In this book I ask 'who decided to bring disability into the mainstream?', as well as 'how did they decide, and why?'. In the shaping of ideas I show that 'who' was sometimes 'what', using conceptualisations from the structure and agency debate. I also give a specific account of who 'they' were. Other writers have said 'Channel 4' did this or that, as though speaking with one voice (see, for example, Alexander, 2015, p. 108). Whilst collective attribution is appropriate in some settings, here where there were conflicting voices, I track down and define who held what kind of power, and which finally held sway. Media power can be sometimes lumped into one imagined place in the public discourse on social change, and also in the past has been referred to rather generally or seen as purely hierarchical. I look closely at this concept of media power and make sense of its manifest operation within Channel 4 at the time of the 2012 Paralympics coverage.

By asking the 'how' element of my question I have been able to follow the enactment of the creative process by individual worker roles, exploring their own freedoms. I investigated beyond just the decision-making into the conscious developing of ideas, themes, and feelings about disability that eventually made it onto the screen. The research shows how programme content often morphs from intended idea into something else altogether via serendipitous moments and, as many of my contributors reflected, something they couldn't quite put their finger on. My empirical evidence pieces together a series of moments that one contributor rather erroneously called 'the perfect storm', revealing further influences and contexts that I have analysed in the light of existing theories and debates.

Why the producers decided things will, at one level, be specific only to this case-study, particularly where there are personal reasons relating to the individuals who contributed. However it is individuals who make up groups and, as a group within their own production sub-culture, the social dimension that affected their enactments as a whole is also very much part of Channel 4's story, and may be something to take account of elsewhere. These machinations under the bonnet of the media production process also inform theoretical implications of other research undertaken by communication theorists as well as by academics working within a broader sociological perspective. By enquiring of disability, what was 'up close and personal' for some, and just a 'deliverable commodity' for others is exposed. In this respect the subject matter is useful as a sample of what agendas and dimensions exist within the production process when offering representations from a mainstream position for the depiction of 'others' in any diversity.

The unique moment of a host nation sporting mega-event affords the opportunity to explore the tension between marginalisation and celebration, invisibility and focus, and inclusion and exclusion as represented in the media coverage. By looking closely at the choices that were made within the production process, with those who constructed these representations for the London 2012 Paralympic Games, my study is able to reveal in detail who and what shapes meanings that are made.

Structure of the book

The upcoming chapters show how much 'othering' is reinforced through the framing of 'extraordinariness', and also conversely, dismantled by closing the gap between 'them' and 'us' for the purposes of selling sport. Drawing on interviews with key players in the production process, I establish what was constructed on purpose, by the UK's media executives and producers, and what was forced by circumstance or influenced by industrial contexts, production infrastructures, and money. 'Disability sport is cool' became part of the publisher-broadcaster's culture as well as being the central framing for onscreen representations across their suite of channels. The decision-making process that created this cultural shift is traced in my study through recollections of the two-year run-up to September 2012 into post-Paralympic decisions, relating to Rio 2016.

Whilst establishing how this 'cool' framing came about, recurring themes of structure, agency, creativity, and commerce emerged. These themes are discussed throughout the upcoming chapters roughly in that order. Naturally the areas do all overlap and command an iterative influence over each other, and they do so too here in my chapters. However, I have separated the themes out broadly into separate sections to enable manageable evaluation and to distinguish their impinging influences over meaning-making. This study contributes to the structure and agency debate and the creativity vs. commerce discussion by exploring the constraints and enablement (see Giddens, 1980) that occurred specifically in relation to the representations that were formed during the 'disability sport' production process.

In Chapter 2, I examine the three research areas of representation, disability, and sport and highlight dilemmas that might arise around the reframing of parasports athletes. In particular I explore how meanings about the 'other' are framed differently in these three contexts and what this might mean for the production of representations. I discuss the Paralympics and disability literature, including the 'supercrip' trope, conflicting ideas about 'inspiration' and 'spectacle', and how the media elevation to sports mega-event status could potentially change pre-existing meanings. This is set in the brief contextualisation of commercial interests within sport that also affect portrayals that make it onto the screen.

With funding for Public Service Media being questioned across the globe, I devote the first empirical chapter, Chapter 3, to the regulation, policies, and industrial context supporting the Channel 4 Television Corporation (C4TVC). Some of this material was presented as evidence to the UK's Communications Select Committee enquiry to help prevent Channel 4 being privatised in 2016 (Parliament, House of Lords, 2016). In particular I look at the organisational and funding structures and the concrete consequences of those structures on the processes of production, including the built-in protection against stakeholder vetoes. The chapter explores the way the parliamentary remit dictated inclusion of a new group into the workforce and also ensured diverse voices being presented onscreen. These edicts clearly affected decisions relating to content, and enabled riskier representations. The unique funding mechanism (which is also protected by the UK's parliamentary regulation) currently forces a certain type of organisational structure with no shareholders, but with associated independent stakeholders. Drawing on my interviews I discuss what happened within that ecology that shaped the onscreen representations of disability for London 2012 and Rio 2016.

Creative human agency, even within the restraints of the existing structures, plays a powerful role in the production of meanings for onscreen content. Chapter 4 explores disability representations and the intentional co-constructions of disability identities by the creative workforce. Attempts were clearly made to avoid ableist narratives. In order to normalise disability, stereotypes and tropes were disrupted, reinforced, and modified to forge the new identities that disabled athletes were given. Critical disability scholars have their own discourse about these framings, and this chapter contributes by exploring how the portrayals were chosen and framed from the producer perspectives, in the pursuit of 'parity', and what their intentions were, focusing mainly on group dynamics and individual agency. Building on the previous chapter's discussion about the regulation of access to employment, a possible correlation is explored between the inclusion of disabled producers and presenters in the workforce and the editorial power exerted to shape the particular meanings of the London 2012 coverage.

With a separate look at creative meaning-making, Chapter 5 explores how the programme formats were used and adapted to reframe disability within the sporting context. I consider the types of representations produced by Channel 4, using these formats, providing insight into who has the editorial power and how much creative freedom they have to use it. As the Games began, an unintended format also emerged that has endured beyond both the London and Rio Paralympics.

Along with the other formats and genres used to shape meanings in the build-up and live coverage, I explain how *The Last Leg* team, who have now taken their programme into the mainstream contexts of politics and satire, consistently blur the 'us' and 'them' distinction, swapping normative places and joking about it. This has been a very successful programme for reframing disability onscreen, closing the gap of 'difference' by introducing a blended team of 'normal' and 'other' characters. In this chapter I again explore, therefore, how access and inclusion into the media production process took a new and creative turn, and in particular during the impromptu formation of what became a late-night 'banter' slot. Their subversive hip-hop theme tune, taken from the *Meet the Superhumans* advertising campaign, has since become the title of the Tokyo 2020 global documentary, extending a cultural influence far beyond that expected for the original 'modified highlights' show.

In the context of 'live' television programming, audience engagement and consumption is a commercial concern. The focus on this commercialism is steered and driven by the corporation's Marketing Department and Chapter 6 is devoted mainly to their efforts. I show to what extent commercial interest and the need for audience growth affected the representations and their promulgation of 'cool'. Some very specific meanings were overlaid over the entire coverage and these were developed and extended again to attract audiences to the Rio Games. This chapter looks particularly at the marketing but also at the branding of the athletes, the borrowing of meanings from other brands to reassure the public, and the rebranding of Channel 4 as 'the Paralympics channel'. My participants made it clear that these elements were designed, at least temporarily, to embed disability into the mainstream. They were also perhaps expected to enhance the consumption of present and future channel inventory as well as change audience perceptions of disability.

Chapter 7 draws together the themes in this book, then explores the application of my findings beyond the representation of disability. Although the focus of this case-study is on portrayals of parasports athletes, the investigation highlights production issues relevant to representations of minority groups more generally. Until now there has not been a detailed television production study of the Paralympic Games, but a focus here, not on the journalism, but on the decision-making process behind the coverage, and its digitally delivered output, is important because the production spaces are where so much power is displayed.

Media representations, or at least their meanings, were noticeably different in 2012, so it has been essential to investigate what the transformational moments were that influenced the encoding stages. This final chapter reviews the internal machinations of the production process that shaped the seminal media coverage, from initial decision to final delivery. I summarise the circumstantial and empirical 'answers' to the questions raised in this book, noting that there was diversity on the inside of the media production amongst the decision-makers, as well as onscreen and that these factors eventually influenced the ableist producers as well.

What kind of media production research?

For the investigation of media production, Mayer (2009) argues that a case-study where something unexpected occurs can be very fruitful in order to observe changes, or differences, that may or may not be recognised by those creating that change. It is a context, she says, which can reveal more about influences on production because something unusual has happened. Therefore, the media coverage of the London 2012 Paralympics is an ideal focus for the investigation of contemporary production and representation and, as a case-study, will complement the work of existing production scholars.

My research is informed by the methodological approach of other production studies that have explored the construction of reality (e.g. Burns, 1977; Newcomb and Alley, 1983; Schlesinger, 1987; Born, 2004; Gitlin, 2005; Caldwell, 2008; Mann, 2009, etc.). I felt the emphasis for my project needed to be, like theirs, mainly face-to-face interviews in order to provide evidence of lived realities. Schlesinger's (1987) *Putting Reality Together*, although focused on newsrooms and not sport, used a line of enquiry and associated methodology that mapped very well onto my own research objectives. His study included personnel interviews at every level across the spectrum of roles, in order to trace the process of meaning-making and illuminate *how* the 'reality' was put together at the BBC. In Schlesinger's case, this was within a single, large institution. I designed a similar research project which would enable me, likewise, to trace meaning-making within the smaller public service broadcaster, Channel 4, and its suppliers. I initially interviewed 23 executives and producers using a semi-structured approach within two years of the production and have since spoken to some of them again as the media landscape continues to change.

As well as interviews, in D'Acci's (1994) study of *Cagney and Lacey*, she gained access to the set, production meetings, files, publicity firms, executive, and audience letters and found out why meanings had been changed in a nuanced way about femininity. Informed by this approach, I knew that I needed to focus on associated material too to understand what had happened at the time when they were constructing meanings, and not just rely on recollections. I was able to track down more detail about why and how meanings about disability were changed for the London 2012 coverage from several associated documents. Meanings were changed from embarrassingly negative to 'cool' for reasons that I was able to investigate through analysis of corporate documents that were written at the inception of the project in 2009 and also from a mindset-changing presentation, called *MENTAL4 the Paralympics*, which was written and delivered by the Disability Executive. She delivered the presentation to the in-house Channel 4 staff first, then to their production partners and presentation teams as well, sending it out to all who missed it, before the coverage began.

My fieldwork was loosely ethnographic in the sense that it involved a form of immersion and time spent with informants. As it was a largely retrospective study there was no intrinsic value in planning to embed myself anywhere for any length of time – I couldn't watch meaning-making as it happened. However, although I was not an embedded observer (see Denzin and Lincoln, 2005) for the preparation of the London 2012 coverage, I was invited to social occasions that allowed me to build relationships with key informants. Influenced by other accounts (e.g. Born, 2004) of the value of participant observation (see also Mayer, 2009), I accepted an invitation, for example, to the Channel 4 Leaving Do for the Disability Executive and was able to meet other further contributors there.

Mann (2009) writes that 'too many production studies are looked at from the top down' (p. 103). In this case, I chose to search for the decision-makers amongst all the production roles in order to obtain a more rounded picture of what actually happened. Snowball recruitment was used with help from my initial participants based on their suggestions of who they thought had influenced the creative and executive decisions that affected onscreen media content. It was essential to discover the influencers from within the group and my earlier career in the industry, including televised sport, proved to be an advantage in gaining good access.

Most of the other production studies that refer to representations and meaning-making have been conducted within newsrooms (see Klinenberg, 2005; Anderson, 2011), or entertainment settings (see Hobson, 2003) rather than within sport. Production studies, of any type, investigate where the control over meaning is exercised (Paterson et al., 2016), and there have been various methods mooted for doing this. Newcomb and Lotz (2002) suggest five levels of possible analysis (p. 26) of which I have focused on the last two. These are 'national and international political economy and policy, specific industrial contexts, particular organisations, individual productions and individual agents' (ibid.).

Rather than taking a separate political economic stance, it was more relevant to my research enquiry to find out about how the specific industrial contexts impinged upon the producers for this individual production, and how they felt the organisational and policy contexts affected their creativity and freedom to work. In order to help find out where control lay I analysed my data broadly at the level of the production and the individual agents. Since I was looking for themes relating to the construction of meaning, my study was based on personal and lived experiences. It was important that I was able to combine the more macro-level institutional perspectives with the micro day-to-day experience of the producers in particular.

In terms of individual influence, Mills (2000) writes that 'from the standpoint of power it is easier to pick out those who count from those who rule' (p. 204). This makes it important to accept that anybody might become important during the analysis stage of the study and not necessarily just because of their decision-making powers. It was also important to find out what was serendipitous and what might be a pattern of practice, belief, or structure. My analysis led me to those whose agency had 'counted' in the eyes of other members of the production teams and how they had come by that power. For example, I discovered that the Disability Executive with a disability of her own, was mentioned by everybody from the Head of Television, to the Video Editor of the *Meet the Superhumans* trailer in Channel 4's subsidiary advertising agency, 4Creative. Nobody left her out of their account which suggests her influence was far-reaching, and universally experienced. It is much more common for diverse voices to have limited reach and very little influence within media organisations (Barnes and Mercer, 2003; Carpentier, 2011) but my analysis was able to highlight the fact and the significance of this organisational and cultural difference for the London 2012 media production very clearly.

As the story unfolded, I found that what are considered 'complex and messy' production and organisational processes (see Blumler and Gurevitch, 1995; Couldry, 2003; Hesmondhalgh, 2013; Lee, 2018) could be untangled. Qualitative data, of course, cannot be manipulated in concrete ways, as quantitative data can (Jensen, 2013, p. 284), but for informing relational, institutional, and theoretical perspectives and dynamics it provided valuable insights.

The main themes that emerged through my analysis relate to organisational and regulatory structures (Chapter 3), the reframing of meanings to provide parity with the Olympians (Chapter 4), the nuanced adaptation of existing programme genres and formats (Chapter 5), and the presence of a powerfully branded marketing strategy to elevate the profile of the Paralympians (Chapter 6). Running throughout these themes was the lived experience of there being 'disability' on the inside of the decision-making team which is important because representations are known to be reflected as well as constructed. The empirical work is explored thematically in the upcoming chapters but first I explore the media histories of spectacle, disability, and otherness as a backdrop to the sports portrayal dilemmas which the editorial production staff were to face.

Bibliography

Aiello, G. and Parry, K. 2019. *Visual communication: understanding images in media culture*. SAGE.

Alexander, J. 2015. 'Superhumanity' and the embodiment of enlightenment: the semiotics of disability in the official art and advertising of the 2012 British Paralympics. In: D. Jackson et al. eds. *Reframing disability?: media, (dis)empowerment, and voice in the 2012 Paralympics*. Oxford: Routledge, pp. 105–120.

Anderson, C. 2011. Between creative and quantified audiences: Web metrics and changing patterns of newswork in local US newsrooms. *Journalism*, 12(5), pp. 550–566.

Banks, M.J. 2009. Gender below-the-line: defining feminist production studies. In: V. Mayer et al. eds. *Production studies: cultural studies of media industries*. London: Routledge, pp. 87–98.

Barnes, C. 1992a. *Disabling imagery and the media: an exploration of the principles for media representations of disabled people: the first in a series of reports*. Halifax: Ryburn Publishing.

Barnes, C. and Mercer, G. 2003. *Disability policy and practice: applying the 'social model'*. Leeds: Disability Press.

Beacom, A., French, L., and Kendall, S. 2016. Reframing impairment? Continuity and change in media representations of disability through the Paralympic Games. *International Journal of Sport Communication*, 9(1), pp. 42–62, available from: https://doi.org/10.1123/ijsc.2015-0077 [Accessed 13 January 2020].

Blumler, J. and Gurevitch, M. 1995. *The crisis of public communication*. London; New York: Routledge.

Bogdanowicz, M., Burgelman, J.-C., Collins, R., Curran, J., Gandy Jr, O.H., Golding, P., Gourova, E., Hanada, T., Harvey, S. and Horwitz, R. 2003. *Toward a political economy of culture: capitalism and communication in the twenty-first century*. Rowman & Littlefield Publishers.

Born, G. 2004. *Uncertain vision: Birt, Dyke and the reinvention of the BBC*. London: Secker and Warburg.

Burns, T. 1977. *The BBC: public institution and private world*. London: Macmillan.

C4TVC. 2009. *Proposal for UK Broadcast Rights*. [Document] London: Channel 4 Television Corporation.

C4TVC. 2013a. *Annual Report 2012*. [Report]. London: Channel 4 Television Corporation.

C4TVC. 2013b. *Diversity Charter*. [Leaflet]. London: Channel 4 Television Corporation.

C4TVC. 2017. *Diversity Charter 360*. [Leaflet]. London: Channel 4 Television Corporation.

Caldwell, J.T. 2008. *Production culture: industrial reflexivity and critical practice in film and television*. Durham, NC: Duke University Press.

Carpentier, N. 2011. *Media and participation: a site of ideological-democratic struggle.* Intellect Online Library.

Communications Act. 2003. London: The Stationery Office.

Couldry, N. 2003. *Media ritual: a critical approach.* London: Routledge.

Curran, J. and Gurevitch, M. eds. 2005. *Mass media and society.* London: Hodder Arnold.

D'Acci, J. 1994. *Defining women: television and the case of Cagney and Lacey.* Chapel Hill, NC: University of North Carolina Press.

Darlow, M. 2004. *Independents struggle: the programme makers who took on the TV establishment.* London: Quartet.

Dayan, D. and Katz, E. 1994. *Media events: the live broadcasting of history.* Cambridge, MA; London: Harvard University Press.

Denzin, N.K. and Lincoln, Y.S. 2005. *Handbook of qualitative research.* Taylor & Francis Online.

Digital Economy Act. 2010. (section 22). London: The Stationery Office.

Du Gay, P. 1997. *Production of culture/cultures of production.* London: SAGE in association with The Open University.

Du Gay, P., Jones, S., and Hall, S. 1997. *Doing cultural studies: the story of the Sony Walkman.* London: SAGE in association with The Open University.

Ellis, K. and Goggin, G. 2015. *Disability and the media.* London: Palgrave.

Frosh, P. 2015. *Selfies the gestural image: the selfie, photography theory, and kinesthetic sociability.* Taylor & Francis Online.

Garland-Thomson, R. 2002. The politics of staring: visual rhetorics of disability in popular photography. In: *Disability studies: enabling the humanities*, pp. 56–75.

Giddens, A. 1980. *Central problems in social theory: action, structure and contradiction in social analysis.* London: Palgrave.

Gilbert, K. and Schantz, O. 2008. *The Paralympic Games: empowerment or side show?* Maidenhead: Meyer and Meyer.

Gill, R. 2007. *Gender and the media.* Chichester: Wiley.

Gitlin, T. 2005. *Inside prime time.* 3rd ed. Taylor & Francis.

Hall, S. 1973. *Encoding and decoding in the television discourse.* Birmingham Centre for Contemporary Cultural Studies, The University of Birmingham.

Hall, S. 1980. Cultural studies: two paradigms. *Media, Culture and Society*, 2(1), pp. 57–72.

Hall, S. 1997. *Representation: cultural representations and signifying practices.* London: SAGE in association with The Open University.

Hesmondhalgh, D. ed. 2006. *Media production.* Open University Press.

Hesmondhalgh, D. 2013. *The cultural industries.* 3rd ed. London: SAGE.

Hobson, D. 2003. *Soap opera.* Chichester: Wiley.

Hobson, D. 2008. *Channel 4: the early years and the Jeremy Isaacs legacy.* London: I.B. Tauris.

Hoggart, R. 1957. *The uses of literacy. Aspects of working-class life, with special reference to publications and entertainments.* London: Chatto and Windus.

Horne, J. 2012. The four 'Cs' of sports mega-events: capitalism, connections, citizenship and contradictions. In: G. Hayes and J. Karamichas eds. *Olympic games, mega-events and civil societies. Global culture and sport.* London: Palgrave Macmillan.

Horne, J. and Whannel, G. 2012. *Understanding the Olympics.* Abingdon, Oxon; New York: Routledge.

IPC. 2014. *Sochi 2014 Paralympic Winter Games.* [Online]. [Accessed 24 May 2018]. Available from: www.paralympic.org/sochi-2014

IPC. 2019. *Change starts with sport: brand platform.* Corporate Document.

Jackson, D. 2013. *2012 Paralympics changed people's perceptions of disability and disabled sport, BU study finds.* [Online]. [Accessed 31 October 2016]. Available from: www.bournemouth.ac.uk/

Jackson, D., Hodges, C.E.M., Molesworth, M., and Scullion, R. eds. 2015. *Reframing disability: media, (dis)empowerment, and voice in the 2012 Paralympics.* Oxford: Routledge.

Jensen, K.B. 2013. *A handbook of media and communication research: qualitative and quantitative methodologies.* New York: Taylor & Francis.

Kidd, J. 2015. *Representation.* London: Routledge.

Klein, B. 2009. *As heard on TV: popular music in advertising.* Burlington: Ashgate.

Klinenberg, E. 2005. Convergence: news production in a digital age. *The ANNALS of the American Academy of Political and Social Science,* 597(1), pp. 48–64.

Lee, D. 2018. *Independent television production in the UK from cottage industry to big business.* Palgrave Macmillan.

Lieb, K. 2016. Pop stars perform 'gay' for the male gaze: the production of fauxmosexuality in female popular music performances and its representational implications. In: *Production studies, the sequel!: cultural studies of global media industries.* London: Taylor & Francis.

Mann, D. 2009. It's not TV, it's brand management TV. In: V. Mayer et al. eds. *Production studies: cultural studies of media industries.* New York; London: Routledge, pp. 99–141.

Mayer, V. 2009. Bringing the social back in: studies of production cultures and social theory. In: V. Mayer et al. eds. *Production studies: cultural studies of media industries.* New York; London: Routledge.

Mayer, V., Banks, M.J., and Caldwell, J.T. 2009. *Production studies: cultural studies of media industries.* New York; London: Routledge.

Mills, C.W. 2000. *The sociological imagination.* Oxford: Oxford University Press.

Murdock, G. and Golding, P. 2016. Political economy and media production: a reply to Dwyer. *Media, Culture and Society,* 38(5), pp. 763–769.

Newcomb, H. and Alley, R.S. 1983. *The producer's medium: conversations with creators of American TV.* Oxford University Press.

Newcomb, H. and Lotz, A. 2002. The production of media fiction. In: *A handbook of media and communications research: qualitative and quantitative methodologies,* pp. 62–77.

Oliver, M. 1990. *The politics of disablement.* London: Macmillan Education.

Orgad, S. 2012. *Media representation and the global imagination.* Cambridge: Polity Press.

Parliament, House of Lords. 2016. *A privatised future for Channel 4? 1st report of session.* [online]. [Accessed 9 December 2018]. Available from: www.parliament.uk/hlcomms-future-of-Channel4

Parry, K. 2010. A visual framing analysis of British press photography during the 2006 Israel-Lebanon conflict. *Media, War and Conflict,* 3(1), pp. 67–85.

Paterson, C., Lee, D., Saha, A., and Zoellner, A. eds. 2016. *Advancing media production research: shifting sites, methods, and politics.* Springer.

Perkins, J. 2002. *The suffering self: pain and narrative representation in the early Christian era*. New York; London: Routledge.

Prendergast, C. 2000. *The triangle of representation*. New York: Columbia University Press.

Pullen, E., Jackson, D., Silk, M., and Scullion, R. 2019. Re-presenting the Paralympics: (contested) philosophies, production practices and the hypervisibility of disability. *Media, Culture & Society*, 41(4), pp. 465–481.

Roche, M. 2000. *Mega-events and modernity: Olympics and expos in the growth of global culture*. London: Routledge.

Saha, A. 2012. 'Beards, scarves, halal meat, terrorists, forced marriage': television industries and the production of 'race'. *Media, Culture and Society*, 34(4), pp. 424–438.

Schantz, O. and Gilbert, K. 2012. Researching the future. In: O.J. Schantz and K. Gilbert eds. *Heroes or zeros? The media's perceptions of Paralympic sport*. Champaign, IL: Common Ground, pp. 237–240.

Schlesinger, P. 1987. *Putting 'reality' together: BBC News*. London: Methuen.

Shakespeare, T. 2013. *Disability rights and wrongs revisited*. Taylor & Francis Online.

Spence, C. 2018. *Transforming lives – London 2012 progress and challenges*. [online]. [Accessed 12 January 2019]. Available from: www.paralympic.org/news/transforming-lives-london-2012-progress-and-challenges

Thompson, E.P. 1963. *Making of the English working class*. Fleet: Gollancz.

Thomson, R.G. 1996. *Freakery: cultural spectacles of the extraordinary body*. NYU Press.

Thomson, R.G. 1997. *Extraordinary bodies: figuring physical disability in American culture and literature*. New York: Columbia University Press.

Thumim, N. 2015. *Self-representation and digital culture*. Basingstoke: Palgrave Macmillan.

Van Zoonen, L. 1994. *Feminist media studies*. New York: SAGE.

Walsh, A. 2015. Out of the shadows into the light? The broadcasting legacy of the 2012 Paralympics for Channel 4. In: D. Jackson, C. Hodges, M. Molesworth, and R. Scullion eds. *Reframing disability? Media, (dis)empowerment, and voice in the 2012 Paralympics*. Oxford: Routledge, pp. 26–36.

Webb, J. 2009. *Understanding representation*. London: SAGE.

Whannel, G. 1992. *Fields in vision: television sport and cultural transformation*. London: Routledge.

YouGov. 2012. *Paralympic Games shifts attitudes towards disabilities*. [online]. [Accessed 12 July 2016]. Available from: www.channel4.com/news

Zoellner, A. 2009a. Professional ideology and program conventions: documentary development in independent British television production. *Mass Communication and Society*, 12(4), pp. 503–536.

Zoellner, A. 2009b. *Creativity and commerce in television production: developing documentaries in the UK and Germany*. Ph.D. thesis. University of Leeds.

Chapter 2

Spectacles of otherness

Media, sports, and disability dilemmas

In the Spring of 2009, the London Organising Committee of the Olympic Games (LOCOG) held a series of focus groups, to establish what interest there may be in the forthcoming UK Paralympics. Run by a clinical psychologist, these groups elicited a particular pattern of responses, after viewing a range of photographs, which flagged up that they might have a problem. The LOCOG Director of Brand, Marketing and Culture, Greg Nugent, explained to me how one particular incident had caused him to rethink their central concept, and later shaped the decision to accept Channel 4's challenger bid for the broadcasting rights over the expected one by the established licence-funded BBC. He remembers that occasion vividly:

> A gentleman from South London stood up, looked at the screen, couldn't see me, and said, 'Listen, mate, I'm going to tell you what we all think – no one wants to watch a fucking spastic play sport [sic.]'. And the room was still, and I think it was quite emotional for everybody because it was true.
>
> (LOCOG Director of Brand, Marketing and Culture, *Interview*, 2019)

It was at this point, he said, that the 'sport first' logic gained precedence over the existing 'disability first' attitude that had prevailed over so much of the previous Paralympic media coverage (which they immediately went back over to check). This conceptual shift, since LOCOG needed to sell seats for the Games and bring a marginalised group into the mainstream, affected the media brief, and their consequent choice of broadcaster, because they needed to 'do something different' in a way it hadn't been done before.

However, according to most of my contributors, there was much argument and a great deal of tension between all the stakeholders, the broadcaster and their associated production companies, once the London 2012 media machine got under way. As this chapter will show, this was largely because mixing disability, something most people do not want, with sport, something that mainstream viewers do want, carries with it inherently problematic conflicts. These conflicts relate not only to types of representation but also to what those representations mean.

Whether or not cultural producers are aware of it, the media portrayal's intersection of disability, sports, and representation scholarship reveals differing theorisations about, for example, 'others', 'inspiration', and 'spectacle'. Bringing them together, as televised parasports does, causes a clash of connotations over ideas of 'courage', 'extraordinariness', and especially the much contested 'superhuman'. For example, disability activists concerned for the welfare of the non-athletic members of their disabled communities, find that normalising elite athletes can work against them (see the 'supercrip' discourse below). But within mainstream sport, elevating high-achieving personalities is expected and perceived as desirable. Similarly, the hyperbole used within normative sports commentary can also be seen as perpetuating an unhelpful caricature for those whose group have suffered from distorted media representation in the past. This is because these notions, stereotypes, and media production tropes derive meanings conferred through differing social histories and contexts.

Whether a television spectacle inspires, or conspires against, those being represented onscreen, depends on how that media content is put together. This, of course, is true for digital and social media too. However, understanding the differing dynamics of representation, whether separating or unifying, as outlined below, is central to understanding 'what' happened, and 'how' and 'why' during the production stage of the 2012 coverage, and even sheds light on those focus groups beforehand. Meanings that differentiate 'us' from 'them' serve slightly different purposes, even when they are apparently framed in a similar fashion, as I will show. The three areas of research also provide differing perspectives on the pressures within the content creation process, relating to power, access, and commercial interests. These conflicts, appearing within the production context and also onscreen, throw into relief creative and commercial agendas, as well as making obvious where structures and agency appear to collaborate or collide.

Within the sub-sections below, I examine respectively the theoretical conceptions of marginality and mainstream 'normality' for each field. In particular I outline previously theorised onscreen representations of the 'stereotyped' other, the disabled 'repulsive' other, and the elite sporting 'inspirational' other, along with how meanings for each have been framed and understood so far. These positions set a reference point for making sense of the empirical material later on, based on previous scholars' key perspectives from the three fields. I also, within each section, summarise some of the known or speculated production dynamics that have been found previously to impinge upon, or enable, the editors' shaping of onscreen content. Within the three subject areas, these are, as I have suggested, concerned with power, access to the workforce, and commercially motivated influences respectively.

Representation and the production of meaning

In this section I show that the main focus for theorists of representation is one of power: power of one group to create meanings about another. This power is exerted behind the scenes and reflected onscreen.

Media representations are described by Hall (1997) as ways in which the media portray 'reality' from a particular set of values, ideology, or other distinct perspective. These representations can apply equally to portrayals of communities, groups, ideas, experiences, relationships, and also, therefore, sporting events (Dayan and Katz, 1994). In order to change perceptions in society, as Channel 4 intended to do, a particular set of realities need to become common sense, and Hall's explanation of how this can happen is helpful. He describes how media representations provide the 'shared meanings' (Hall, 1997, p. 3) that help 'us' understand our cultural practices and more specifically identify who we are in relation to 'others' or 'them'.

A safe distance from 'them'

The key elements of representation, according to Hall (1997), are the setting up of difference or 'otherness', by creating boundaries of 'us' and 'them', whilst reducing individual realities to known stereotypes in order to fix meanings that will communicate to an audience. Hall argues that 'otherness' is something that occurs when editorial power is in the hands of a 'normal' group who seek to maintain a *safe distance* between themselves and the 'others' (ibid.). This safe distance appeared to be reduced, during the London 2012 Paralympic coverage, by bringing the Games from the margins into the mainstream. It follows, from Hall's perspective, therefore, that the place to look for a substantial change in depictions of 'other', should be at the 'normal' producers who changed the parameters.

A central concept, offered as a framework for thinking about the making of television representations, is that representations generally come about as *reflections* of existing society or are deliberate *constructions* of a changing reality (Hall, 1980; 1997). These constructions and reflections are hammered out in creative spaces to make onscreen representations that provide the viewer with a sense of shared meanings. Producers, who make meanings, may or may not be conscious of their role as reflectors of existing realities when constructing paradigms or new framings for change and may feel they hold a neutral standpoint (Born, 2004). However Hall's (1973; 1980; 1997) cultural understanding of the process includes the notion of reflecting existing social realities, and therefore reflecting what is considered as 'normal'. This matters when looking at the media production workforce as a microcosm of wider society, as this study does and Born also did with her ethnographic study of the BBC (Born, 2004, p. 10).

The notions of reflection and construction provide a clear indicator that research should also be focused on the attitudes and beliefs held within the media organisation, as well as on other influencing factors, especially as any existing social realities are likely to transfer into onscreen representations. Media producers, within their microcosm, bring their own meanings to bear during the editorial process and I explore this aspect of Hall's theory (1980; 1997), particularly in Chapters 4 and 5, to argue the correlation between the make-up of the workforce and who they consider 'others' to be. The sense of an agreed norm has a direct bearing on how to represent 'them' and how to construct their identities as different from 'us'.

Embedding the values of outsiders, not for but *by* the minorities being represented, is explored in, for example, the fields of education, health, and organisational management (Hart, 1992; Tritter and McCallum, 2006; Cummings and Worley, 2014) using engagement models based on Arnstein's (1969) theoretical ladder of citizen participation. This tracing of power has been extended into media production (Cammaerts and Carpentier, 2007; Carpentier, 2011) to measure some forms of consultancy and presentation but not as yet to consider the make-up of the production workforce itself. Born (2004) connects the lack of promotion for minorities within production teams with under-representation onscreen, considering these two situations to be 'linked failures' (p. 10). I address this potential correlation, or linkage, in the latter part of Chapter 4, in relation to Channel 4 and their disability programming output. The linked relationship between 'normal' producers and their representations of whom they consider to be 'others' affects why certain representations are made, dependant on the agreed viewpoint of the ones with editorial powers.

A constructed spectacle of the caricatured 'other'

Making a spectacle of 'others' is achieved through stereotyping, by deliberately exaggerating familiar imagery to set apart the group with more power from the group with less power. These forms of representation shape culture as what we think of as normal is re-educated, and this happens, according to Giddens (1989), by reinforcing 'the values the members of a given group hold' (p. 31). Who is in that group is clearly an important indicator in the process of understanding how certain representations end up onscreen. What they choose to portray is more often taken up by textual analysts but is nevertheless connected to production (Campion, 2005; Ahmed, 2007a; Caldwell, 2008; Kellner, 2011; Saha, 2012), validating an exploration of stereotyping during that process. The continuing questions of who decides and what affects their decisions are addressed in this case-study, in direct relation to the operation of editorial power to create a spectacle of stereotyped others.

A correlation between who the producers are and what they portray is also highlighted starkly by the disability theorists, whom I introduce below, and additionally noted in the Paralympics literature. The key point is that a spectacle is made of 'others' because the others are different. This difference can be used as a form of entertainment for the mainstream group (Garland-Thomson, 2002), as well as providing a distancing mechanism to protect those not being depicted (Hall, 1997; Howe, 2008a). Identities of 'us' are reinforced by knowing whom we are not, in relation to these contrasted stereotyped 'others'. The idea of making a spectacle of 'them', including any respective purposes and connotations, is developed further in the disability section below and also, slightly differently, in the sports section that follows on.

In more detail, representation, generally, establishes and embeds a 'norm' from which other groups are differentiated and the distance from that norm determines their relative value. For example, black, female, gay, immigrant, disabled, and welfare 'scroungers' are expressions of 'other' groups in relation to the appearance and/or greater (perceived) function of the white, middle-class, employed, heterosexual male standpoint (see Said, 1979; Davis, 1995; Ross and Sreberny, 2000; Schell and Rodriguez, 2001; Butler, 2011). Particularly, the power used to reduce the excluded 'other' group naturalises the normalcy of the culture from which it is being produced and acts as an exclusion mechanism.

A feature of previous BBC Paralympic coverage had been the use of largely non-disabled producers to form representations of disabled athletes (BBC, 2011). Scholars of representation suggest that editorial power in the hands of those who consider themselves 'normal', when depicting 'others' of any group, results necessarily in excluding, reductive, or negative representations (Prendergast, 2000; Webb, 2009; Kidd, 2015). Understanding this mechanism of power over others, to ascribe lower value and reinforce distance, forces the questions, in my own research, directly towards *who* had control over *why* the London 2012 coverage was substantially more inclusive.

Use of power is intrinsic to defining 'otherness', with reductive stereotyping used as a form of exclusion or even violation. The media representation is understood as an imposed caricature, therefore, or at the very least an over-simplification (Hesmondhalgh, 2013) rather than a negotiated reality, conveying nuanced meanings within its portrayal. According to Hall (1997), strategies for stereotyping are designed to fix meanings for as long as possible (p. 259) but, he established, new meanings can be grafted onto old ones. This distinction between representation and meaning is an important one to be aware of when establishing what happened in the case of Channel 4's parasport athlete depictions. Hall (ibid.) goes on to point out that, even with reductive stereotypes, meanings are not fixed, or else there would never be any change (p. 259). Active choice-making, for example over imagery, reflects existing inequalities in power relations, as well as potentially creating new ones, since the chooser of the imagery is defining meanings for and about the 'other'.

In order to interrogate this power, production studies, such as the one featured in this book, are essential for understanding the process of representation. Inequality in editorial power has particularly been seen as a form of social oppression within disability studies (Barnes, 1992a; Oliver and Barnes, 2016). Portrayals are understood to have been designed to manipulate emotional response (Shakespeare, 1994; 2013; Garland-Thomson, 2002) and to make the able-bodied feel better (Longmore, 1987). Whilst stereotyping is inevitable and useful for communicating known ideas quickly, both in drama and factual output (Fiske, 1987; Fiske and Hartley, 2003), the way that meanings are redrafted needs further investigation. I explore the construction of new meanings in detail in Chapter 4.

Meanings are constructed to appear as 'reality' and carried out by the creative production teams, whether by diverse, minority group, or not. Each has their own viewpoint and reasons for asserting their perspective. Whether reflected or constructed, or both, the creative media process includes the assembling and projection of words, pictures, and other media as a form of multi-media language (see Saussure, 1974; Barthes, 1977; Baudrillard, 1994) to convey the object, person, idea, identity, or other concept to an audience. Therefore, the decision-makers creating meanings within each of these areas need to be included in any production research on the meaning-making process.

One of the chief ways televisual meanings are achieved is through the use of these multi-media forms of language (as developed by Williams, Du Gay, Hall, etc.). Signs are often analysed to decipher such 'othering' textually (drawing on the works of, for example, Barthes, 1973, and Saussure, 1974, to do that, but see also Parry, 2010). A necessary additional question this 'othering' raises must also be, 'who has access to the workforce, and with what associated editorial powers to shape the language that makes these significations?' It is a powerful role that can shape society to denote any group, or type of person, as 'other' at all and only some participants in the production process have enough power to produce these distinctions. In the upcoming chapters I examine the power associated with certain roles to try to understand how social change can be brought about through constructing representations that change audience perception.

Hall's (1973) theory of both 'encoding' by producers and 'decoding' by audiences has spawned criticisms and refinements about the subjectivity of the audience decoding elements (Morley, 2006; Ross, 2011). Decoding has been considered limited as a 'semiological concept' (Wren-Lewis, 1983, p. 179) and the model in general has been critiqued. However, Hall makes a usefully important point about the encoding stage where, in addition to there being intended and preferred meanings, there is also a 'dominant meaning' creatively produced. He describes this creativity as:

> The work required to enforce, win plausibility for and command as legitimate a decoding of the event within the limit of dominant definitions in which it has been connotatively signified.
>
> (Hall, 1973, p. 124)

It is therefore important to question a variety of agents about their impact on the generation of dominant meanings, however problematic these meanings are to locate, measure, and define (e.g. Lewis, 2005). Within my research I observe how the significations of mega-event sport were used to position the Paralympics for a favourable decoding by the television audience. Another question posed is whether 'winning plausibility', in this case, was a central challenge faced by the sports producers, and potentially the Marketing Department, in order to legitimate the previously marginalised elite athletes. I address this question directly in Chapter 6.

Current work by other scholars continues to validate Hall's constructionist paradigm (e.g. Chimba and Kitzinger, 2010). Kidd (2015) notes that more recent academic studies (see also Prendergast, 2000; Webb, 2009) have tended to focus on textual analysis and audience responses. She additionally points out that continued exploration of the production process is still important, to investigate the mechanisms of representation (Kidd, 2015, p. 2). Thumim (2015) also calls for 'specific instances' (p. 57) of media production to be examined to understand the power of those undertaking the mediation of 'others'. Some scholars have considered a focus on representation as outdated and lacking in impact (Harris, 2006), but this critique is largely addressing the subjective nature of much textual analysis (Steyn, 2016). My study looks at representation from the encoding position. It is clear that studying how and why representations are constructed at the point of production remains an important and relevant complementarity to reading texts, as the producer intentions for those onscreen representations of 'others' also provide insight into cultural production.

The key understanding, therefore, of the televisual representations made by producers, is that power is used to depict 'others' in order to create a safe distance from 'them' for those who are 'normal'. Whether this distance is 'safe', is more problematic with depictions of disability as I outline below.

Disability studies and the Paralympics

A key representation issue in disability studies, Shakespeare (1998; 2013) argues, is that the able-bodied are more threatened by portrayals of disability than they are by other depicted anomalies because of the risk of becoming disabled themselves. Disability therefore makes uncomfortable viewing. We may develop a disability either sooner or later, at the onset of illness, by unexpected accident or inevitably in old age (ibid.). Other forms of difference, such as race and gender, are less threatening (Mitchell and Snyder, 2014), both onscreen and off, because they do not normally suddenly, or gradually, affect us. For race and gender, and possibly sexual orientation, the 'normal' position remains a safe and not too remote position from which to view the 'other' (Prendergast, 2000). Therefore, because of the uncomfortable underlying threat to 'us', media representations of disability are understood to be, amongst disability scholars, distinctly more problematic.

In this section I show how meanings about disability are informed by our past cultural history as well as our own potential futures, beginning with an inherited historic sense of *revulsion* (Elias, 1978). Then I show how, either invisibility altogether from the screens, or the use of 'the overcoming super-crip' representation, have been adopted to avoid that sense of revulsion. I also outline how scholars in the disability field have disagreed about the 'medical' and 'social' models, as part of a historic schism, at least amongst the British theorists (see Oliver, 2013; Shakespeare and Watson, 2001). My argument is that both of these perspectives still relate to and affect media production.

There is agreement amongst disability scholars that 'medical' meanings about disability are used onscreen generically to benefit the non-disabled (e.g. Longmore, 1987; Garland-Thomson, 2002). The primary 'social model' media production issue for disability theorists is lack of access into the production workforce finding that access has been denied both onscreen and off, for most parts of the production team. Scholars (Barnes, 1992a; Corker and Shakespeare, 2002; Barnes and Mercer, 2010; Goodley, 2013) have noted in particular that disabled practitioners are not normally present to shape more positive meanings about disability.

Revulsion, invisibility and supercrips

Whilst meanings are generated, as already established, by a shared common-sense understanding about 'them' (Hall, 1997), meanings can also be rooted in a familiar and shared historic context. Many years ago Elias (1978) identified that depictions of disability, or extreme difference, often trigger revulsion in the spectator or audience, and as we might now add, the digital consumer too. He argued that the source of this cultural revulsion, to certain forms of disability, stemmed from the post-medieval 'civilising process' that historically trained our prevalent perceptions of acceptable bodily function and control. The spectacle of the disabled 'other', therefore, carries an extra meaning of being repulsively different. Davis (1995) traces the construction of 'normalcy' for 'us', through the nineteenth century, where he notes that 'the terrain of the body' (ibid., p. 48) is scrutinised for difference of any kind (see also Ahmed, 2007b). This is one of the ways that we have defined who we are in relation to others, by checking for bodily differences. Since noticing bodily differences is something that cannot be avoided whilst watching the Paralympic Games, attempts at normalisation could be a particular challenge.

Revulsion, Davis says, is a learned response, becoming an action on a societal level producing discrimination and marginalisation (1995, p. 13).

These deeply ingrained historical prejudices pervade literary and artistic representations of disability as they did in the days of the Ancient Greeks and Romans. The antidote to revulsion on television has been not to depict disability at all, rendering it invisible (Davis, 2005), unless fascination or intrigue dictate the need to include it (e.g. Barnes, 1992a; Negrine and Cumberbatch, 1992; Haller, 1995; Darke, 2004). Historically, 'freaks' were paraded and celebrated for their difference in a way that was designed to invoke revulsion and construct distance away from them, for the 'normal' public majority (Davis, 1995).

The Olympic and Paralympic sporting events also include a parade of athletes, with the athletic body as a central focus. What makes this parade problematic, when televised, is that depictions of able-bodied and depictions of disfigured or 'different' bodies, even if framed the same televisually, do not carry the same connotations because of their differing historic contexts. Over time, spectacles of disability have triggered repulsion in the mainstream audience (Elias, 1978; Davis, 1995) whilst perceptions of Olympian bodies, as I show in the next section, have been of perfection and beauty. These conflicts of meaning make the Paralympian bodies harder to represent as watchable, because of the paradox of the predisposed meanings about physical difference already in place (Purdue and Howe, 2012, see also Pullen et al., 2019). There are also varying degrees of acceptability, such as athletes in wheelchairs (Hardin and Hardin, 2004), because they look like 'normal' people who sit down too and the military wounded (Brittain and Green, 2012), because they were like 'us' once, and have had an accident.

In relation to onscreen depictions, there are two key paradigms about disability that activists and academics have debated over recent decades, since the inception of a formalised field of disability studies in the late 1970s (see Hunt, 1966; UPIAS, 1976; Finkelstein, 1980; Oliver, 1983). The key discussions for understanding media representations of disability come from these two theories, and their relative weight is unbalanced in onscreen depictions. One, the 'medical' model, reflects the depictions that are normally seen on television and the other, the 'social' model, which is less often depicted, but offers potential reasons why this reflection may be so. The first perspective, more explicitly known as the 'bio-medical model' (Barnes and Mercer, 2003), focuses on 'disability' as a malfunction of the individual. The second, the 'social model' (Oliver, 1983), argues that the focus of (dis)ability should be on the ableist society that creates disabling barriers (see also Barnes and Mercer, 2003). It should be noted that there is also a North American Social Model (Smith and Bundon, 2018) that is more individually focused, as well as an emerging body of work within Critical Disability Studies (CDS) that embraces, amongst other models, the Human Rights and Social Relational Models (see Thomas, 2007). These are important bodies of work but are not the focus of this research.

Representations of disability in the media so far, scholars have found, are typically reflections of the individual impairment approach to disability (Oliver and Barnes, 2016) which is seen across many film genres too as a medicalisation perspective. This bio-medical perspective highlights the condition of the impaired individual as a 'personal tragedy' whilst emphasising 'courage' if negative circumstances have been overcome. Stigma, and the sense of being wrong, were famously articulated by Hunt (1966) as a predominant representation with discriminatory meanings. Television portrayals consistently portray 'disability' in this way (Barnes and Mercer, 2003) with the 'disabled' seen as flawed able-bodied people. The key theme of 'having to overcome or fix a disability', with triumph or failure narratives, arises repeatedly in disability studies of representation (Hunt, 1966; Barnes, 1992c; Thomson, 1996; Goggin and Newell, 2003; Purdue and Howe, 2012) and the corresponding tropes are firmly embedded in the 'medical model' approach to disabled 'others'. Triumph and failure narratives are of course a central tenet of sport, although losers disappear from the screen almost immediately. Even so, according to Rees et al.'s (2019) systematic analysis of elite para-athlete media portrayals from pre-Salt Lake to post-Rio (2001 to 2017), the medicalisation explanatory paradigm continues to be present within a range of journalistic media output, although there is an increasing athleticism element as well.

Being extraordinary at something, for a disabled person, has not been celebrated televisually for its own sake, purely as an achievement, but only as part of fixing an anomaly by compensating for impairment (Darke, 2004; Gilbert and Schantz, 2012). It is, therefore, possible to anticipate the difficulty producers might have in celebrating disabled elite athletes as mainstream because their achievement has now to do two things. It has to vindicate their impairment as a parasports athlete, and based on past histories, eradicate it at the same time, for the benefit of the able-bodied. Various stereotypes have been used to reinforce this pre-2012 'overcoming' positioning (Shakespeare and Watson, 2001; Darke, 2004) and these categories have clearly persisted (Goggin and Newell, 2000; 2003; Barnes, 1992a; Oliver and Barnes, 2016; Kearney et al., 2019).

Arguably, reliance on the 'bio-medical model' has led to the recurrent use of these categorised stereotypes, tropes, and narratives. As a background for this study the most relevant are the 'pitiable and pathetic' condition (also particularly utilised by charity advertisers, see Hevey, 1992, p. 5) and the opposite to this underclass, the 'super cripple', overachieving to be acceptable. When disability features at all, being 'subhuman' or 'superhuman' consistently remain the binary narrative also used in the press. A content analysis, undertaken by the Glasgow Media Group of print representations of disability, compares newspapers from 2004–2005 with newspapers from 2010–2011, and concludes that most portrayals and references to the physically impaired are related to their 'burden on society' (Philo, 2012, p. 9). The other predominant representation conveys the meaning 'triumph over adversity' (ibid., p. 8) with 'super cripple' references being found in both periods. In 2012, these superhuman and subhuman narratives ran alongside each other, and even alternated, as perceived by Crow (2014) who says of the press, 'now that the Paralympics is over, the benefits juggernaut rumbles on' [no pagination].

Further types and tropes, in a much-quoted list of negative disability representations (see Barnes, 1992a), are mainly sinister and villainous in connotation, or legitimise ridicule using caricatures of functional difference. These other categories occur mostly in fiction, usually as a means of progressing the plot, and also are used in other forms of literary and visual representation as signifiers of difference that reinforce 'normality'. What is significant across all genres of media production is that cultural meanings are attached to people with impairments consistently portraying them as 'deficient, not quite normal or perhaps not fully human' (Barnes and Mercer, 2010, p. 168). The London 2012 Paralympics coverage appeared to be, and billed itself as, an exception to this pattern, and as such is a uniquely rich resource for investigation into how and why changes in meaning are actually made.

Disabled imagery, in addition, has tended to exist in either the margins of the television schedule (Goggin and Newell, 2000), or around the periphery of the central programme subject (Darke, 2004). The Paralympics coverage, as mainstream 'normal' programming, had to be framed in a way that would dismantle existing disability depictions and audience expectations in order to create new meanings. Meanings relating to 'freak' (Garland-Thomson, 2002), or 'superhuman' (Silva and Howe, 2012) are theoretically nuanced at this intersection and could be the cause of conflicting editorial judgements. In the light of this literature, it is necessary to discover more about which of these contexts has more power to prevail over meanings.

I trace the creative decision-making process that producers went through to make these shifts in the upcoming chapters. More research is needed to explore whether it is possible to be depicted as 'different' without being the 'other', and this study contributes to that. It is also not clear whether tropes from one included 'acceptable' group can be successfully mapped onto a previously excluded 'unacceptable' group. In televisual terms, this should be straightforward, but, as this chapter demonstrates, in theory might create different meanings. The dilemmas thrown up by historical revulsion (Elias, 1978; Davis, 1995) alongside repeated visual caricatures of disability (Barnes, 1992c; Darke, 2004), within the context of familiar mainstream TV (Fiske, 1987), make the decoding of dominant sporting meanings less predictable. Entrenched meanings conditioned by existing framings, therefore, would potentially be hard to dismantle.

Inspiration porn or sporting inspiration?

Historically I have shown that there is a tension between how disability is typically represented and how elite athletes are typically represented. This makes the Paralympics coverage, as a sporting event for disabled elite athletes, all the more important to research. The sports section below outlines the inspirational cohesive framings that Channel 4 would have had at their disposal. These clash with the way that disability has been portrayed on television so far, raising the question as to why the producers would choose to blend these positive and negative framings in 2012. Until now, disability studies have shown that typically media portrayals still mainly focus on lack of function and helplessness (Smith and Thomas, 2005). Why this has changed is an important question that my empirical chapters take up and address.

Prior to the London 2012 media coverage, Silva and Howe (2012) interrogated the value of the 'supercrip', or 'superhuman', representation that occurs in the Paralympics, and suggested an openness to difference could be thought out and presented in other ways. The authors question whether the 'supercrip' representation of Paralympic athletes fulfils the International Paralympic Committee's requirement for 'empowerment' (IPC, 1989) or whether it is in fact a form of *dis*empowerment. Their premise is that overemphasis of a 'super' difference actually helps to preserve a *safe distance* for the 'normal' observer whilst undermining the 'normal' prowess of these athletes with impairments. There is a conflict here between the historic understanding of disability representations as repulsive or invisible (Barnes, 1992a; Goggin and Newell, 2003; Davis, 2005), and an understanding, which I discuss in the next section, of the inspirational and visible sporting tropes (Horne and Whannel, 2012). It seems clear that further research needs to be conducted to clarify the motivations and purposes of producers constructing such representations.

Meanings are highlighted by Silva and Howe (2012), in their textual study of Paralympic representations, whilst discussing the reinforcement of 'achievement syndrome' (p. 2). They explain that using the 'supercrip' narrative creates a meaning that 'the impaired are successful *in spite* of their disability' (see also Hardin and Hardin, 2004). This predominant meaning suggests a query in editorial judgement that a disabled producer might have, over, for example, one of the sports editors. That disabled people are cast as 'heroes or zeros' has been well established in previous research (Brittain, 2010; Schantz 2012), however in sport, so are athletes also winners or losers. What this might mean is that the disadvantage embedded in the 'disability' meaning may not perhaps be intended as a disadvantage in the sports representation.

This discrepancy raises questions of power. Whose editorial judgement holds sway and what are the considerations? Established uses of disability representation arguably makes the celebrating of Paralympic athleticism harder to frame. The question of how to overcome a sense of revulsion and dismantle existing tropes for an imagined audience is something I explore in Chapter 4. I analyse the intersection of associated meanings and the cross-pollination of mainstream tropes within the different programme formats to see how they were used and to what purpose in the formats chapter, Chapter 5.

It is only recently that much academic interest has been taken in the media coverage of the Paralympic Games at all (Gilbert and Schantz, 2008) and most of this research has either analysed broadcast and print output for its meanings or focused on audience reception. At the time of writing there are only two published media production studies on the Paralympics. The first (Howe, 2008b) was undertaken in the print newsroom at Athens in 2004 and the second (Pullen et al., 2019) explores production decisions for Rio 2016 as part of a larger project including texts and audiences.

Howe's (2008b) work focused on the production of printed texts rather than broadcast television or digital platforms. He noted that images were carefully mediated for a target audience. Howe embedded himself as a newspaper reporter to study media production ethnographically within the journalists' habitat. He found that 95 per cent of the reporters, in 2004, were able-bodied and that they constructed meanings of 'purity' with charitable and patronising undertones, during the production stage, using only positive representations. Here, again, as Born (2004) had done (p. 10), Howe makes a link between the use of able-bodied producers in direct relation to the tone and framing of ensuing media representations. The relationship between mediator and mediated representations is also central to this study.

Howe (ibid.) noted additionally that amongst print journalists in the Media Centre at Athens the 'triumph over adversity' narrative was being gradually superseded by a greater focus on sport (ibid., pp. 141–143). This continued to happen in 2012 too, with the sport making the front as well as the back pages of the national newspapers. The reason given for choosing to break away from a content analysis approach to Paralympic representational studies was because he wanted to examine the control of information. By 'researching the lived experiences of the media production processes' (ibid., p. 135) he sought to understand how the image of elite sport for the disabled was 'properly managed' (ibid.). His own researcher perspective was that of a former Paralympic athlete, my perspective comes from being a former BBC television production practitioner, who has had the experience of broadcasting national sport output.

Existing theoretical insights, from my discussion so far, suggest that simply applying familiar media production processes, even from the field of inspirational sport, below, may not solve underlying revulsion to a minority group with visual disfigurements. However, Bournemouth University's

(Jackson, 2013) audience research suggests that it did so. Their findings reinforce my suggestion that further exploration is therefore needed to examine the overlaying tropes and common televisual representations that were used to unite an audience as opposed to separate them.

Increasingly spectacular representations (Haller, 1995; Orgad, 2012), alongside a clearly selective omission process (DePauw, 1997), are the embodiment of the 'emphasise' or 'ignore' attitudes that emerge within both the disability and sports literature. Although this may be oversimplified, Gilbert and Schantz (2012) suggest that there are really only two main attitudes to Paralympic sports that are taken up by the media. The first is to ignore the event completely, as NBC have done in the past, by not transmitting 'live' coverage, or to overlook elements by selective representation of the more normal looking sequences (e.g. not swimming events). The second is to 'construe the myth of the supercrip, the freaky cyborg or the hero who overcame his terrible fate' (Schantz, 2012, p. 8, but see also Hardin and Hardin, 2004; Berger, 2008; McGillivray et al., 2019). There has not been much in between to normalise visibility without extremity.

The reductive attitude towards event selection is perhaps a reflection of the stereotypical representations of disability across other genres of television programming, in that the Paralympic Games has also historically over-represented the wheelchair-based events (Schantz and Marty, 1995). The physical motor impairments have been found to be the predominant representation upsetting the able-bodied public the least, and the wheelchair symbol, as recorded across other television genres, the least 'repulsive' of these (see Barnes, 1992a). Triumphing over disability is not, however, the same as triumphing in sport, and negotiations over the distinctions in meaning, as I have already suggested, throw production issues and editorial judgement-making into relief.

According to Barnes and Mercer (2003), there is now a strong emphasis on the reality that the social world is organised by an able-bodied majority. Additionally, a combined 'biopsychosocial' approach (World Health Organization, 2001) confirms that impairments and a full range of other factors affect a person with unusual appearance or impaired function (Barnes and Mercer, 2003, p. 14). There is a normative implication in this approach that the status quo will continue. This defining emphasis raises a question for television production, however, that I take up in the chapters that follow, asking whether media representations should necessarily also be made by the organising able-bodied majority. Based on the unfairness of 'othering' and distancing, as described in the representation section, and media invisibility, or sense of 'revulsion', observed by disability scholars above, perhaps media productions ought to be made by those who have experience of what is being represented. This is a familiar discourse, too, with other diversities.

The 'social model' and access to production

Having established that the medical/individual narrative has remained the virtually unchallenged dominant discourse within the media, it has historically been the 'social model' (Oliver, 1983) which has dominated arguments within the academic discipline. This model challenges the location of power and powerlessness and identifies the nature of disabled identities as socially constructed. Studies have focused the direction of disability theory away from simply the medical condition of the individual and towards the able-bodied societies that are perceived as excluding and constructing 'disabled' others (e.g. Finkelstein, 1980; Oliver, 1983; Barnes, 2004). In spite of this social focus, the literature shows media portrayals have generally represented these situations as barriers less often and generically point to the individual medical predicament as the disabling factor or point of blame (e.g. Darke, 2004). This may be a reflection of the make-up of the workforce, as intimated above, and is a question that scholars have wanted to address (Barnes, 1992b; Haller, 1995).

Where the 'social model' does seem to still apply is within the production process. This model is not particularly depicted onscreen as a representation of disablement, compared to the 'medical model' of individual tragedy, but society's disabling barriers have been identified as restricting access into the media production process (Barnes 1992b; Oliver and Barnes, 2016). This identification demonstrates the continuing importance and validity of the 'social' model paradigm, in spite of some saying that the concept has run its course (Shakespeare and Watson, 2001), at least in its current form (e.g. Thomas, 2007; Berghs et al., 2019). The inference is clear, that social exclusion in wider society has also affected access to mainstream television programme making, other than, perhaps, tokenistically, as a 'consultant'. I explore this role of consultant as it occurred for my participants and evaluate the influence, or not, on final onscreen outcomes for 2008 and 2012, where some of the same people were used by different companies to different effect.

A major criticism of media representations generally is that they are created mainly by able-bodied people who overlook the social barriers that others say are the really disabling factors (Haller, 1995; 2010). In addition to attitudes, the 'social model' highlights infrastructures that are created for the consumption and use of the able-bodied group to the exclusion of disabled 'others'. The way society is organised at a macro level, applies equally, of course, to the micro levels of television production and associated marketing. My research therefore investigates whether any of the disabling social barriers also occur within the media production process, and within the organisational structures, rather than, as disability theorists have mainly done, amongst the audience and society at large.

In order to establish how disability is represented and what perpetuates such commonly negative representations, Barnes' (1992a) study remains important and relevant. The fundamental reason for onscreen stereotyping has been clearly understood and defined by one of the founders of disability studies. He says in that report, 'Disablist imagery will only disappear if disabled people are integrated at all levels into the media' (ibid., p. 21). Barnes mooted a potential correlation between onscreen representation of 'others' and their involvement in the production process as the conclusion to his classic list (1992a) of prevalent disability tropes and stereotypes. The paper insisted that 'there must be more effort to recruit disabled people to work in mainstream media organisations' (ibid.) in order to get rid of 'disablist' imagery (as distinct from images that could neutrally include physically impaired people). Twenty years later disablist imagery noticeably changed at the 2012 Paralympics pointing clearly, in the light of Barnes' research, towards the need for an investigation of the media organisation. My research, therefore, ensures that knowledge is generated about the organisation and the potential integration, or not, of disabled producers.

Recent textual studies have discussed whether these 'new' representations are really new, or indeed helpful (e.g. Hibberd, 2015, pp. 100–102; Ellis and Goggin, 2015). These are valuable contributions, although an understanding of representations of disability will still benefit from an exploration of the production context, as Barnes suggested, and as my study takes up. Whether change is indeed down to the integration of disabled people within the workforce is an important line of enquiry. Barnes does not go on to interrogate at what level of integration within the media organisation those disabled producers would need to be, to make any difference to the imagery. A key reason, Barnes (1992a) says, for needing this access, and to be included in the workforce, is to reduce 'corporate ignorance about disability [...] since those who experience disability daily have little or no say in how they are presented on television or in the press' (ibid., pp. 6–7).

This is a similar observation to the one made by Born (2004) about the under-representation of ethnic minorities at the BBC (p. 10). Make-up of the workforce is clearly flagged up as integral to the construction of onscreen depictions, within the field of disability studies, as it has been amongst production and cultural industry scholars more generally. In the following chapters I take up this issue by exploring this integration issue throughout all levels of the Paralympic production, to assess the extent of its influence, amongst other impinging factors. If the workforce is mixed between able-bodied and disabled, which criteria are applied and what are the constraints? I address these issues throughout the upcoming chapters.

In this section I have flagged up the lack of access to production for those with disabilities as potentially key to detrimental onscreen representations (Barnes, 1992a). I have also explored the reasons for the historic sense of revulsion, onscreen invisibility, and supercrip representations that have prevailed to date in representations of disability. Unlike watching representations of race or gender from a 'safe' distance, something unexpected can happen to suddenly make 'us' disabled, and if not and we live long enough, disability scholars note that we eventually become disabled anyway (Shakespeare, 1994). Therefore disability is not a 'safe' topic for viewing, and there would be considerable risks for producers in making it more visible or positively watchable. I have shown how, historically, watching disability on television, with its associated meanings of pity and tragedy, has been considered uncomfortable and unsafe viewing. How disability is typically represented differs enormously from how elite athletes are typically represented, as I will outline below. Trying to marry the depictions of impairment with the meanings of celebrated sport is one that has not been attempted by Paralympic 'side-show' (Gilbert and Schantz, 2008) TV coverage before. Given the difficulty of this, my study asks why Channel 4 would choose to risk elevating and reshaping the London 2012 Paralympic Games coverage into an international, highly visible sporting mega-event.

Televised sports mega-events

Neither revulsion nor invisibility have had a place in inspirational high-profile international televised sport. The research shows that sport has its own tropes and framings along with its own mainstream audiences who understand its televisual conventions and shared meanings (Roche, 2000; Horne and Whannel, 2012). Additionally, in the field of sport, audiences are bought and sold (Horne, 2007). In this section I explore the arguments that a sense of collective identity is central to the representations of international athletes on television, and that the spectacle of the athlete is there for us to be drawn *towards* (Hayes and Karamichas, 2012) rather than to be kept at a safe distance *from*. I outline how social cohesion is understood to be a key component of global mega-events and how the short-term disruption of the special event broadcasts has a direct bearing on how we feel about what we watch in this context. Marketing and commercialisation are also key focuses for sports television coverage, especially amongst the producing decision-makers (Horne, 2007; Horne and Whannel, 2012). I outline below some of the key understandings from this research field that have a direct bearing on how to understand the producer intentions, and influencing factors over them, for the production of the London 2012 Paralympics coverage.

In order to understand the meanings that can be derived from onscreen sports representations, the context, format, and genre need to be established, as some of these come with meanings and assumptions built into them (Billings, 2008). For the first time the Paralympic Games was treated, in 2012, as an international mega-event. Arguably, this in itself will have reframed the identity of the Paralympians. There has been much debate about whether mega-events are purely driven by economics or whether they serve a greater purpose for reinforcing collective identities (Whannel and

Tomlinson, 1984; Maguire, 1993; Dayan and Katz, 1994; Billig, 1995; Roche, 2006; Hayes and Karamichas, 2012) through a sense of 'communitas' (Katz, 2009), national identity, and cultural affinity (Gellner, 1983; Smith, 2003). The sense of 'us' (Herzfeld, 2005; Bauman, 2001) is developed within this particular context of international sporting mega-event, for reasons I develop below.

By mega-events I am using Maurice Roche's definition of 'large-scale cultural [including commercial and sporting] events, which have a dramatic character, mass popular appeal and international significance' (Roche, 2000, p. 1). Horne (2007) adds a prerequisite to the definition, that the event is televised and broadcast in many countries around the world (p. 33). The term is largely used in relation to sporting events but not exclusively so. It is more significant that the event interrupts daily schedules and routines. Dayan and Katz (1994) point out that, whether they be a coronation, conquest, or contest, mega-events are particularly considered to be an opportunity for 'hegemonic manipulations' (1994, p. 5), able to frame both narrative and spectacle on a global scale (see also Katz and Dayan, 1986). It is important therefore to examine the decision to elevate the 2012 Paralympics to mega-event status and establish not only why this was done but what difference it made to framings and subsequent perceptions of disability.

Mega-event framing, developed during the production process, sets up the feel that 'the whole world is watching', broadening the reach and authenticity of its meanings (ibid.). This occurs to such an extent that Whannel (2008), after Beijing 2008, referred to the Olympic Games as one of the 'institutions through which we define ourselves as a global collectivity' (p. 199). The mega-event is a platform, therefore, for defining who is included as 'us', and by implication who is excluded, whilst also refining and reflecting collective values. A sense of *collective* 'shared meanings' (Hall, 1997) has been the hallmark of large-scale media events since the inception of its kind in the UK when TV sets were first purchased to watch the coronation in 1952 (Billig, 1995; Katz, 2009). The important point is that in this setting the shared meanings are about who we *are* rather than who we are *not*. It may be that the embedding of a diversity group with a transformation agenda into a unifying collective history moment such as an international sporting event is a crucial part of bringing a minority into the mainstream. It certainly makes that moment of attempted inclusivity an important one to study.

Representations created in sporting contexts have also been studied in relation to the Olympic Games (beginning with Riefenstahl's famous film *Olympia* (1938) representing the Aryan race at the 1936 Berlin Games) and the football World Cup (Roche, 2000; Hayes and Karamichas, 2012). The collective 'sense of connection' (Marshall et al., 2010, p. 267) comes about through the projection of 'liveness' which is represented by a 'seamless mix'

(Whannel and Tomlinson, 1984, p. 34) of replays, inserts, pre-recorded interviews, and special effects. Although a lot of it isn't technically live, the linking with others is a meaning that is made through the constructed representation of 'liveness'. Dayan and Katz (1994) have called this powerful and mediated representation of the Olympics a 'social integration of the highest order' (p. 15). Arguably this socially integrated space is ripe for embedding common-sense ideas of identity, of who we are in relation to 'others'. It follows on, therefore, that any act of borrowing tropes from the Olympics would include the borrowing also of the shared embedded meanings about 'our' identity.

At the time of the London Paralympic Games, press coverage connected the meanings and excitement attributed to it with the context and momentum carried over from the two previous media mega-events in the same year. Later research also confirms this beneficial momentum (Wood, 2013). The first of these media events, although not a coronation per se, was a Royal Jubilee, and the second, the London Olympics, including its massively successful British medal-haul, could arguably be seen as a conquest as well as contest. These events may have set the scene for a potential 'cultural shift' that might not have been possible otherwise, based on the sense of collective national identity and shared values that can be communicated on such occasions (Horne and Manzenreiter, 2006).

Sports nationalism and 'our team'

As established, elevating the treatment of the Paralympic Games to mega-event status, with round-the-clock 'live' sports coverage puts it on a par with the World Cup and the Olympic Games in terms of televisual spectacle (Roche, 2000; Hayes and Karamichas, 2012). This status, in itself, arguably has a direct impact on meaning-making since those represented are automatically positioned within the mainstream. A key part of the media framing is the extraordinary spectacle of elite 'others'. However, celebrity sport is designed to inspire and to get 'us' to root for 'them' and identify with either the national team or the individual being represented (Billings, 2008). The team in turn represent 'us', our nation, or our aspirations. This two-way identification means the *extreme* 'spectacle of the inspirational other', in this context, has an almost polar opposite effect to the extreme spectacle of revulsion analysed by disability scholars. The gap between 'them' and 'us' is closed rather than widened because, rather than providing a safe distance, the sporting spectacle draws us in. This dynamic seems to be at odds with the normal function and use of extreme caricatures or stereotypes.

Extraordinary achievement is focused upon but for inspirational reasons rather than distance-creating ones. Olympic parity and success were aimed at in 2012 by the television producers and also by the British Paralympic

Association (BPA) and LOCOG. However, Longmore (1987) argues that representations of successful disabled people, including under the guise of entertainment, are seemingly used to reassure the non-disabled audience (p. 66) rather than inspire others with impairments. Since the 2012 Paralympics, Haller and Preston (2016) re-asserted the consideration that the disabled subject is purely a media construct to confirm normalcy. Calling the 2012 Paralympics coverage 'inspiration porn' (ibid., p. 53), as Stella Young (2014) the disability activist had done, they based their argument on a shift away from subject to object, asserting that objectification occurs when:

> One whose struggle against systemic barriers is converted into a moment of reflection and encouragement for the nondisabled to better themselves.
>
> (ibid.)

If the coverage is encoded and framed as Olympian, however, this suggests other contextualised meanings might also be intended. Olympic athletes are also objectified, but not necessarily for the same reasons, and this raises the question of whether parity is indeed possible. Certainly it raises the question of what parity, for those who are different, might mean. In Chapter 4 I address how producers considered that and what influenced the decisions they made about it.

The key difference in 2012 was the alignment of these 'superhumans' with ableist Olympic representations. Understanding the influences that brought about that shift is an important part of my investigation. The super-athlete in the Olympic setting is considered successful because of their inspiring efforts (Wenner, 1998), with triumph not intended as a 'triumph over tragedy' (Barnes, 1992a, p. 13; Oliver, 1996). Instead the triumph over their own ordinariness propels them into celebrity culture and this is not therefore necessarily seen as a distancing trope for mainstream sports athletes.

Within this extraordinary or 'freak' setting, revulsion seems to be the preferred meaning for one group (according to Brittain, 2010; Schantz, 2012; Silva and Howe, 2012) and inspiration (consistently since Riefenstahl's film in 1938) the preferred meaning for the other group. Resolving the two sets of meanings, or even managing them, could therefore potentially be problematic during production. Whether or not the producers were aware of the need to dismantle the negative historic associations or, indeed, whether they consciously chose to borrow from the positive ones, is a question that I address in the upcoming chapters. There would undoubtedly be different agendas affecting the decision-makers and this particular intersection between disability and sports representation provides an opportunity to better understand the editorial dynamics of media production.

Commercialisation, marketing, and branding

The other scaling-up process connected to the Paralympic Games, in addition to Olympic-style spectacularisation, has been the increasing *commercialisation*. Since it was first officially staged at Rome in 1960 the Paralympics has been treated as a side-show to the Olympics (Gilbert and Schantz, 2008) at least until Barcelona in 1992. Brittain (2012) noted in his summary of disability sport media portrayals that, from Barcelona onwards, there has been a sharp increase in media coverage, both in broadcast hours, and in the breadth of countries providing air-time and column inches. Because the media value of sports coverage has become increasingly 'determined by the size and composition of its audience' (Maguire, 1993, p. 38), scholars argue that representations of events and athletes have consequently been changing, becoming more and more spectacular for commercial purposes (Tomlinson and Young, 2006).

Whilst sport in general has been developing its celebrity culture to increase its saleable commodity value to sponsors and advertisers, the Paralympics has been at an inevitable disadvantage. This is because the pervading representation in sport is of an ideal physicality which DePauw (1997) concludes is an able-bodied masculine perfection, for both men and women, including 'aggression, independence, strength and courage' (p. 421). Attractive body appearance is central to the media agenda for sport (Rowe, 1999) which has resulted in marginalisation of the Paralympic Games (Gilbert and Schantz, 2008) and until 2012 a selective representation of only a handful of 'acceptable' events. This begs the question, why change that now? Why would the Paralympics suddenly be of commercial value?

From a production perspective, Zoellner (2009) points out that the multi-platform environment needs the amplification of the ordinary to the extraordinary simply to attract a distracted audience's attention (p. 528). This idea brings the benchmark for normalisation into question as even the mundane is spectacularised to compete for commissioning into the multi-platform environment. Much of the scholarly concern with the super-extraordinary misrepresentation, within the disability and Paralympic fields (DePauw, 1997; Silva and Howe, 2012), does not yet take into account this new environmental pressure. In what follows, my study addresses these questions and establishes some reasons that will be useful for comparative research in other contexts.

According to other production studies, commercial value to the broadcaster occurs on several levels that we ought to pay attention to, particularly the presence of marketing. Mann (2009) notes the commercial tension over creativity when she suggests that the singular 'auteur' voice, as an industry paradigm for meaning-making, is now obsolete. She makes the point that a 'six-pack of execs' (2009, p. 99) is now needed to run spinoff digital content and promotions since they are 'managing a brand and not just a TV show' (ibid.). This raises the question of the role of execs at Channel 4, and whether they had any impact on the programme content or meaning-making more generally than just their promotional material. In Chapter 6 I discuss the role of Channel 4's marketing team in relation to the 2012 Paralympics entire coverage.

As well as the marketing drive, other production researchers have highlighted brand awareness amongst public service broadcasters away from the field of televised sport. Brand influence can occur at channel level and also for types of content, and this is another factor in the meaning-making process established by both Buckingham (1987) and Born (2004). In his study of a BBC soap, Buckingham (1987) suggests that the BBC commissioned *EastEnders* in the first instance to get rid of the unwanted 'Auntie' image and reshape the brand of the BBC. Buckingham here establishes that the existence of the soap as well as its content creation are primarily there to serve a commercial agenda. Born (2004) later established, in more detail, through her ethnographic research, that the distinct channel brands within the organisation, namely BBC1 and BBC2, are conceptualised differently from each other by creatives, beyond the generic Auntie image, and that depictions and meanings are chosen to be delivered uniquely through each of them. BBC3, which has moved to digital streaming only, is clearly branded and targeted for a younger consumer, even more so.

It is worth considering, therefore, whether Channel 4 also had a commercial or brand agenda for choosing to host the Paralympics, and whether this possible agenda also shaped the content. The channel idents during the Games included the strapline 'Channel 4 – The Paralympics Channel', both in 2012 and then again in 2016 during the Rio coverage, signifying a brand awareness amongst the producers. I address questions of branding and channel identity in the industry chapter, Chapter 3, and the marketing chapter, Chapter 6.

Typically, branding is seen as a tool of marketing, but Banet-Weiser (2012) has argued that the social meanings and significance attached to brands extends their influence beyond normal commercial business models. Davis (2013), too, is concerned that the promotion of ideas and meanings surrounding more complex uses of brands is producing a promotional culture that is harder to identify. He associates these promulgated ideas with influences over representations and the identity shaping of 'others' (ibid., p. 4). With this in mind, I examine the internal culture of the organisation throughout each of my chapters, in case meanings were shaped by changes taking place there.

Beyond sport, other television scholars have also shown that both creativity and commerce are influencing programme output in increasingly complex and messy ways, in order to secure an audience or reinforce brand loyalty (e.g. Grindstaff, 2002; Caldwell, 2008; Banks, 2009; Mayer, 2011). To what extent these are affected by the political economy, with its associated regulations and macro structures, can be examined from inside the production process alongside, as this case-study does, a tracking of the individual decision-makers and what affected them personally.

Televised sport, as a highly commercialised product (Wenner, 2009), is potentially affected by all of the concerns highlighted by the scholars discussed above. Because sport is inclusive and relies on ability, or ableness (Rowe, 2003), certain editorial aspects of the production process will necessarily be highlighted whilst creating acceptable sports representations for 'others' who are normally, by contrast, disabled, excluded, and stigmatised. There are two particular ways of managing stigma that Goffman (1963) has theorised which are pertinent to this study and may provide insight for any of the potential editorial dilemmas that would occur with televising disability sport. Both theories relate to settings of 'mixed contact' (p. 14) where the abnormal person or group is in close proximity with 'normals'. With diversity programming this close contact happens both away from the cameras and also onscreen.

The first, 'disclosure etiquette' (ibid.), defines the conceal or reveal dilemma faced by those who are stigmatised, when amongst those who are not. Goffman asserts that moments of proximity produce the dilemma of whether to show or hide 'difference' in order to be treated normally. With normalisation as a goal of the Paralympic production, I ask whether this dilemma emerges amongst the Channel 4 producers representing the stigmatised group onscreen.

The second idea from Goffman surrounding stigma management relates to a specific anomaly in the 'othering' process. Whilst marginalised groups generally mix amongst their 'own', sometimes these groups can include an honorary 'wise' outsider (1963, p. 19). According to Goffman, these 'normal' people are included because of some connection they have with the 'othered' group and the net result is that the 'wise' one tends to *normalise* the stigmatised because they spend time around them and the others do not mind them being there (ibid., pp. 31–32). This has the effect of reframing meanings for those within that group and leaves open the question of whether the dynamic extends also to affecting television audiences should that Wise One dynamic be presented on the television screen. The Paralympic sports coverage appeared to include some examples of this anomaly in the chatty satire programme format, *The Last Leg*, and this question is addressed in Chapter 5. Drawing on Goffman, I also observe stigma management by the producers in other ways throughout all my empirical chapters.

Conclusion

The three bodies of representation, disability, and televised sports research, that I have outlined above, provide intersecting debates on representation of bodily difference and the framing of 'meanings'. In terms of production, the scholars suggest that representing others is a matter of power: the power to reduce a person or people to a set of characteristics from which we may feel a *safe distance* from them. Additionally, disability scholars have established that production is largely carried out by the able-bodied and that representations of disability are negatively produced to benefit the non-disabled. Within sport, depictions of the 'other' are much more relatable. The debates indicate that athletes are set up as inspirational heroes whom we can identify with and root for. With all three of these processes occurring at once for the Paralympic Games the intersection both theoretically and in practice provides an important focus.

As this chapter has shown, there is a considerable production risk in attempting to close the gap between 'us' and 'them', in relation to disability. The mixing of something we do want with something we do not want is conflicted, such that meanings are trickier to encode. The LOCOG focus groups in 2009 highlighted this particular challenge and this book investigates to what extent producers tried to change the inherently negative positioning and how they were able to successfully market an unwanted attribute.

Finally, the purpose of examining representation at the point of media production is to gain a better understanding of the media producers' role in meaning-making and how meaning is made through a series of linked decisions. The power of representation, in relation to cultural production and theories of social change, is that the media is able to 'effectively manage the understanding that the public has of the world' (Howe, 2008b, p. 135). Since 'us' and 'them' mean different things for the team supporting audience, the diversity voyeur and the charitable or patronising viewer, the role of those that frame these meanings needs to be scrutinised in some depth. There are unanswered questions that this review of the intersecting histories reveals in particular in relation to the representation of marginalised groups, with no detailed research into the televisual media production setting of Paralympic sport yet undertaken. Disability theorists have suggested in no uncertain terms that the under-representation of disabled media producers in the workforce affects the meanings that appear onscreen. Was this the difference with the host nation television coverage of London 2012?

Another question to ask is whether the 'superhuman' trope has merely been showcased yet again, albeit in this unusual Home Games context, and for whose benefit? Did the depictions *mean* the same as previous versions of the trope, and if not, why not, and how was that achieved? Was this down to the personnel involved at the production stages or did the diktats of the public service remit, and other structures, constrain or enable their creativity? Which underlying commercial pressures impinged on these decisions or was it just the way that the elite athletes were marketed? Equally, was the level of involvement, by disabled 'others' on the inside of production, somehow different than, for example, within the BBC for Beijing 2008 and previous Paralympic coverage? Shaped by the debates discussed in this chapter I address these empirical and theoretical queries in what follows.

Bibliography

Ahmed, S. 2007a. The language of diversity. *Ethnic and Racial Studies*, 30(2), pp. 235–256.

Ahmed, S. 2007b. A phenomenology of whiteness. *Feminist Theory*, 8(2), pp. 149–168.

Arnstein, S.R. 1969. Ladder of citizen participation. *Journal of the American Institute of Planners*, 35(4), p. 216.

Banet-Weiser, S. 2012. *Authentic TM: the politics of ambivalence in a brand culture*. New York; London: New York University Press.

Banks, M.J. 2009. Gender below-the-line: defining feminist production studies. In: V. Mayer et al. eds. *Production studies: cultural studies of media industries*. London: Routledge, pp. 87–98.

Barnes, C. 1992a. *Disabling imagery and the media: an exploration of the principles for media representations of disabled people*. Halifax: Ryburn Publishing.

Barnes, C. 1992b. Disability and employment. *Personnel Review*, 21(6), pp. 55–73.

Barnes, C. 1992c. Images of disability on television. *Disability, Handicap and Society*, 7(4), pp. 385–387.

Barnes, C. 2004. Disability, disability studies and the academy. In: J. Swain et al. eds. *Disabling barriers – enabling environments*. 2nd ed. London: SAGE, pp. 306–389.

Barnes, C. and Mercer, G. 2003. *Disability policy and practice: applying the 'social model'*. Leeds: Disability Press.

Barnes, C. and Mercer, G. 2010. *Exploring disability*. Chichester: Wiley.

Barthes, R. 1973. *Mythologies*. New York: Paladin.

Barthes, R. 1977. *Image, music, text*. Illinois: Fontana Press.

Baudrillard, J. trans. Glaser, S.F. 1994. *Simulacra and simulation*. University of Michigan Press.

Bauman, Z. 2001. *Community: seeking safety in an insecure world*. Cambridge: Polity Press.

BBC. 2011. *Paralympics 2008*. [online]. [Accessed 12 July 2016]. Available from: http://news.bbc.co.uk/sport

Berger, R.J. 2008. Disability and the dedicated wheelchair athlete: beyond the 'supercrip' critique. *Journal of Contemporary Ethnography*, 37(6), pp. 647–678.

Berghs, M., Atkin, K., Hatton, C., and Thomas, C. 2019. Do disabled people need a stronger social model: a social model of human rights? *Disability & Society*, 34(7–8), pp. 1034–1039.

Billig, M. 1995. *Banal nationalism*. London: SAGE.

Billings, A.C. 2008. *Olympic media: inside the biggest show on television*. London: Routledge.

Born, G. 2004. *Uncertain vision: Birt, Dyke and the reinvention of the BBC*. London: Secker and Warburg.

Brittain, I. 2010. *The Paralympic Games explained*. London: Routledge.

Brittain, I. 2012. British media portrayals of Paralympic and disability sport. In: *Heroes or zeros: the media portrayal of Paralympic sport*. Champaign, IL: Common Ground, pp. 105–113.

Brittain, I. and Green, S. 2012. Disability sport is going back to its roots: rehabilitation of military personnel receiving sudden traumatic disabilities in the twenty-first century. *Qualitative Research in Sport, Exercise and Health*, 4(2), pp. 244–264, DOI: 10.1080/2159676X.2012.685100

Buckingham, D. 1987. *Public secrets: EastEnders and its audience.* London: British Film Institute.

Butler, J. 2011. *Gender trouble: feminism and the subversion of identity.* London: Routledge.

Caldwell, J.T. 2008. *Production culture: industrial reflexivity and critical practice in film and television.* Durham, NC: Duke University Press.

Cammaerts, B. and Carpentier, N. 2007. eds. *Reclaiming the media: communication rights and democratic media roles.* Intellect Online Library.

Campion, M.J. 2005. *Look who's talking: cultural diversity, public service broadcasting and the national conversation.* London: Nuffield College.

Carpentier, N. 2011. *Media and participation: a site of ideological-democratic struggle.* Intellect Online Library.

Chimba, M. and Kitzinger, J. 2010. Bimbo or boffin? Women in science: an analysis of media representations and how female scientists negotiate cultural contradictions. *Public Understanding of Science*, 19(5), pp. 609–624.

Corker, M. and Shakespeare, T. 2002. *Disability/postmodernity: embodying disability theory.* London: Continuum.

Crow, L. 2014. *Summer of 2012: Paralympic legacy and the welfare benefit scandal.* Unpublished.

Cummings, T. and Worley, C. 2014. *Organization development and change.* Stamford, CT: Cengage Learning.

Curran, J. and Gurevitch, M. 2005. *Mass media and society.* 4th ed. London: Hodder Arnold.

Darke, P.A. 2004. The changing face of representations of disability in the media. In: J. Swain et al. eds. *Disabling barriers – enabling environments.* 2nd ed. London: SAGE, pp. 100–105.

Davis, A. 2013. *Promotional cultures: the rise and spread of advertising, public relations, marketing and branding.* Chichester: Wiley.

Davis, L.J. 1995. The construction of normalcy. In: L.J. Davis, ed. *The disability studies reader.* 4th ed. New York: Routledge, pp. 3–16.

Davis, N.A. 2005. Invisible disability. *Ethics*, 116(1), pp. 153–213.

Dayan, D. and Katz, E. 1994. *Media events: the live broadcasting of history.* Cambridge, MA; London: Harvard University Press.

DePauw, K. 1997. The (In)Visibility of DisAbility: cultural contexts and 'sporting bodies'. *Quest.* 49(4), pp. 416–430.

Du Gay, P., Jones, S., and Hall, S. 1997. *Doing cultural studies: the story of the Sony Walkman.* London: SAGE in association with The Open University.

Elias, N. 1978. *The civilizing process: the history of manners.* London: Blackwell.

Ellis, K. and Goggin, G. 2015. *Disability and the media.* London: Palgrave.

Finkelstein, V. 1980. *Attitudes and disabled people: issues for discussion.* New York: International Exchange of Information in Rehabilitation.

Fiske, J. 1987. *Television culture.* London: Methuen.

Fiske, J. and Hartley, J. 2003. *Reading television.* New York; London: Routledge.

Garland-Thomson, R. 2002. The politics of staring: visual rhetorics of disability in popular photography. In: *Disability studies: enabling the humanities*, pp. 56–75.

Gellner, E. 1983. *Nations and nationalism.* Oxford: Blackwell.

Giddens, A. 1989. *Sociology.* Cambridge: Polity Press.

Gilbert, K. and Schantz, O. 2008. *The Paralympic Games: empowerment or side show?* Maidenhead: Meyer and Meyer.

Gilbert, K. and Schantz, O. 2012. An implosion of discontent. *Heroes or zeros.* Champaign, IL: Common Ground, pp. 225–236.

Goffman, E. 1963. *Stigma: notes on the management of spoiled identity.* Harmondsworth: Penguin.

Goggin, G. and Newell, C. 2000. Crippling Paralympics? Media, disability and Olympism. *Media International Australia incorporating Culture and Policy,* 97(1), pp. 71–83.

Goggin, G. and Newell, C. 2003. *Digital disability: the social construction of disability in new media.* Lanham, MD; Oxford: Rowman & Littlefield.

Goodley, D. 2013. Dis/entangling critical disability studies. *Disability & Society,* 28(5), pp. 631–644.

Grindstaff, L. 2002. *The money shot: trash, class, and the making of TV talk shows.* Chicago, IL: University of Chicago Press.

Hall, S. 1973. *Encoding and decoding in the television discourse.* Birmingham Centre for Contemporary Cultural Studies, The University of Birmingham.

Hall, S. 1980. Cultural studies: two paradigms. *Media, Culture and Society,* 2(1), pp. 57–72.

Hall, S. 1997. *Representation: cultural representations and signifying practices.* London: SAGE in association with The Open University.

Haller, B. 1995. Rethinking models of media representations of disability. *Disability Studies Quarterly,* 15(2), pp. 26–30.

Haller, B.A. 2010. *Representing disability in an ableist world: essays on mass media.* Louisville, KY, The Advocado Press.

Haller, B. and Preston, J. 2016. Confirming normalcy: 'inspiration porn' and the construction of the disabled subject? In: *Disability and social media.* Routledge, pp. 63–78.

Hardin, M.M. and Hardin, B. 2004. The 'supercrip' in sport media: wheelchair athletes discuss hegemony's disabled hero. *Sociology of Sport Online-SOSOL,* 7(1).

Harris, G. 2006. *Beyond representation: television drama and the politics and aesthetics of identity.* Manchester; New York: Manchester University Press: Distributed exclusively in the USA by Palgrave.

Hart, R.A. 1992. *Children's participation: from tokenism to citizenship.* Florence: UNICEF International Child Development Centre.

Hayes, G. and Karamichas, J. 2012. *Olympic Games, mega-events and civil societies: globalization, environment, resistance.* Basingstoke: Palgrave Macmillan.

Herzfeld, M. 2005. *Cultural intimacy: social poetics in the nation-state.* 2nd ed. London: Routledge.

Hesmondhalgh, D. 2013. *The cultural industries.* 3rd ed. London: SAGE.

Hevey, D. 1992. *The creatures time forgot: photography and disability imagery.* London: Routledge.

Hibberd, L. 2015. Provoking a public service: Paralympic broadcasting and the discourse of disability on Channel 4. In: D. Jackson et al. eds. *Reframing disability? Media, (dis)empowerment, and voice in the 2012 Paralympics.* Oxford: Routledge, pp. 94–104.

Horne, J. 2007. The four 'knowns' of sports mega-events. *Leisure Studies*, 26(1), pp. 81–96.

Horne, J. and Manzenreiter, W. 2006. Sports mega-events: social scientific analyses of a global phenomenon. *Sociological Review*, 54(Suppl. 2), pp. 1–187.

Horne, J. and Whannel, G. 2012. *Understanding the Olympics*. Abingdon, Oxon; New York: Routledge.

Howe, P.D. 2008a. *The cultural politics of the Paralympic movement: through an anthropological lens*. Abingdon, Oxon; New York: Routledge.

Howe, P.D. 2008b. From inside the newsroom: Paralympic media and the 'production' of elite disability. *International Review for the Sociology of Sport*, 43(2), pp. 135–150.

Hunt, P. 1966. *Stigma: the experience of disability*. London: Chapman.

IPC. 1989. *Vision mission and values*. [Online]. [Accessed 24 May 2014]. Available from: www.paralympic.org/IPC

Jackson, D. 2013. *2012 Paralympics changed people's perceptions of disability and disabled sport, BU study finds*. [Online]. [Accessed 31 October 2016]. Available from: www.bournemouth.ac.uk/

Katz, E. 2009. The end of television? *The Annals of the American Academy of Political and Social Science*, 625, pp. 6–18.

Katz, E. and Dayan, D. 1986. Contests, conquests, coronations: on media events and their heroes. In: C.F. Graumann and S. Moscovici eds. *Changing conceptions of leadership*. New York: Springer Series in Social Psychology, pp. 25–53.

Kearney, S., Brittain, I., and Kipnis, E. 2019. 'Superdisabilities' vs 'disabilities'? Theorizing the role of ableism in (mis)representational mythology of disability in the marketplace. *Consumption Markets & Culture*, 22(5–6), pp. 545–567.

Kellner, D. 2011. Cultural studies, multiculturalism, and media culture. In: *Gender, race, and class in media: a critical reader*. 3rd ed. Thousand Oaks, CA: SAGE, pp. 7–18.

Kidd, J. 2015. *Representation*. London: Routledge.

Lewis, D. 2005. Against the grain: black women and sexuality. *Agenda*, 19(63), pp. 11–24.

Longmore, P.K. 1987. Screening stereotypes: images of disabled people in television and motion pictures. In: A. Gartner and T. Joe eds. *Images of the disabled, disabling images*. New York; London: Praeger, pp. 65–78.

Maguire, J.A. 1993. Globalization, sport development and the media/sport production complex. *Sports Science Review*, 2(1), pp. 29–47.

Mann, D. 2009. It's not TV, it's brand management TV. In: V. Mayer et al. eds. *Production studies: cultural studies of media industries*. New York; London: Routledge, pp. 99–141.

Marshall, P.D., Walker, B., and Russo, N. 2010. Mediating the Olympics. *Convergence: The International Journal of Research into New Media Technologies*, 16(3), pp. 263–278.

Mayer, V. 2011. *Below the line: producers and production studies in the new television economy*. Durham, NC: Duke University Press.

McGillivray, D., O'Donnell, H., McPherson, G., and Misener, L. 2019. Repurposing the (super)crip: media representations of disability at the Rio 2016 Paralympic Games. *Communication & Sport*. Online.

Mitchell, D.T. and Snyder, S.L. 2014. *Narrative prosthesis: disability and the dependencies of discourse*. University of Michigan Press.

Morley, D. 2006. Unanswered questions in audience research. *The Communication Review*, 9(2), pp. 101–121.

Oliver, M. 1983. *Social work with disabled people*. London: Macmillan, for the British Association of Social Workers.

Oliver, M. 1996. *Understanding disability: from theory to practice*. Basingstoke: Macmillan.

Oliver, M. 2013. The social model of disability: thirty years on. *Disability & Society*, 28(7), pp. 1024–1026, DOI: 10.1080/09687599.2013.818773

Oliver, M. and Barnes, C. 2016. *The new politics of disablement*. London: Palgrave Macmillan.

Olympia. 1938. [film]. Leni Riefenstahl. dir. Berlin: GmbH [de].

Orgad, S. 2012. *Media representation and the global imagination*. Cambridge: Polity Press.

Parry, K. 2010. A visual framing analysis of British press photography during the 2006 Israel-Lebanon conflict. *Media, War and Conflict*, 3(1), pp. 67–85.

Philo, G. 2012. *Bad news for disabled people: how the newspapers are reporting disability*. [Online]. Glasgow: University of Glasgow.

Prendergast, C. 2000. *The triangle of representation*. New York: Columbia University Press.

Pullen, E., Jackson, D., Silk, M., and Scullion, R. 2019. Re-presenting the Paralympics: (contested) philosophies, production practices and the hypervisibility of disability. *Media, Culture & Society*, 41(4), pp. 465–481.

Purdue, D.E.J. and Howe, P.D. 2012. See the sport, not the disability: exploring the Paralympic paradox. *Qualitative Research in Sport, Exercise and Health*, 4(2), pp. 189–205.

Riefenstahl, L. 1938. See *Olympia*.

Roche, M. 2000. *Mega-events and modernity: Olympics and expos in the growth of global culture*. London: Routledge.

Roche, M. 2006. Mega-events and modernity revisited: globalization and the case of the Olympics. *The Sociological Review*, 54(2_suppl), pp. 27–40.

Ross, K. 2011. But where's me in it? Disability, broadcasting and the audience. *Media, Culture and Society*, 19(4), pp. 669–677.

Ross, K. and Sreberny, A. 2000. Women in the house: media representation of British politicians. In: *Gender, politics and communication*, pp. 79–99.

Rowe, D. 1999. *Sport, culture and the media*. Buckingham: Open University Press.

Rowe, D. 2003. *Sport, culture and media*. McGraw-Hill Education.

Saha, A. 2012. 'Beards, scarves, halal meat, terrorists, forced marriage': television industries and the production of 'race'. *Media, Culture and Society*, 34(4), pp. 424–438.

Said, E.W. 1979. *Orientalism*. Hertford: Penguin Modern Classic.

Saussure, F., trans. Bally, C., Sechehaye, A., Reidlinger, A. and Baskin, W. 1974. *Course in general linguistics*. Revised ed./introduction by Jonathan Culler. ed. London: Owen.

Schantz, O. and Marty, C. 1995. The French press and sport for people with handicapping conditions. In: I. Morisback and P.E. Jorgensen eds. *Quality of life through adapted physical activity*. Oslo: Hamtrykk, pp. 72–79.

Schantz, O. and Gilbert, K. 2012. *Heroes or zeros? The media's perceptions of Paralympic Sport*. Champaign, IL: Common Ground.

Schell, B.L.A. and Rodriguez, S. 2001. Subverting bodies/ambivalent representations: media analysis of Paralympian, Hope Lewellen. *Sociology of Sport Journal*, 18(1), pp. 127–135.

Shakespeare, T. 1994. Cultural representation of disabled people: dustbins for disavowal? *Disability and Society*, 9(3), pp. 283–299.

Shakespeare, T. 1998. *The disability reader: social science perspectives*. London: Cassell.

Shakespeare, T. 2013. *Disability rights and wrongs revisited*. Taylor & Francis Online.

Shakespeare, T. and Watson, N. 2001. The 'social model' of disability: an outdated ideology? In: *Exploring theories and expanding methodologies: where we are and where we need to go*. Bingley: Emerald Group Publishing Limited, pp. 9–28. https://doi.org/10.1016/S1479-3547(01)80018-X

Silva, C.F. and Howe, P.D. 2012. The (in)validity of supercrip representation of Paralympian athletes. *Journal of Sport and Social Issues*, 36(2), pp. 174–194.

Smith, A. 2003. *Chosen peoples*. Oxford: Oxford University Press.

Smith, B. and Bundon, A. 2018. Disability models: explaining and understanding disability sport in different ways. In: *The Palgrave handbook of Paralympic studies*. London: Palgrave Macmillan, pp. 15–34.

Smith, A. and Thomas, N. 2005. The 'inclusion' of elite athletes with disabilities in the 2002 Manchester Commonwealth Games: an exploratory analysis of British newspaper coverage. *Sport, Education and Society*, 10(1), pp. 49–67.

Steyn, J. 2016. Vicissitudes of representation: remembering and forgetting. In: *Challenging history in the museum: international perspectives*. Surrey: Ashgate.

Thomas, C. 2007. *Sociologies of disability and illness. Contested ideas in disability studies and medical sociology*. Palgrave Macmillan.

Tomlinson, A. and Young, C. 2006. Culture, politics, and spectacle in the global sports event: an introduction. In: A. Tomlinson and C. Young eds. *National identity and global sporting events: culture, politics and spectacle in the Olympics and the Football World Cup*. Albany: State University of York, pp. 1–14.

Thumim, N. 2015. *Self-representation and digital culture*. Basingstoke: Palgrave Macmillan.

Tritter, J.Q. and McCallum, A. 2006. The snakes and ladders of user involvement: moving beyond Arnstein. *Health Policy*, 76(2), pp. 156–168.

UPIAS. 1976. *Fundamental principles of disability*. Disability Online.

Webb, J. 2009. *Understanding representation*. London: SAGE.

Wenner, L.A. 1998. *MediaSport*. London: Psychology Press.

Wenner, L.A. 2009. *Sport, beer, and gender: promotional culture and contemporary social life*. Southampton: Peter Lang.

Whannel, G. 1992. *Fields in vision: television sport and cultural transformation*. London: Routledge.

Whannel, G. 2008. *Culture, politics and sport: blowing the whistle, revisited*. London: Routledge.

Whannel, G. and Tomlinson, A. 1984. *Five ring circus: money, power and politics at the Olympic Games*. London: Pluto.

Williams, R. 1983. *Culture and society, 1780–1950*. Columbia University Press.

Wood, C. 2013. *One year on: a review of the cultural legacy of the Paralympic Games*. London: Demos.

World Health Organization. 2001. *International classification of functioning, disability and health: ICF short version.* Geneva: WHO.

Wren-Lewis, J. 1983. The encoding/decoding model: criticisms and redevelopments for research on decoding. *Media, Culture and Society*, 5(2), pp. 179–197.

Young, S. 2014. *Stella Young, inspiration porn, and the objectification of disabled people.* Available from: https://disabilityvisibilityproject.com/2014/10/16/stella-young-inspiration-porn-and-the-objectification-of-disabled-people/

Zoellner, A. 2009. Professional ideology and program conventions: documentary development in independent British television production. *Mass Communication and Society*, 12(4), pp. 503–536.

Chapter 3

Riskier representations

Channel 4's public service broadcast model

The domestic Paralympics media coverage, for Sydney 2000, Athens 2004, and Beijing 2008, produced for the UK in Northern Europe, was supplied by the licence-funded and globally renowned BBC. But for London 2012, when the UK was the host nation, it rather surprisingly wasn't, and that decision had ramifications for what was to appear onscreen.

For each cycle of the Games, the IPC sells the broadcasting rights of the Paralympics to broadcasters all around the world. Each of those broadcasters buys the rights to stream or broadcast the Paralympics in their territory, including the broadcaster in the host territory, who has to bid for it. Other countries also have access to the live event feed that can be shown within their own territories, giving an opportunity for them to reinforce their own national and cultural narratives through their programming around that feed.

It is often, therefore, Public Service Media (PSM) or state-controlled media that will bid for these quadrennial rights (which is perhaps why take-up of the Paralympics in the United States had historically been so poor). However, the global reach of that domestic coverage is limited, as the media offered by the host broadcaster, even on their digital streams, is geo-blocked beyond their own national borders. Therefore the reader of this chapter, from outside the UK, may not be aware that it was Britain's niche public service provider, Channel 4, who created the host nation mass media content for the Games, that the IPC described as the 'game-changer'.

The public service, free-to-air TV network was considered to be a 'challenger brand' (see Morgan, 2009) to the BBC, much as the Paralympics had been to the Olympics. One of the key decision-makers for the broadcasting rights bid, Greg Nugent, discussed this dynamic for creating change with me, saying he felt that Channel 4 was therefore uniquely placed to break new ground (*Interview*, 2019). This chapter explores the industrial contexts surrounding some of the ways in which they were able to do that.

In the UK, Channel 4 is renowned for its risk-taking and was designed to be that way from its inception (Burns, 1977; Brown, 2007). The facility for taking risk was uniquely built into the corporation's fundamental structures (see Harvey, 2003; Darlow, 2004) and in this chapter I argue that this industrial context particularly enabled risky representations. Drawing on interviews and documentary analysis, I will show how risk-taking was facilitated by Channel 4's organisational, financial, and regulatory structures and how this taking of risk enabled ground-breaking onscreen representations of disability. Born (2004) asks of the BBC, 'what kind of an organisation is [it], and why does it matter?' (p. 67). Her answer applies equally well to Channel 4 that, 'above all, it matters because it affects what is made' (ibid.). Both organisations are public service broadcasters, and both have a parliamentary remit that regulates the quality and content of their programming. In Channel 4's case this regulation includes taking risks both with programmes and also with the workforce.

In addition to the public service remit I found two other external and internal structures that also affected what was made and this chapter is devoted to examining and analysing the impact of all three on the 2012 Paralympics media coverage. Critical political economy theorists, particularly of media production and communication (e.g. Mosco, 1996; Garnham, 2005; Wasko et al., 2011; Dwyer, 2015; Murdock and Golding, 2016), have made an urgent call for research to analyse the way meaning is made, incorporating economic dynamics but with a broader scope (Murdock and Golding, 2016, p. 5). The need, they say, is to illuminate the connections between 'the concrete practices of production and the wider organisational and economic shifts that shape them' (ibid.). In particular this research perspective strives to go 'beyond structural features to assess the consequences for daily practice' (ibid.). They have gone as far, in the past, as describing these as 'concrete consequences' (Golding and Murdock, 2000, p. 84) and I draw out clear concrete examples in the discussion that follows.

Utilising this perspective, I use my research findings to show that the unique *funding mechanism* of Channel 4 had a direct bearing on risk-taking, for the acquisition of the Paralympic project in the first instance, and by providing protection against attempted risk-associated stakeholder vetoes regarding innovative representations of disability. The financial organisation also created a need for corporate sponsors, whose presence and finances stabilised other risks. I then show how the *organisational structure* facilitated flexibility amongst the various decision-makers to enable risk-taking with the framing of onscreen disability portrayals. Whilst the Channel 4 *parliamentary remit* will be a repeating theme throughout this book, in this chapter I look specifically at two effects of its power, to facilitate innovative risk-taking and to take risks with the make-up of the production workforce (*Digital Economy Act*, 2010, Section 22).

The remit also protects a public service mandate into which is built a commercial motivation (Harvey, 1994). None of the other channels available in the UK, whether terrestrial or via satellite, has a public service remit that includes developing new talent as well as shaping society's attitude through education without being accountable to either the government, a Board of Governors, or shareholders (ibid.). This makes Channel 4's business model a unique focus for researching influential structures and the relationships between these that, either directly or indirectly, affect the creative process. I begin with the funding mechanism, then the organisational structure before discussing the impact of the parliamentary remit below.

Funding mechanism

In this section I will show how the funding mechanism that is part of Channel 4's business model, enabled, rather than constrained, risk-taking. Firstly, I show how the decision to broadcast the Paralympics as 'live' mainstream sports coverage was influenced by the way that programmes were funded. With Channel 4, the advertising revenue pays for next year's programming and this dictates the make-up of Channel 4's schedules based on the need for income generation. I show how an emerging schedule deficit prompted the selection of the Paralympics to fill a gap. Secondly I highlight how the security and structure of the funding mechanism gave power to the producers at Channel 4 seeking change, to resist the attempted vetoes by external stakeholders of the newly realistic depictions of disability. Thirdly this section explains how the addition of necessary corporate sponsors helped to stabilise some of the risks that were being taken by Channel 4.

The three dominant broadcasting organisations in the UK have each been defined by their funding mechanisms, namely the licence fee for BBC, subscriptions for Sky, and advertising revenues for ITV. Channel 4 is structured differently, being publicly owned but commercially funded. It has been defined more by its output irrespective of the funding model, which has changed already once, since its inception in 1982 (Darlow, 2004). Doing things differently at Channel 4 was the mantra of everyone that I interviewed, as understood by their remit, and the *difference in the funding model* particularly had a bearing on the representations of disability that made it to the screens during the Paralympic Games of 2012. It also had a bearing on the fact that the Channel 4 coverage happened at all.

When I walked into the office of Kevin Lygo, who had been Head of Channel 4 Television at the time of their bid for the broadcasting rights for the Paralympics, his opening comment demonstrated that financial considerations were central to why he had chosen the Paralympics and bid for the broadcasting rights. He initially said, when casting his mind back to 2009, 'I do remember it had something to do with *Big Brother*' (Head of Television, *Interview*, 2015). He then recalled saying to his team at the time:

> You won't have *Big Brother*. Do you understand? It's going to be a
> fucking nightmare without *Big Brother*? [sic.] Get real! Get ready for a
> very cold wind especially in the summer.
>
> (Head of Television, *Interview*, 2015)

This live production had been a huge show that almost redefined the channel
when it arrived, being the first in the UK of its, since much-copied, genre.
Whilst other executives, as I will show later, were concerned about the
channel brand and reputation, also, curiously, in relation to *Big Brother*,
for the primary decision-maker at the inception of the project, this was still
very much driven by the funding mechanism. He told me:

> It was all up to me as to what I did with the £700 million or whatever
> it was that I spend every year, so in the scheme of things, you know I
> wish I could remember, 25 million – whatever it was, in the scheme of
> things [not much]. It was one of those bloody great holes in the sum-
> mer [schedule] anyway and money had come free because *Big Brother*
> wasn't there and also it is 2009 for 2012. It is great to say, I don't
> remember anybody saying anything other than 'oh that's a good idea'.
>
> (Head of Television, *Interview*, 2015)

Lygo clearly did not regard the acquisition of the broadcasting rights as
much of a risk 'in the scheme of things'. He simply had to shell out a small
portion of his budget to fill the schedule and it was 'all up to me', he said.
The Paralympics provided Lygo with a solution to a deficit problem and
his thinking for a solution was, 'It's going to be hours and hours of telly,
it's going to be an event, it's going to be "live"' (ibid.). The value of 'live
sport' (which continues to deliberately give the appearance of being 'live'
even when it is pre-recorded and edited), for a commercially funded broadcaster, is that it holds the audience for the advertising breaks (Wenner,
1998; Horne, 2006). I take up the strategy of purchasing sport audiences
further in Chapter 6. What is significant here is that the Paralympics was an
opportunity he could buy. In this interview with the chief decision-maker,
disability, as yet, had not been mentioned.

As the controller of the schedule with money to burn, and money to
recoup, he demonstrates his consideration and calculation of the risk:

> We thought that if we're going to do this, it is only two weeks actually
> on the air – and I know what the BBC will be like – they will be compla-
> cent. It will be the same as they have always done it, they won't be pay-
> ing much money for it – it wasn't viewed very heavily – but for us, you
> know, why wouldn't you get 2 million viewers, type thing? And that is
> fine for Channel 4 anyway, and it is so beautifully public service and
> we can pick up the coverage and tell the stories. [We could] redesign it;

being that we would not only show a lot more of the events than ever before – I mean I can't remember but – I mean five or six times more!

(Head of Television, *Interview*, 2015)

It was in Lygo's thought processes, therefore, to purchase 2 million viewers and fill the hole left by *Big Brother*. This is a significant motivation, distinct from a desire to change perceptions about disability, that influenced the decision to broadcast the Games. Richeri (2003) stresses the importance of highlighting 'how financial organisation acts on the creation and circulation of content and its meaning' (p. 131). Channel 4's Head of Television, in this instance, had the money available and makes it clear there was a financial consideration affecting the acquisition of the London 2012 Games. He explained to me that Channel 4 relies for its funding, largely, on its advertising revenues to provide the commissioning budget for the following year. Therefore, the schedule needs to be full and consistently attracting an audience that advertisers will want to advertise to. In this case, the funding mechanism directly affected the creation and later circulation of the Paralympic Games coverage – which went on to achieve an unexpected 11.8 million viewers for the opening ceremony (C4, 2013) making the circulation significant too.

It was Lygo who introduced *Big Brother* to the screens in 2000 and it was he who axed it a decade later. It may therefore have been a personally or politically motivated decision to prevent the 'cold wind' he predicted for that summer in such a risky way. Garnham (1995) writes that:

A delimited social group, pursuing economic or political ends determines which meanings circulate and which do not, which stories are told about what, which arguments are given prominence and what cultural resources are made available to whom.

(p. 65)

In this case, the initial determinant for the meanings that were then to circulate about Paralympic athletes in 2012 did indeed have economic roots and possibly political ones. The first reason was embedded into the structure of Channel 4 but the second was personal and serendipitous. Later, his successor, is recalled by others to have thought this project a 'financial disaster', but could do nothing about the inherited deal as it was signed and sealed in 2009. This serendipitous moment, then, and the risk taken, set the course of all that was to follow, making an understanding of how it came about all the more important to understand.

No shareholders

Channel 4 exists in a unique production setting, even though commercially funded, because it is publicly owned and therefore does not have shareholders. This is a crucial part of being able to take unfettered risks, allowing Lygo the autonomy to achieve the following, as he put it:

> We do our pirate thing of stealing it from the BBC, we'll do it properly, we are genuinely committed to the promotion of disability and the community – and it hits the sweet spot of Channel 4.
>
> (Head of Television, *Interview*, 2015)

Opting to outbid the BBC to buy an audience has a slight risk attached to it, but it would have been much harder to persuade a board of directors seeking dividends, or shareholders looking to make a profit for themselves, to agree with his idea. Lygo considered that transmitting 'hours and hours' of disability sport was a risk worth taking. Purely commercial operators may well not have agreed with this. Without the funding mechanism in place for the channel, Lygo may not have been allowed, by others with vested interests, the freedom to bid for the broadcasting rights, and audience perceptions about disability might still be where they were in 2011. The outcome that was BAFTA-winning and caused a cultural shift in attitudes towards a minority (BDRC, 2012) was one of the 'concrete consequences' (Golding and Murdock, 2000, p. 84) of Channel 4 being set up the way that it was. Sir Jeremy Isaacs, founding CEO of Channel 4, told me that the way the Paralympics coverage unfolded and what it achieved, by taking so many risks, was derived directly from the 'DNA of the channel' (Former CEO, *Interview*, 2015) that he had helped design at its inception.

The second way in which risks were protected and enabled is again down to the absence of shareholders. There were two groups of stakeholders that vehemently objected to the *Meet the Superhumans* advertising trailer, in particular an eight second sequence in the middle. This included soldiers caught in an explosion, a car crash, and a maternity hospital 'bad news' scene. The Channel 4 shock depictions challenged existing ideas about disability being only about 'others', with the potential for the audience to feel less safe about their own identities. I discuss this conflict in the next chapter, on representations, but need to establish here that this segment is what most of my participants considered the defining lynchpin for the new framings of disabled sportsmen and women. If the funding mechanism had not been in place, to prevent a veto from outside voices, creative risks would have been compromised and the opportunity to shape new meanings potentially lost. Objection letters were written, including from the Head of the International Paralympic Committee, who according to the Disability Executive 'kicked up an absolute storm about it' (*Interview*, 2015) but as the in-house Chief Marketing and Communications Officer told me 'it was our money' (*Interview*, 2014) so they took the risks and transmitted the portrayals anyway.

Whilst it is tempting to imagine that it was solely in their capacity as a public service broadcaster that Channel 4 was inspired to take this risky path, the Business Director makes it clear that the financial structure also dictated what they could do. He compared the models operated by the BBC with their own at Channel 4. Whilst both broadcasters have a public service remit, it was other considerations that affected and enabled the risks that they did take. He explained:

> The BBC are very different because everyone pays a tax or whatever you want to call it, so everyone owns a bit of the BBC so you can't push the boundaries too far because you are going to be speaking to a very small part of your big audience. Channel 4 can do all that stuff, it's why it was set up in the first place. There have been very few opportunities for Channel 4 to flex those muscles since *Big Brother* so the Paralympics was a perfect opportunity to actually reassert why the channel was set up in the first place. And to go 'you know what, this is exactly – only Channel 4 could do what we [can] do with the Paralympics, literally only Channel 4 could do that' – because the BBC would NEVER do a 90-second trail showing people being blown up in a car with a Public Enemy hip-hop track.
>
> (Business Manager, *Interview*, 2015)

Murdock and Golding assert that economic dynamics define the key features of communication processes (Golding and Murdock, 1991, p. 19) and Channel 4's Business Director demonstrated a clear understanding of this dynamic. He particularly told me:

> ITV are driven by profit, they are a business. If people don't [love it], they don't get their ratings, if people don't feel good about it, if people watch less ITV – that can't ever be their strategy because they'll die as a business in the longer term.
>
> (Business Manager, *Interview*, 2015)

Mosco (2009) argues that, beyond purely economic and political aims, mass media institutions are predisposed 'to advance social life as opposed to simply having commercial purposes' (2009, p. 4). However it is clear, from the above interview, that ITV are not in a position to advance social life by taking risks with their audience, because they will then 'die as a business'. The uniqueness of Channel 4's funding mechanism therefore shaped and protected the creative processes associated with meaning-making and the reshaping of attitudes towards disability. Retaining autonomous editorial judgement is something that Channel 4 were able to do, according to the Head of Television, Chief Marketing and Communications Officer and the Business Director, as I have shown above. My assertion is that being free to take financial risks and creative ones was a key factor in being able to change perceptions in society.

It is clear from existing scholarship (Richeri, 2003; Wasko et al., 2011; Dwyer, 2015) that meaning-making should specifically be analysed from the perspective of the way the finances are organised, which this study also does. The power of stakeholder veto is an important one, particularly in relation to minority group representations, and absolutely needed to be resisted in this case. Many of my participants either associated the element of risk with their channel brand (see Chapter 6) or referred to risk as stemming from the remit (see below). My argument here is that it was the unique *funding mechanism* of Channel 4 that ensured they had full editorial judgement and control over other vested interests, and these powers facilitated the risk-taking. This second 'concrete consequence' of the business model on the Paralympic Games was that Channel 4 could prevent outside stakeholders (the British Paralympic Association and the International Paralympic Committee) from stopping *them* taking risks with the representations that might have challenged public feeling. There is more detail about this in upcoming chapters.

Corporate sponsors

The third influence that the funding arrangements had on the London 2012 Paralympic media coverage was the inbuilt extra necessity of finding additional corporate sponsors. Funded entirely by the previous year's advertising revenue, it was of huge importance to Channel 4, who had paid a lot for the broadcasting rights, to sign up corporate sponsors as marketing companions, with their financial contributions essential to offset the production budget. Had the corporation been funded by subscriptions, or from the annual licence fee, Sainsbury's and BT would not perhaps have been brought on board. Meanings were affected by the sponsors they chose, as well as budgets. The Project Leader for the Paralympics noted that the particular combination of niche broadcaster, Channel 4, partnered with a 'major' supermarket chain, Sainsbury's, and a 'massive' telecommunications company, BT, was a deliberate choice of hers (Project Leader, *Interview*, 2016). Although choices like these are not always obvious from the outside, Corner (2013) considers strategic selection a naturalised process (p. 57) for political purposes and for the propagation of powerful messages. Certainly, these brand alliances were powerful message carriers for Poulton. As Project Leader she considered the strong combined network she had created as vital for the success of the Paralympics coverage and the meanings they would be able to project.

Channel 4 chose these two companies' differing visions to add richer content and meaning for the wider mix of television audiences that they were expecting, after putting the sponsorship deals out to tender. Films and inserts were made by, and for, both companies and these were also transmitted throughout the other programming across the schedule. Kerr (2018) has found that other potential sponsors thought they were too late to be included. In fact the key decision-maker intentionally selected the specific two only, on purpose, for strategic reasons. Poulton chose these two, because of the funding they brought with them, but also because Sainsbury's had a 'wholesome' approach which she wanted to blend with BT's outlook that was 'a little more edgy' (Project Leader, *Interview*, 2016). I discuss other aspects of these sponsorship arrangements in Chapter 6 as part of the marketing and branding initiative. However, I include them here because these two companies were needed not only for funding, but also to add value and enhance the reach and specific messaging of the media coverage. Here again, this is another example of meanings and circulation being driven by underlying financial organisation (see Richeri, 2003; Murdock and Golding, 2016).

In this case, 'wholesome' and 'edgy' were added to a 'niche public service' framing and distributed as a blended meaning via two differing types of national networks beyond the television environment. These 'horizontal lines of communication' (see Castells, 2011, pp. 1976–1977), personally selected by Poulton, had far-reaching consequences across Britain with initiatives taking place in schools, supermarkets, and on billboards across the UK. All these initiatives fed into the television coverage of the 12 days of the Paralympics. This situation suggests that theories of connectivity and consequence need again to be updated, to include wider networked business practices, for example, using even supermarket networks, to consolidate meanings within media production.

It was a huge vision, set out at the beginning before production began, that the Paralympics should no longer be a poor second cousin to the Olympics, as it had been perceived on the BBC. However, in televisual terms, there was no corresponding budget to match that aspiration. My final point about these corporate sponsors is that the two partner organisations contributed, on Poulton's recollection, £1 million each towards the production costs. This extra money enabled the risk of attempting visual parity with the Olympic Games. I suggest that the additional cameras, and camera angles, needed to achieve the Olympic-style media coverage created by Channel 4, were a vital ingredient in the normalisation process of disability. The effect on meanings that were made by these additional resources, alongside other attempts as Olympic parity, are discussed more fully in later chapters, but were hugely significant for the visual representations of normality.

Other production studies (e.g. Silverstone, 1985; Grindstaff, 2002) have also noted how important the right camera positions are to create recognisable and familiar meanings, and Channel 4 needed to supplement the existing ones as these were insufficient for a mega-event sports treatment. More than one of my contributors observed that without the corporate sponsorship deals the high quality of Channel 4's television coverage could not have been achieved. Channel 4 has the freedom to engage in commercial activities to fund its production budgets (Harvey, 1994) and the selection of the two chosen partner brands therefore had a direct impact on creativity and content delivery, and arguably the ability to woo the BBC Olympic audience across to Channel 4.

The beleaguered Rio 2016 Games, by stark contrast, even though it was hosting high-profile Brazilian Paralympian athletes for its home audience, suffered financial cuts in July 2016. The Rio Organising Committee felt that they couldn't afford any extra expense, so only 13 of the 22 sports had live TV feeds supplied by the OBS (Olympic Broadcasting Service). This clearly did not achieve parity with the mainstream Olympic broadcasting for the parasports athletes, nor could they have afforded the 'money shot' (Grindstaff, 2002) extra trackside cameras that Channel 4 used some of their corporate sponsorship for. Opportunities for athlete endorsements to help fund their training and advertising revenues were also consequently lost. It is, of course, easy for better resourced Northern European countries to be more inclusive, and afford nuanced output, nevertheless the flow of money, or lack of it, can be seen to have a direct consequence for minority representations and diverse (in)visibility onscreen. The conditions for funding media production therefore matter if marginalised 'others' are to be sustainably included within the mainstream.

From the above London examples drawn from my empirical material, I have shown that the funding mechanism performed a structural role directly affecting the overall media coverage of 2012, and also the construction of nuanced meanings. The way the finances are organised within the business model of Channel 4 explicitly facilitated the taking of risks, and provided editorial autonomy over outside stakeholders. This same mechanism included a requirement to reach out to external sponsors, who brought other powers of persuasion and brand messaging along with their financial backing. In this case decisions were made with care and judgement but it does not necessarily follow that in other cases this combination of roles, resources, and revenue pools would be as sensitively handled. It does help that Channel 4 is a small organisation with a lot of cross accountability, and this is discussed further below.

Organisational structure

In this section I will show how the organisation of Channel 4, particularly as it compares to the much larger licence-funded BBC, meant that people had to double up, be flexible, and work in ways that actually increased the risks that they could take. I will also show how it gave them the ability to discuss different approaches. Born (2004) in her study of the BBC, discusses the loss of vertical integration in that structure (p. 132).

A comparison, here, with Channel 4's more fluid organisational structure and flexible ecology will show how the differing production environments do affect decisions made and levels of risk that can be taken with framing and programme content.

Creativity and commerce, as one might expect, were symbiotically linked in the case of the London 2012 Paralympic Games. Changing dynamics were traceable throughout my interviews, reminiscent of the 'marriage' between commerce and creativity described by Hesmondhalgh (2013, p. 249), in the field of popular music. The inherent tensions of this relationship within the television production process are exacerbated when a client relationship is introduced, but, as I discovered, those tensions can also enhance creativity and make the ground for new ideas more fertile.

The success of the funding combination with sponsors, discussed above, relied heavily on 'client management', or as the Project Leader put it in this case, a 'healthy positive collaborative engagement' with Sainsbury's and BT, who were their clients. Poulton had to carefully handle Sainsbury's queries about, for example, the hip-hop street framing of their shared Paralympian actors, or the 'close-up lingering' on Jonnie Peacock's artificial leg, and she managed to keep the clients on side. Elliott (1972) stresses the importance of investigating 'the organisational setting and the social context' (p. 144) in which programme production takes place. It is true here that for Channel 4, as a publisher-broadcaster, these external relationships were key to their ability to create meaningful content. The channel's autonomy, according to my research evidence, remained intact for these partnerships in 2012. In spite of having cultivated friendly relationships, ultimate editorial power was written into the contracts in favour of Channel 4 (Commercial Lawyer, *Interview*, 2015). The evidence from my contributors suggests that in-house power was retained in all of the collaborations, to maintain the creative freedom Channel 4's remit protects.

Freedom to take creative risks was essential to framing a disabled group who might be potentially considered repulsive (see Chapter 2), in order for them to be acceptable to the 'normal' audience in the mainstream television schedules. The 1990 *Broadcasting Act* asserts the need for Channel 4 to make programmes that *ITV* would not make. This has a definite risk implication. Yet within the organisation, most of my participants saw themselves as making something that in fact *the BBC* would not make. This may be an artificial comparison in the sense that only the BBC had ever produced the Paralympics before for the UK, and with a different brief. However the key dimension of comparison was consistently the level of 'risk' rather than the subject matter itself. In all bar one of my cases the contributors vocalised the creative freedom as being something they felt was unique to Channel 4. The only dissenter was an outsourced independent sports producer, for whom disability was not on his radar. His sports provision, widely used by many broadcasters, carries, in his opinion, no risk in any case.

The BBC has a large workforce of thousands that has layers of management, committees, and procedures to inhibit impromptu decisions (Burns, 1977; Schlesinger, 1987; Silverstone, 1985; Born, 2004). By contrast, Channel 4 is very small with less than 800 employees (Chief Marketing and Communications Officer, *Interview*, 2014). One of their business managers utilised Channel 4's distinctive organisational arrangement to extend the possibilities for portrayals of disability within their media coverage. He worked closely with the Channel 4 Disability Executive throughout and they both separately spoke of the battles they had gone through together. It was a distinctive element of their project that the teams pulled together where necessary. On one occasion, when an academic researcher was brought in to advise, telling them 'not to show people the stumps', the Disability Executive told me she had resisted. As she recalled in our interview:

> It wasn't just me, it was everybody in the room, all the producers, said, 'No, wait a minute. Well that's not how we're going to do it, because Channel 4 doesn't do programmes like that and we've got a remit to bring disability into the mainstream and to make people familiar with it'. You don't make them familiar with it by not showing it.
> (Disability Executive, *Interview*, 2015)

They were able to retain their creative power in this situation because they were all together in one room. It was not a question of memos passing across desks and sub-committees, an entrenched practice that Born (2004) noted at the BBC. This same situation with the academic acted as a catalyst for the Chief Marketing and Communications Officer who said for him the pronouncement that people needed to be treated gently was 'a red rag to a bull' (*Interview*, 2014). The team continued on their track of redefining how to present disability to the public, possibly with even more intent, or as they started to say themselves, 'Channel 4-style'. At different levels within the organisation, individuals felt they had autonomy and this permeated down from the Head of Channel 4 Television. He said:

> I think there is something gloriously unaccountable about Channel 4 and so when it's working well, in the job I had, you could just do anything you wanted and you don't really see it that way at the time, but nobody would ever tell you 'don't do this' or 'do do that'.
> (Head of Television, *Interview*, 2015)

Historically this had been the case too, as Sir Jeremy Isaacs explained to me in a telephone interview, 'no one could say no to us' (former CEO, *Interview*, 2015) because this power was built into their structure as an organisation, on purpose.

As well as the freedom of autonomy there was also considerable freedom to communicate powerful feelings both onscreen and off. There were several emotive and passionate expressions used by the decision-makers. One had been that 'red rag to a bull' experience when the researcher came in to brief their collective ranks. Another hugely significant one, that may have partly set the trajectory for the project, was what the Project Leader called her 'fire in the belly' moment. This decision to do even more for disability sport was, as the academic advice had been, triggered by someone whom she disagreed with, who wanted to sideline disability and make it invisible. The impact, though, comes from the multiple roles of the person she passed it on to, Tom Tagholm, Channel 4's Network Creative Director, who was also the film maker of the *Meet the Superhumans* ad. This was how she explained it:

> Tom contacted me on Wednesday afternoon just to get a perspective on what I wanted the marketing trail to have. It just so happened that, that Saturday night, I had been to a dinner party down in a West Sussex pub, and I met, face on, the ugly, ugly, ugly [sic.] face of disability discrimination and it was disgusting and I was really upset by it. It was so black and white, and the person who said it was so unaware of the offence that they would have caused anybody. So when I met with Tom that week I was still really riled by that, and I relayed to Tom in great detail this story about this woman, who said, at the school fundraiser, that this man [a parent with one arm] 'had had the gall to walk around without a jacket over his arm' and how offensive she had found it, and everyone had wanted to run home and hide. I relayed that story to Tom that day and later said 'I hope I really fired you up with that story' and he said 'yes you did'. It was very timely.
>
> (Project Leader, *Interview*, 2016)

This timely moment was a serendipitous piece of the jigsaw that my participants helped me piece together, defining why they took so many risks and did so much more than the BBC had done before (bearing in mind also that this was a Home Games opportunity this time). Poulton went on to tell the woman, who was a friend, what she thought as she was so angry, before leaving promptly. However, the person whom she next told, moved between roles, as several of them did. He was the Head of 4Creative, the influential marketing arm of Channel 4, but then his role became one that could directly shape onscreen representations. He explained that he was unable to secure the Hollywood Film Director he was hoping for, to direct the trailer (anecdotally thought by others to be James Cameron who directed the '*Titanic*'), although that had been his hope at the start. I discuss Tagholm's role in a later chapter but the important organisational issue here is that, due to clashing timetables, he ended up directing the film himself. This multi-functioning role meant that, according to him, he could pass

Poulton's 'fire' directly into the tone, texture, and feel of the film. There were no other layers of creatives, producers, or planners between his shared exchanges with Poulton and the finished piece.

It has been common practice within the commissioning model that an idea, once pitched, is often taken over (e.g. Dornfeld, 1998; Redvall, 2013). Concepts are watered down or changed (D'Acci, 1994; Lieb, 2016) as they are passed through the creative labour roles. Worse still, ideas are now more often strategised rather than inspired, as one of Zoellner's (2016) contributors argues:

> In development it's completely idiotic to say 'Well, I think this topic is interesting, I want to make a film about it'. Total idiocy, one shouldn't even think like that. You have to think about what broadcaster, what slot, what fits into that slot and we try to develop something that fits.
>
> (p. 151)

Born (2004) likewise found that:

> Whereas in the previous, vertically integrated BBC, channels and production departments sat side by side in Television and Radio and cooperated in planning the output, now a streamlined commissioning apparatus based in Broadcast and backed by teams of market analysts and strategists would determine channel strategies and schedules, to be filled by Production as required.
>
> (p. 132)

This diktat by analysts and strategists did not happen in Channel 4's case. There was not a top-down directive to 'do a disability sports event' or anything to satisfy 'the strategy and planning apparatus'. At Channel 4, although there had been a hole in the schedules left by *Big Brother*, it seemed serendipitous that the arrival of the Paralympics opportunity fitted this bill. Many of my contributors felt it had happened somewhat organically.

What they did with the opportunity was more creative because of the organisational set-up and fluidity between roles. Tagholm was able to take creative risks based on the fundamental structure of Channel 4's organisation. The structure, in this case, facilitated multiple conversations that cross-fertilised between teams, and as I will show in Chapters 4 and 6, enabled considerable innovation and risk.

This individual passing on of vision, passion, and even fury, was more exposed and open in the Channel 4 setting than the BBC, as the Project Leader felt she wanted to tell me two years after the event:

> It was never a harmonious project. There was a huge amount of tension because we all wanted to do such a brilliant, brilliant job of it – and because unlike the BBC or ITV we didn't have a 100 strong sports department which is what the BBC have, that is what ITV have. We

were just a disparate group of individuals and we, as a result, had to go out and seek the input and advice of a lot of people and we did that by getting advice from former Paralympians. Ade Adepitan was a central person for us. We assembled a project team of about 30 or 40 people from within the channel and [some] other external people.

(Project Leader, *Interview*, 2016)

Because the group was so small, it was possible to communicate quickly and easily, and not just about her fire and her passion. She continued:

So there was this tension, because…[when we]…reported back at our regular forums we'd have one end of the table going, 'we need cameras in the dressing room we need cameras underneath them as they are diving off the blocks. We need cameras with them in the athletes' studio' – and then the other end of the table are going, 'it's not possible, we don't have that access'. 'Well, we've got to get that access!'

(Project Leader, *Interview*, 2016)

Without the inhibiting nature of an overbearing infrastructure, it seems that creative freedom to take risks arose, particularly for example, with the recurring camera position topic. The visual representation of 'showing the stumps' came to be a key trope that I explain in the next chapter but it was considered by many to be an extremely risky decision. It was facilitated by these early discussions. This group were not simply a sub-committee as they might have been at the BBC. These conversations came out of necessity, close proximity, and doubling up within the production roles. The infrastructure wasn't there for risks to be played down or minimised, mainly because the organisation was so small, as the Project Leader realised shortly after putting in the bid for the broadcasting rights:

Martin [the Commercial Lawyer] rang me in January and said 'we bloody won it', and what was ironic was that we won one of the biggest sporting events in the world, but we didn't have a sports department!

(Project Leader, *Interview*, 2016)

At first this may seem like a challenge, but one of the production managers stressed how the manageable scale of Channel 4's organisation had made a positive difference to their working practice. We were discussing whether it would have been any different if the BBC had won the licence for it. Having worked for both companies his response is significant:

I do quite a bit of stuff for Red Bee [with the BBC]. I have done in the past. And they're a bit more by committee. They're very, very – I mean Channel 4 is not quite the same as it used to be. It's slowly getting a little more watered down. They even say, I mean comparatively – with all the BBC jobs I've done, it's just like 100 people coming and there's so many departments and layers. Maybe sometimes it's good. But in my experience, that many opinions is only going to have one effect. And that is to water an idea down. Unless you've got one person who overall is brave and sort of says, 'Guys, alright, we have to…' and has got a vision of something. Then it will come through. But I don't know. I mean it's hard to say, if it had gone purely down the agency route then there's all that other stuff coming into it, and that worry and angst, which we just didn't have to worry about. We really didn't. I think we just didn't have those extra voices. There was very few [sic.]. There was not tons of input coming in from other people.

(Production Manager, *Interview*, 2014)

Attitudes were shaped in these more intimate settings and this may have had a bearing on how they were able to change so much, compared to the BBC. The last Paralympic coverage of theirs had included only a late-night package of highlights (BBC, 2011), and, whilst obviously not a fair comparison with host nation coverage, may have reflected an attitude that still remains on their Disability Sports webpages:

It is impossible to change everyone's perceptions on the subject of disabled sport. But when it comes down to the ability of people to have their senses opened to the possibility of learning about it, then it's worth trying.

(Hudson, 2004)

Being 'open to the possibility of learning about it' and having 'their senses opened' did not successfully happen four years later with the Beijing 2008 BBC coverage either. But it did with the London 2012 Channel 4 coverage. Whilst this study also explores other contributing factors, the producers felt a key reason was risk-taking. Ideas grew and developed, my contributors refer to 'conflicts' and 'arguments', 'tensions' and even 'battles', but their communications were open and 'epiphanies', 'flips', and 'tipping points' were all repeatedly mentioned. The BBC did offer live coverage in their bid for 2012 but were still rejected by the Organising Committee, according to Nugent (ex-LOCOG Director of Marketing, *Interview*, 2019). Because of the scale of the BBC, the silo mentality of their sports department and other creative departments may have meant that real innovation could never have taken place there. Born (2004) unearthed bureaucracy, internal career manoeuvrings, personal rivalries, and arrogance, during her time at the BBC. What was strikingly different with the Channel 4 creatives was their regularly getting together, apparently on an equal footing. I discuss a key staff 'away day' in detail in the next chapter which affected their internal culture. Here I need to make a structural comparison between what happens when departments are insulated from one another, and when they are not.

There was a pivotal creative moment for Channel 4, which was experienced by the producers at one of these group days away. Contributors told me they suddenly and simply decided to 'remove disability from their thinking' and get excited about the project as if they were doing the 'real' Olympics (something they could never afford). It was only at this point that the project was taken seriously by those creatives present. One of the Business Directors, Kuba Wieczorek, explained the moment:

> There were a couple of internal things that we had organised that I think made us realise that it was a phenomenal creative opportunity. We had a couple of away days in August 2011, two big away days, and then – we sort of – we've analysed at 4Creative that, as a creative opportunity, it was just huge because, just because we all sort of realised that the creative benchmark was so low – that disabled athletes were never treated as real athletes – they were always massively patronised in terms of how they were portrayed in advertising especially. And, you see, we were sort of talking very much about Channel 4's remit – and that hold that Channel 4 has in society – and the two things sort of just came together at that time really.
>
> (Business Director, *Interview*, 2015)

Out of this, the biggest marketing push in their history was born, affecting content, the athletes, the public, and public discourse. Initially the attitude from within the creative production team had been that this project was one that *no one* really wanted to get involved with. It involved liaising with several groups of stakeholders which made it 'rather grubby' according to the 4Creative Business Director. He also said that Channel 4 had initial reservations relating to both themselves and the likely outcomes.

He recalled:

> It ended up infinitely a far larger project than any of us anticipated – so how it started was, it was actually relatively modest and small when 4Creative were first briefed. And I think that is largely due to just the sort of preconceptions we had at Channel 4, but also that society had in general, about disability sport.
>
> (Business Director, *Interview*, 2015)

This was before what he called their 'tipping point':

> After that away day we stopped making a distinction between disabled sports and able-bodied sport. We banned that phrase...we banned that distinction.
>
> (Business Director, *Interview*, 2015)

This is a far cry from the BBC's earlier view that 'when it comes down to the ability of people to have their senses opened to the possibility of learning about it, then it's worth trying' (Hudson, 2004). Banning the phrase 'disabled sport', even amongst the producers was a crucial tipping point for the production team. Paralympics representations were reframed from the inside of the organisation, through personnel changing their own views, and this process was facilitated by the broadcaster's flexible organisational circumstances. Paralympic scholars have since analysed and noted a change in media positioning for athletes at both the 2012 and 2016 Games (e.g. Hodges et al., 2015; McGillivray et al., 2019) and, from the point of view of these pioneering producers, that repositioning started at a Team Away Day. At least the realisation of the need for it did, as they cross-fertilised ideas and experiences that are discussed further in Chapter 4.

Channel 4's internal culture changed as they collectively banned the word 'disability' from their own discourse. This, Wieczorek said, acted as a switch, raising the excitement within the team. I noticed that it resurfaced in his body language as he recalled this moment in our interview. More importantly their group dynamic helped spawn a new trajectory for the entire project away from disabled, special, 'also-rans' to authentic representations of elite athletes. According to Hesmondhalgh (2013), and Banks (2009), 'symbolic meaning' shapes cultural values and comes from the people who hold the 'decision-making-and-breaking powers' (Banks, 2009, pp. 88–89) in above-the-line roles. What is significant about Channel 4 is that they could all sit in one room, making collective decisions seeming to share the sense of risk as a point of group identity.

If there were internal rivalries of the kind that Born (2004) noted, then they diminished during the project. Because of the publisher-broadcaster model there are no long-term production roles to be protected or preserved. Actual programme making is outsourced and this affects the dynamics. It may also, project by project, make them riskier as an organisation. There *was* a rivalry across different roles and levels of editorial decision-making amongst the range of my participants, but this was a channel rivalry with the BBC. The Commercial Lawyer passed comment to me, in a corridor one day when I was leaving the Channel 4 building, that 'of course Channel 4 only exists to snap at the heels of the BBC' but, even so, a desire to do something *better* than them, as well as something *different* to them, was a recurring theme. Jacka (2003) writes that the need for public service broadcasters (PSBs) is over, given the multi-channel options available to air niche or minority programming in other places. However, her argument perhaps overlooks a suggestion that emerges from my research, that a creative tension exists and is developed through more than one channel having a PSB requirement. It provides healthy competition, encourages risk-taking, and forces diverse programming into *mainstream* schedules. For Tokyo 2020, Japan's sole public service broadcaster, NHK, will be undertaking the coverage, as they have since 1964, but with no other PSB to snap at their heels, will their representations be as they were, or as they could be now?

It may be that, following Paris 2024, the BBC will broadcast the Paralympics again, but now 'the genie is out of the bottle', as C4's Head of Marketing put it, they will not be able to pass it off as an afterthought. Indeed they may not even want to, now that the risks have already been taken and broader audience acceptance received. The BBC employed Alison Walsh, the Disability Executive, as a Diversity Officer in their own team, after Channel 4 broadened their version of the role but did not offer her this new contract in 2015. Whether or not she was able to achieve the same goals by taking similar risks, within their different structure, would make interesting further research.

In the case of London 2012 it does seem that the unique Channel 4 business model, with its flexible organisation and fluid editorial roles, facilitated certain key decisions and lots of smaller ones. Individual personalities made a difference, as Chapters 4, 5, and 6 will show, but the range and profile of diverse representations were collectively derived, as many of my participants acknowledged, because they were all 'part of the team' that took risks. In this section I have shown that this 'team' were organised in ways that facilitated operational freedom and provided room for ideas to germinate, culminating in collective risk-taking and innovation. They attributed much of their courage to 'the remit' below.

Parliamentary remit

In the final part of this chapter, I show that there were two distinct directives, associated with risk, that were used by Channel 4 that helped to shape the outcome of their 2012 Paralympics production. The first of these government remits is to make 'innovative' programmes (Communications Act, 2003, c.21) whilst reflecting *in the content*, the diversity of the wider public. The other risk is situated in the Digital Economy Act (2010) in Section (22), part 4 of the revisions for Channel 4, where they are expected to recruit new and untried talent. Channel 4 did both and went further by training new disabled talent, thereby reflecting diversity *offscreen* as well. One of the concerns of some political economists of communication (e.g. Golding and Murdock, 1991; Mosco, 1996; Garnham, 2006) has been to observe the mutual influences of media systems and regulations and how they operate within the processes of production. These two parliamentary regulations applying to the commercially funded publicly owned public service broadcaster had a direct impact on Channel 4's media coverage of the Paralympic Games, by legislating risk, as I will show.

The noticeable sense of rivalry between Channel 4 and the BBC comes in part from their shared remit to public service, as public service broadcasters who have to represent diversity onscreen. In the previous section there are examples of this rivalry, and sense of competition. One of the ways of 'beating the BBC' has been to invoke their Channel 4 remit for 'risk'. One of their channel idents at the time affirmed the value of this distinction by carrying the slogan 'born risky' (C4, 2013). This account, of the bid writing stage, demonstrates an understanding of the uniqueness of Channel 4's remit and how that affects its position in the broadcasting field:

> There were lots of people involved and Julian [Bellamy] was the architect of that at the time and I remember those meetings. Alison Walsh's job was to get disability onto the agenda at every point that she could, and I remember us all sitting in the room thinking 'oh my god we could do something really exciting here' and we had all this anecdotal evidence saying the BBC have been doing the Paralympics for years and they never do it properly [sic.].
>
> (Project Leader, *Interview*, 2015)

There was a keen sense of competition here that goes beyond their 'snapping at the heels' role. Schlesinger (1987) asked of the BBC 'how is [it] affected by the state and by competition in the media industries?' (p. 12). It is clear from this interview material that Channel 4 were considerably affected by both the state, via the parliamentary remit, and its closest competitor. It seems feasible that there was a motivation for Channel 4 to use the remit to 'beat the BBC', based on the similarity in detail, in this account here, with how the coverage ended up:

> They give hours and hours and hours and hours to the Olympic Games – and then they just do a one-hour highlights of the Paralympics and, you know, they never show the bodies up close, they don't celebrate disability they just do a polite nod to it...and this was our chance to do it 'different'. So we wrote a very bold bid that talked about how we would go further than any broadcaster had gone before, and we would really show disability in its true light and we would attempt to normalise it.
>
> (Disability Executive, *Interview*, 2015)

It was this bold bid that fixed later actions; many oppositional viewpoints that would have dulled the effectiveness of the coverage were resolved because certain things were laid down in the bid and therefore were non-negotiable. Risks were written into it. Incoming executives were not happy with the unprecedented marketing budget allocation, but it could not be changed (see Chapter 6). The LOCOG chief asserted that he did not need there to be any disabled presenters onscreen, but the Disability Executive, Alison Walsh, was able to protect them, because their inclusion was written into this document, by her.

The remit for 'innovation' was used as a central argument and as a heading within the document. It was a vision to normalise disability by taking innovative risks and was offered as follows:

> Our coverage will pull no punches. We will never be patronising, and we will bring a rawness and intimacy to the coverage that hasn't been seen on television before.
>
> (C4TVC, 2009)

They built the remit requirement into the pitch for the broadcasting rights, perhaps in order to succeed, or to beat the BBC. The uniqueness of Channel 4, as defined by the remit, was written into every page, and felt by all whom I interviewed. There was a sensed culture of 'Channel 4ness', that indirectly shaped the programme content, because they knew they had a mandate for it.

I found during my season of interviews that this shared awareness of the remit did indeed permeate the organisation. Golding and Elliott (1979) link newsroom practices with occupational ideologies and here too, the sense of 'Channel 4ness' and duty to the remit were bordering on the ideological amongst the workforce. The ability to satisfy the parliamentary remit, including the hiring of higher risk new staff, and doing what others dare not, for risk of loss of funding, is intrinsically linked to the business model of Channel 4. The risk-taking edgier remit is part of the DNA of the channel but it is also part of their culture. Born (2004) speaks of the BBC as a microcosm of society, and the mini-culture defined by Channel 4's remit, was palpable amongst the people and in the office spaces that I met them in.

The tension between creative and commercial decisions as a publisher was clear and they were looking for all sorts of things when, according to Lygo, 'the Paralympics flared up in front of us'. Actually the Commercial Lawyer had received a phone call from LOCOG asking them directly to pitch for the broadcasting rights, but the suggestion when it reached the top executive did 'hit the spot'. Their sweet spot, it emerged, is when all the remit directives are in place. This was experienced and identified by some participants as a collective identity, or feel, and more explicitly, a brand image. I discuss the brand image of Channel 4 in Chapter 6. In all cases the sense of innovation and risk gave them confidence to branch out and do things differently.

However framed, whether government mandate, corporate culture, or brand awareness, the executives and producers mainly understood the structural undercurrents to decisions they were making that affected representations of disability. Within this context James Walker, the Head of Marketing (before he became Controller of Marketing and Media) revealed their 'making a difference' paradigm that was held in tension with those undercurrents:

> We have to fund ourselves, we don't have a licence fee, so we have to fund ourselves. But we do have a licence to take risks and some will

come off and some won't come off, and ultimately, ideally, we wanted the thing [the Paralympics] to pay for itself but our primary objective was not to, we didn't – this wasn't a commercial decision. This was a decision based on 'could we change something significant in the world?' You know, 'could we actually do something really worthwhile?' And, yes, it would benefit our brand and our reputation on top of that but you know, clearly within our aims, we wanted to change attitudes to disability and to disability sport – and a by-product of that would be people feeling that Channel 4 had done some good and done something worthwhile, and we did manage to get significant sponsors to help us.

(Head of Marketing, *Interview*, 2014)

How they then treated the project was very much affected by the remit, to represent the diversity within society and make innovative programmes about them. Although I have split the funding mechanism, organisation, and remit legislation for analytical purposes, in this chapter, it can be seen from Walker's perspective that in fact they are much more intertwined.

This first of the two remit elements that introduced risk, not taken by other channels, was considered to be a mandate, that made my interviewees feel secure because it was legislated by government. They were proud to be taking risks, because they were meant to be. In this way the innovative parliamentary remit became part of the occupational ideology (see Golding and Elliott, 1979) that directly affected methods of operation and decisions about production (a question raised by Golding and Murdock, 1991, p. 19). My contributors also felt secure, taking risks with ideas about representation, as the upcoming chapters on disability representation, formats, and marketing will show.

The second remit element involving risk had probably an even more profound effect on the production of the Paralympics media coverage. Indirectly this will also have had an impact on the available meanings for audiences as they would have been affected by differences onscreen. The *Digital Economy Act* (2010) stipulates that Channel 4 'must support the development' of 'people involved in the making of innovative content' as well as 'people at the beginning of their careers' (Section 22, iv). Fulfilling a diversity quota at the same time was a way of satisfying multiple requirements at once, for new talent and disabled talent. As well as being an equality issue for the physically impaired to be able to access mainstream employment, the onscreen presence of disabled television presenters also affected meanings for the viewer. Seeing deformity onscreen in a mainstream setting (Prendergast, 2000) rather than as a spectacle to be peered at by 'normal' people (Goffman, 1963), meant that mental defences against difference could be breached and the 'other' unexpectedly included within the popular culture (see Hall, 2012, p. 261).

Two slides for the in-house Production Teams (see next chapter for more details) mention this and gave producers this advice, 'It's when viewers happen on disability when they least expect it, that we can really open eyes, stretch minds and change attitudes'. Likewise, 'We've had greatest impact when we have perfectly cast disabled contributors in favourite shows, rather than making disability the focus. Channel 4 [has] led the way in getting disabled people into peak-time popular shows' (C4TVC, 2011).

The Paralympics paradox (Purdue and Howe, 2012), celebrating ability in spite of disability, is that disability *is* the focus, in the sense that it is the qualifying entrance requirement for the athletes to compete. How to treat the apparent contradiction of meanings within the Paralympics has been handled differently, with almost no risk, by the BBC. Channel 4 chose to invoke their high-risk 'new talent' mandate, having spent £500,000 developing and training new disabled talent. Ade Adepitan, who the Project Leader had said was 'key', was able to make a direct comparison between the two approaches:

> Initially when Channel 4 approached me about taking on the Paralympics, I didn't see them as a correct fit. But I think that was me going against my principles because I didn't – I wasn't open minded enough to think 'oh look they've got some potential here'. And it's only when I started working with them that I thought 'absolutely, of course, this would work with Channel 4 because they're risk takers. That's what they're about, they're about taking risks, they're about doing things differently, they're about going against the norm'. So they were perfect and no disrespect to the BBC, the BBC is probably too establishment to have taken those kind of risks. They probably worry too much about offending people in middle England to be able to have done something like *The Last Leg* or to have had myself, a black disabled guy and Clare Balding someone who is out as a gay woman presenting the main show. It wouldn't have happened on the BBC because they would have been worried about all the *Points of View* letters they would have got. And so that's probably what made Channel 4 the perfect fit for it.
>
> (ex-Paralympian/TV Presenter, *Interview*, 2015)

It was a huge battle for the London 2012 team to get the sports producers to allow disabled presenters onto their sporting coverage. Alex Brooker, who is physically impaired and has moved from sports journalist to *The Last Leg* celebrity, told me, 'We were an unknown quantity going onto the television, because no one had seen how we could operate in a stressful live environment. It was a big gamble that everyone was taking'. It is a gamble that some of the sports producers had not wanted to take, and had there been shareholders, for example, power may have been wielded to stop the inclusion of 'rookie' presenters with six months' training taking on a sporting occasion that was being marketed at elite sport mega-event level. As Channel 4 were the client, however, they made the final decision. Brooker went on to say:

> The BBC never would have done what Channel 4 did. They wouldn't have taken the risk. And if they had have, then it would have been 'Yeah, we'll have you on [as a presenter] but it's paying lip service to it'. There's no way the BBC would have run the 'Meet the Superhumans' campaign and there's no way the BBC would have shown – I've seen the BBC coverage of Beijing. It was the highlights. It was second-rate [sic.]. The production was second-rate, whereas Channel 4 treated it as a flagship event. And that was the difference and I think, you know – as great as the BBC are, they wouldn't have let us do it.
>
> (TV Presenter, *Interview*, 2016)

Brooker was not the only one to associate risk with Channel 4, suggesting that even for outside production staff on short-term contracts their culture and distinctive remit was clearly communicated. The BBC had used disabled presenters as pundits, to give advice about their specialism, but not elevated them to full presenter status, speaking on behalf of the viewer. These decisions were taken here under the shadow of a parliamentary act asking them to take risks with new talent. Deborah Poulton, the Project Manager, highlighted just what a risk it had been, professionally:

> What we did was extremely challenging. We didn't just use our disabled talent that we discovered, to be pundits, we also recruited disabled TV talent with little or no experience and turned them overnight into live sports broadcasters and that was an incredibly dangerous and risky and bold thing to do. I think we were extremely lucky that we pulled it off [laughs]. It was nerve wracking, extremely nerve wracking.
>
> (Project Leader, *Interview*, 2016)

Undergirding all this risk was the clause in the remit, which it appears they took further than was required, by representing the minority population within the production as well as within the programme content. For 2012 they trained up onscreen talent; for Rio 2016 they also recruited production trainees as well. Participation at any level of society has been difficult for disabled people and the disabling barriers highlighted very much initially through the UK 'social model' scholarship (e.g. Finkelstein, 1980; Oliver, 1983; Barnes and Mercer, 2003) and more recently through emerging critical disability paradigms (see Thomas, 2007; Goodley, 2013). The risk, insisted upon by the remit, is to take on new talent, but Channel 4 took on the 'double whammy' (Chief Marketing and Communications Officer, *Interview*, 2014) of new, untried personnel who were also from the untapped disabled talent pool.

The use of pundits, who give their expert opinion on camera, is an extremely low-risk policy, as the main presenter can easily take back the reins. However, to train the pundits to be the presenters was a risk that the BBC had never taken. Pundits are simply referred to, whereas presenters are part of the programme. The BBC websites still refer to the same people that Channel 4 used, as 'advisors' or 'experts' (e.g. BBC, 2008), as accessories to the anchors for the show. The remit for Channel 4 expressly advises the use of new talent, but they still had a choice over the level of participation. My interviews suggest that there is a narrowly defined point at which power is shared between both the consultant and the producer, just beyond tokenism where risks begin to be taken (see Arnstein, 1969; Carpentier, 2011). The BBC referred to their 'pundits' for expert analysis, allowing them slots of time to make comments, before taking back control of the programme. This is a common format in sports programming anyway (see Horne, 2007; Whannel, 2008). Channel 4, however, allowed the disabled presenters to share the onscreen time with 'able' presenters, making teams that had equal status as onscreen personalities. The Project Leader, Poulton, described these set-ups as a 'risky but refreshing mix'.

It is a central finding of this research that offscreen, these 'rungs of participation' (Arnstein, 1969, p. 93) were scaled higher than normal and that people with disabilities were included with executive function and power to shape production. Suggestions and advice, that outsiders commonly give, do not carry much weight as they are seemingly listened to, but do not change anything (ibid.). At this level of 'participation', the relationship seems to be collaborative but only if what the 'consultant' says agrees with what the key decision-makers were going to do anyway. Such gestures of consultancy have been understood as tokenistic (Cammaerts and Carpentier, 2006), whereas the less frequent higher level of participatory power occurs when what the consultant suggests *changes the decisions* that are taken. Ade Adepitan was one of the 'pundits' from the BBC's 2008 coverage who crossed over to Channel 4 for the 2012 Games. He contrasted his experiences at both places, as an ex-Paralympic athlete, highlighting the differing level of involvement he experienced, and the way he was treated by executives:

I was invited to a meeting and [...] met with the bosses at the time of Channel 4, Kevin Lygo and Julian Bellamy. And that impressed me straightaway the fact that they invited me to a meeting to meet the people at the very top of their organisation. I think I can barely remember counting on one hand the amount of times I met the top or the big boss at the BBC. So straightaway that made me believe that these guys really wanted to do something special with the Paralympics. And they basically asked me for a lot of advice on how it should be portrayed and what needed to be done. And the main thing I said, you know, I said people understand a little bit about the sport, but what they don't know about is the athletes. And I said I feel we need to give the athletes a personality.

(ex-Paralympian/TV Presenter, *Interview*, 2015)

He went on to say 'I wanted us to have athletes on billboards. I wanted Nike, all the big brands to be interested. And I think in a way we started to get there and I really think the *Superhumans* campaign played a big part. I helped push that a little bit as well'. This level of access and influence is something that Adepitan felt was unique to Channel 4's 'set-up'. He didn't think NBC or FoxTV 'would do it with the same freedom that Channel 4 did it'. Nor was he given that much voice at the BBC, he observed.

That defining participatory point, where the 'consultant' has a voice, but the producers do what they were going to do anyway, occurs regularly in documentary film, as Dornfeld (1998) found. In his study specialist advisors could make suggestions that may or may not be taken up. The element of risk, however, occurs, he argues, when you give the participating person *executive* power. This is exactly what Channel 4 did with Alison Walsh, the Disability Executive. Her role had been to devise and manage the Disabled Talent Strategy, but from 2010 and for the duration of the Paralympics they also gave her a senior editorial role, with power over *all* the commissioning editors (Disability Executive, *Interview*, 2015). As well as directing content and having the final editorial say, which was not always popular, she helped change the make-up of the workforce and led the initiative to achieve this. It seems significant that Walsh was actually asked about 'the social model' (Oliver, 1983) at her job interview in 1995, and when the Paralympic opportunity came up she embedded as many disabled practitioners into the workforce and onscreen as possible, of those she thought were good enough. The upcoming chapters are full of evidence that employment choices made a difference – to the meanings that were circulated about disability within the teams and, most markedly, as a direct consequence, onscreen.

Conclusion

Drawing on a critical political economy of communications perspective, that understands media institutions to be makers of meanings, this chapter has illuminated inherent connections between Channel 4's external and internal structures and the production of the reframed parasport representations for the London 2012 Paralympic Games. The financial structure enabled an audacious bid, provided autonomy over resistant stakeholders and engendered stabilising and lucrative corporate sponsorship deals. Additionally, the size and make-up of the organisation facilitated creative relationships with fluid roles, and those who held those roles felt they were able to take greater risks than their counterparts would have been able to at the BBC.

Because they did not work in silos, the media creators were motivated to draw on their innovative sub-culture and utilise creative tensions to forge something new.

The parliamentary remit, that directs both channels towards minority programming, insists that Channel 4 takes risks with innovative content and should also risk employing new talent in the workplace. Channel 4 did more than that and recruited and trained new disabled talent, who made up 50 per cent of the onscreen presenters for the London 2012 coverage. They then increased their self-imposed quota to 75 per cent, including personnel across the entire workforce in all roles for the Rio 2016 Paralympics. This chapter therefore evidences that the industrial context in which the producers were situated, structurally facilitated risk-taking with disability both within production and with representations onscreen. Creative agency was thereby both enabled and enhanced.

As well as increasing visibility of disabled presenters, representations were framed with newly inclusive meanings for the minority group of elite athletes at the London 2012 Paralympic Games. The next chapter looks at the agents who brought about changes to those meanings, including what they did and how and why they did it.

Bibliography

Arnstein, S.R. 1969. Ladder of citizen participation. *Journal of the American Institute of Planners*, 35(4), p. 216.

Banks, M.J. 2009. Gender below-the-line: defining feminist production studies. In: V. Mayer et al. eds. *Production studies: cultural studies of media industries*. London: Routledge, pp. 87–98.

Barnes, C. and Mercer, G. 2003. *Disability policy and practice: applying the 'social model'*. Leeds: Disability Press.

BBC. 2008. *The 2008 Beijing Olympics and Paralympics on the BBC*. [online]. [Accessed 12 July 2016]. Available from: www.bbc.co.uk/pressoffice

BBC. 2011. *Paralympics 2008*. [online]. [Accessed 12 July 2016]. Available from: http://news.bbc.co.uk/sport

BDRC. 2012. *Viewers feel more positive towards disabled people*. Available from: http://bdrc-continental.com/opinions

Born, G. 2004. *Uncertain vision: Birt, Dyke and the reinvention of the BBC*. London: Secker and Warburg.

Brown, M. 2007. *A licence to be different: the story of Channel 4*. London: BFI.

Burns, T. 1977. *The BBC: public institution and private world*. London: Macmillan.

C4. 2013. *Born risky: Channel 4*. [online]. [Accessed 15 May 2017]. Available from: www.youtube.com

C4TVC. 2009. *Proposal for UK Broadcast Rights*. [Document] London: Channel 4 Television Corporation.

C4TVC. 2011. *MENTAL4 the Paralympics*. [PowerPoint]. London: Channel 4 Television Corporation.

Cammaerts, B. and Carpentier, N. 2006. *Reclaiming the media: communication rights and democratic media roles*. Intellect Books.

Carpentier, N. 2011. *Media and participation: a site of ideological-democratic struggle*. Intellect Online Library.

Castells, M. 2011. *The rise of the network society: the information age: economy, society, and culture*. Chichester: Wiley.

Communications Act. 2003. (c. 21. pt.3) London: The Stationery Office.

Corner, J. 2013. *Theorising media: power, form and subjectivity*. Oxford University Press.

D'Acci, J. 1994. *Defining women: television and the case of Cagney and Lacey*. Chapel Hill, NC: University of North Carolina Press.

Darlow, M. 2004. *Independents struggle: the programme makers who took on the TV establishment*. London: Quartet.

Digital Economy Act. 2010. (Section 22). London: The Stationery Office.

Dornfeld, B. 1998. *Producing public television, producing public culture*. Princeton, NJ; Chichester: Princeton University Press.

Dwyer, P. 2015. Theorizing media production: the poverty of political economy. *Media, Culture and Society*, 37(7), pp. 988–1004.

Elliott, P. 1972. *The making of a television series: a case-study in the sociology of culture*. Brighton: Constable.

Finkelstein, V. 1980. *Attitudes and disabled people: issues for discussion*. New York: International Exchange of Information in Rehabilitation.

Garnham, N. 1995. Political economy and cultural studies. *Critical Studies in Mass Communication*, 12(2), pp. 62–71.

Garnham, N. 2005. From cultural to creative industries: an analysis of the implications of the 'creative industries' approach to arts and media policy making in the United Kingdom. *International Journal of Cultural Policy*, 11(1), pp. 15–29.

Garnham, N. 2006. Contribution to a political economy of mass-communication. In: *Media and cultural studies*. Malden, MA: Blackwell, p. 201.

Goffman, E. 1963. *Stigma: notes on the management of spoiled identity*. Harmondsworth: Penguin.

Golding, P. and Elliott, P.R.C. 1979. *Making the news*. Longman Publishing Group.

Golding, P. and Murdock, G. 1991. Culture, communications and political economy. *Mass Media and Society*, 2(1), pp. 15–32.

Golding, P. and Murdock, G. 2000. Culture, political economy and communications. *Mass Media and Society*, 3, pp. 82–87.

Goodley, D. 2013. Dis/entangling critical disability studies. *Disability & Society*, 28(5), pp. 631–644.

Grindstaff, L. 2002. *The money shot: trash, class, and the making of TV talk shows*. Chicago, IL: University of Chicago Press.

Hall, S. 2012. *Representation: cultural representations and signifying practices*. 2nd ed. London: SAGE in association with The Open University.

Harvey, S. 1994. Channel 4 television: from Annan to Grade. In: *Behind the screens: the structure of British television in the nineties*. London: Lawrence and Wishart, pp. 92–117.

Harvey, S. 2003. Channel 4 and the redefining of public service broadcasting. In: *The television history book*. London: BFI, pp. 50–54.

Hesmondhalgh, D. 2013. *The cultural industries*. 3rd ed. London: SAGE.

Hodges, C.E.M., Scullion, R., and Jackson, D. 2015. From aww to awe factor: UK audience meaning-making of the 2012 Paralympics as mediated spectacle. *Journal of Popular Television*, 3, 195–211.

Horne, J. 2006. *Sports in consumer culture*. Basingstoke: Palgrave Macmillan.

Horne, J. 2007. The four 'knowns' of sports mega-events. *Leisure Studies*, 26(1), pp. 81–96.

Hudson, E. 2004. Athens advances Paralympics. [Online]. [Accessed 24 May 2014]. Available from: http://news.bbc.co.uk/sport1

Jacka, E. 2003. 'Democracy as defeat': the impotence of arguments for public service broadcasting. *Television & New Media*, 4(2), pp. 177–191.

Kerr, S. 2018. The London 2012 Paralympic Games. In: *The Palgrave handbook of Paralympic studies*. London: Palgrave Macmillan, pp. 481–505.

Lieb, K. 2016. Pop stars perform 'gay' for the male gaze: the production of faux-mosexuality in female popular music performances and its representational implications. In: *Production studies, the sequel!: cultural studies of global media industries*. London: Taylor & Francis.

McGillivray, D., O'Donnell, H., McPherson, G., and Misener, L. 2019. Repurposing the (super)crip: media representations of disability at the Rio 2016 Paralympic Games. *Communication & Sport*. Online.

Morgan, A. 2009. *Eating the big fish*. 2nd ed. New Jersey: Wiley.

Mosco, V. 1996. *The political economy of communication: rethinking and renewal*. London: SAGE.

Mosco, V. 2009. *Political economy*. Wiley Online Library.

Murdock, G. and Golding, P. 2016. Political economy and media production: a reply to Dwyer. *Media, Culture and Society*, 38(5), pp. 763–769.

Oliver, M. 1983. *Social work with disabled people*. London: Macmillan, for the British Association of Social Workers.

Prendergast, C. 2000. *The triangle of representation*. New York: Columbia University Press.

Purdue, D.E.J. and Howe, P.D. 2012. See the sport, not the disability: exploring the Paralympic paradox. *Qualitative Research in Sport, Exercise and Health*, 4(2), pp. 189–205.

Redvall, E.N. 2013. *Writing and producing television drama in Denmark: from the kingdom to the killing*. Springer.

Richeri, G. 2003. Broadcasting and the market: the case of public television. In: A. Calabrese et al. eds. *Toward a political economy of culture: capitalism and communication in the twenty-first century*. Lanham, MD: Rowman & Littlefield Publishers.

Schlesinger, P. 1987. *Putting 'reality' together: BBC News*. London: Methuen.

Silverstone, R. 1985. *Framing science; the making of a BBC documentary*. California: BFI.

Thomas, C. 2007. *Sociologies of disability and illness*. London: Palgrave Macmillan.

Wasko, J., Murdock, G., and Sousa, H. 2011. *Introduction: the political economy of communications: core concerns and issues*. Wiley Online Library.

Wenner, L.A. 1998. *MediaSport*. London: Psychology Press.

Whannel, G. 2008. *Culture, politics and sport: blowing the whistle, revisited*. London: Routledge.

Zoellner, A. 2016. Detachment, pride, critique professional identity in independent factual television production in Great Britain and Germany. In: M. Banks, B. Conor, and V. Mayer eds. *Production studies, the sequel!: cultural studies of global media industries*. London: Taylor & Francis, pp. 150–163.

Chapter 4

Normalising disability

Mega-event media parity for the 'superhuman' supercrips

As holders of the broadcasting rights to the Tokyo 2020 and Paris 2024 Paralympic Games, Channel 4 has a continuing platform to change the conversation about disability within the UK, having provided a broader repertoire of acceptable media representations from London 2012 onwards. This chapter focuses on how those pattern-breaking representations came about, drawing on interviews with the television producers who constructed them. But first, it is worth observing some of the routes the ensuing conversation has taken.

Since domestic media coverage of the Games varies widely from country to country it follows that meanings about disability and difference will vary too, reflecting national cultural contexts. Further, meanings are then decoded and reshaped across the world's online and social media platforms beyond the influence of the primary media producers. For example, the UK host nation sports broadcaster introduced athleticism and a performance focus to its televised and digitally streamed content, as this chapter will show. But some journalists reporting on it, and digital consumers commenting in the public sphere, still echoed the historically entrenched medicalisation and overcoming tragedy narratives that were previously associated with disability (see Rees et al., 2019; French and Le Clair, 2018), in spite of the producers trying to move the public beyond those framings.

Now that the Paralympic Games is becoming accepted as a showcase for spectacular sporting achievement, the media coverage does have an extra influence over these discourses in terms of visibility and mainstream positioning. For example, medal-winning success stories (or dramatic disqualifications) can be seen on the front pages of the national press, rather than the back pages, because these form the underpinnings of televised sports mega-events (Roche, 2000). Women's sport and disability sports have this in common, that they often do not feature on the back pages either, unless something spectacular has happened, but media producers have the power to change this. For both London 2012 and for Rio 2016, sporting nationalism was found to be part of the media conversation within the UK print media (McGillivray et al., 2019), but with their newspapers also carrying the 'supercrip' tragedy element alongside the sports narratives. The Canadian press were also similarly predisposed (Maika and Danylchuk, 2016) throughout their 2012 coverage.

This turn from disability sport to world class athletics, however, has sparked another strand of discussion around whether the newly spectacular framing for the Paralympic Games might be counter-productive (see Braye et al., 2013) for the social change agenda, in the way that the more negative portrayals were previously. McGillivray et al. (2019) highlight the following:

> The hyping of disabled athletes into superhuman status by Channel 4 only deepens our wounds, inflicted by continual assaults on our daily lives. It truly seems that the only acceptable disabled person is a Paralympian—and then only for a few weeks.
>
> (p. 22)

Normalising difference for elite parasports athletes may not be having the intended outcome, therefore, for everyone in wider society with a disability, but that discourse lies outside the scope of this research. It is the producers' intentions, and the pressures upon them, that are the subject of this book and, according to my participants, their intentions were to actively dismantle unhelpful tropes and caricatures and move inclusive depictions forward. It is clear that the conversation is changing within the public discourse, with the UK charity Scope finding that 'seventy two per cent of disabled people felt the 2012 Games had a positive impact in societal attitudes to disability' (Claydon, 2015, p. 37). However, changing the conversation about the broadcasting of 'disability' has not come about easily, and not without many difficult conversations behind the scenes, that I discuss below.

The last chapter demonstrated some of the structural influences on Channel 4's Paralympic media coverage, exploring the industrial context that shaped decisions that had concrete consequences for onscreen representations and the production of meaning. Now this chapter examines the individual attitudes and actions of the production personnel, as they sought to renegotiate meanings of disability through their specifically selected televisual portrayals. Whilst attempting to normalise disability the common theme amongst the producers was to provide parity for the Paralympians with 'us', normal human beings, and also with our super-elite Olympic athletes. As Chapter 3 has already shown there were conflicts and resolutions, and executive powers exercised, in order to achieve new representations that were then able to challenge audience perceptions. Specific instances of those conflicts are now examined, where creative and executive powers of judgement were used, arguing that it was predominantly the pursuit of 'parity' that drove the personal decisions at the level of production.

According to my contributors, there were two representational dilemmas the producers faced, which I have divided into the two sections below.

The first was whether to 'show the sport' or 'show the stumps'. Visual representations were constantly reviewed and discussed in terms of parity with others, from differing perspectives. The second dilemma at that time was which stereotype to promote, and with what meanings attached, again for the same reason, in order to give Olympic parity to an unusual sub-set of elite athletes. The shaping of meanings involved challenging, reversing, or tweaking existing stereotypes. This is a powerful mediation role for producers, and a role that still needs scrutiny (see Silverstone, 2005; Livingstone, 2009; Thumim, 2015, p. 57). Would it be possible to communicate that these elite Paralympic athletes were 'extraordinarily human', 'extraordinarily good at sport', and 'extraordinarily different' all at the same time? These dilemmas, at the intersection of representation, sport, and disability, were exacerbated by the existing tropes and meanings resonating from the respective media histories that I have outlined in Chapter 2.

During this chapter I analyse the relationship between these media histories and my participants' dilemmas around communicating new meanings. To recap briefly, and as elaborated in Chapter 2, making a 'spectacle of the other' (Hall, 2012) is commonly achieved by selecting some extreme characteristics for a group of people and de-humanising that group with a reductive stereotype, to provide 'us' with a 'safe distance' (ibid.) from 'them'. This situation is transformed for athletes in the context of televised sport, where we seek to identify *with* 'them' whilst they win or lose sporting competitions *for* 'us' (Whannel, 1992; Dayan and Katz, 1994; Roche, 2000). The entertaining televisual spectacle of international sports competitions includes multiple tropes that help attract large audiences (Rowe, 2011) and the coverage is a desirable commodity for a television network to therefore purchase. Unfortunately, spectacles of disability, however, do the opposite to spectacles of sport, and do not attract the same audiences. As noted in Chapter 2, historically, parades of disability have invoked revulsion in the spectator (Elias, 1978; Barnes, 1992; Davis, 1995; Garland-Thomson, 1997; Gilbert and Schantz, 2008; Schantz and Gilbert, 2012). Televisual representations intended to avoid revulsion have normally minimised obvious disability by not showing it on camera, or cropping it from the frame (Shakespeare, 1999; Brittain, 2012).

It is possible to see from these representational issues that media coverage straddling disability and elite international sport would inevitably engender challenges that could surface during production. This chapter investigates specific instances of conflicting attitudes catalysing both individual and collective agency. The moments outlined reveal how certain meanings are preferred and chosen and what happens to bring about their construction at the encoding stage (see Hall, 1973; 1980). How these representations are then framed, utilising different programme formats, will be the subject of the next chapter, Chapter 5.

The sections that follow explore the micro decisions that were made to normalise representations of the disabled athletes onscreen. Drawing on personal interviews, and some associated internal training materials, I discuss the dilemmas around visual representation, and the meanings and stereotypes that were constructed, from the details supplied by my participants. The vast majority of decisions, that were taken at the role level of the individual producers or creatives, were driven by the felt need to deliver 'parity', of some sort. Historically, of course, and more broadly within the three research areas, there has been no such parity. However, as I will show, these histories shed considerable light on the underlying dilemmas the producers faced. Excerpts from my interviews, below, demonstrate how those working for Channel 4 handled these underlying opposing dimensions, and produced a new range of representations that other producers now, post-2012, have at their creative disposal.

'Show the stumps' or 'show the sport?'

Whether to expose or conceal disability on camera is the theme of this first section. The dilemma was that whilst strong visual representations play a huge part in the successful close-up portrayals of televised sport (Howe, 2008), looking at physical disability onscreen is uncomfortable (Garland-Thomson, 1997; Corker and Shakespeare, 2002). There were outsourced sports producers who wanted to get on with their job of sport 'as usual', giving the coverage parity with any normal sport. This would naturally involve underplaying the physical bodily differences in order not to detract from the sport. At the same time there were Channel 4 employees who wanted to take risks with the media profiles of the disabled athletes, showing them 'up close and personally', providing creative treatments they would consider equal with their channel's other 'risky' programme making, providing parity in that way.

Whilst for many the issue was which to do, 'show the stumps' *or* 'show the sport', or which to show first, the Commercial Lawyer, from the outset, saw the perspectives equally:

> Our view was that you couldn't and shouldn't disentangle the two and that there was something, an extraordinary thing, happening here and it was right to reflect that.
>
> (Commercial Lawyer, *Interview*, 2015)

Not being able to disentangle the physical differences from the extraordinary sportsmanship was an essential ingredient, he felt, to the whole project. By contrast, attempts to separate the sport from the athletes' physical impairments was an adverse pressure initially applied by the International Paralympic Committee (IPC), one of the stakeholders, who, like the British

Paralympic Association (BPA), objected to the 'in-your-face' approach and kept telling the production teams and commissioning editors not to focus on the disability. Walsh, as the advisor on disability, with a disability of her own, told me she repeatedly had to respond to them:

> Actually, if you do that, you separate it. You make it as a sort of special [event]– you know, disabled people are like a different species then. You're not being true to the athletes; you're not treating them like any other athletes then.
>
> (Disability Executive, *Interview*, 2015)

Parity, in Walsh's argument, is between the disabled athletes and any other athletes. The goal to achieve status parity with the Olympians had been a firm objective for her, and Channel 4 had promised it in the bid that she had helped to write, to LOCOG for the broadcasting rights in 2009. The Disability Executive also did not want them to be treated like 'a different species' and this humanising concern was central to many of the team throughout the decision-making process.

Paralympic scholars (Gilbert and Schantz, 2012) have argued that the media, if it 'carefully thought through' the visibility and invisibility of its athletes, could arrest people's current perceptions of disability. Their argument continues:

> Everything which is not standard in terms of the body is often hidden by the sports media, as they are responsible for the ideas and concepts which are selected for the consumer of sports.
>
> (p. 241)

Although those who are 'not standard' are of course, human, it is commonly agreed that the prevalent conceptualisation for disabled 'others' in the media is either subhuman (see Haller, 1995; Garland-Thomson, 2002) or superhuman (e.g. Purdue and Howe, 2012). Because people with disabilities are so often depicted as subhuman (see also Philo, 2012), academic writers have complained that the Paralympics would always be a 'side-show' (Gilbert and Schantz, 2008). Clearly, in 2012, the Paralympics was not a side-show, garnering, for the opening ceremony, the highest audience figures, 11.8 million, in over a decade for the host nation television rights holders (C4, 2013). The blend of 'showing the stumps' as well as 'showing the sport', was a separate way of humanising the athletes intentionally to give them parity. Visually depicting the athletes as *actually* human in this way, rather than either subhuman or superhuman, was a new conceptualisation.

Walsh felt that communicating this normal humanity for the physically impaired was part of the job that Channel 4 had employed her to do. In her capacity as Disability Executive, she had the strategic role of shaping the representations of disability onscreen, as well as promoting disability within the organisation offscreen. She, herself, had been a keen rower until contracting rheumatoid arthritis which brought her own sporting career to an end. The reach of Walsh's powers was extended for the duration of the 2012 Paralympics production schedule over the other editorial positions as well as the content. It was clear, from the general tone of comments from Walsh's colleagues, that she operated with determination to bring disability into the mainstream, as if it was 'normal'. She tried to achieve this by offering them parity with everyone else, Olympic athletes and normal human beings alike. Berger and Luckman (1979), discussing social constructions, once pointed out that 'he who has the bigger stick has the better chance of imposing his reality' (p. 127). Channel 4, perhaps as a differentiation from the BBC previously, gave this role, and this editorial stick, to someone with a disability.

It is important to raise the distinction here between normalisation and parity. What is normal is what is *expected*, whereas parity constitutes *equal treatment* (Stevenson, 2010). This distinction matters for the following reason. It is not *expected* to see 'stumps' and close-ups of anatomical differences on television (other than programmes about that), but if the disabled athletes were to be treated *equally* with Olympians, then close-ups are part of the drama, and part of the way that those Olympic athletes would normally be televised. Offering equal visual treatment was a way of normalising the athletes and changing what could be expected onscreen in the future. This combination was seen as 'natural' for Walsh, and she brought personal experience of disabling physical impairment, with a corresponding sense of what ought to be normal or equal, to her professional role, within the organisation.

Most of my contributors wanted to 'show the stumps' onscreen. There is lots of evidence that having a disabled voice on the inside of the production helped reshape the culture and attitudes within the production and marketing teams. Walsh was a key proponent of the revealing disability viewpoint. At pre-training days, hosted for multiple creative teams, she wrote and delivered a special presentation called *MENTAL4 the Paralympics* (C4TVC, 2011). The MENTAL acronym stood for Mainstream; Everyday Everywhere not Exceptional; New; Talent; Audience; Love, Listen and Laugh. An example from that, of the editorial control over the emphasis strategy states:

> [We need] clever editing with disabled presenters or reporters – make it look natural, and we want to see the disability, not shoot to hide it.
>
> (ibid.)

The reason for insisting on this strategy was not simply to 'show the stumps', but to provide a parity with other presentational tropes. There are particular televisual styles used in sport to introduce and also depict elite athletes, including the Olympians (see Whannel, 1992). Channel 4 wanted to create the same televisual representations that would be normative for this other group of elites. Specifically, the Olympic athletes are depicted using uninhibited and impactful close-up visuals (Jhally, 1989) with brutally honest commentary, and Walsh did not want the Paralympians to be treated as a 'different species' (the tone of the commentary is discussed further in Chapter 5). By being *treated* differently, as they had been historically, their actual differences were being masked onscreen. There was a sense, this time, for 2012, that the Paralympians should be treated exactly like Olympians, as if that was natural, however much of a shock this might be for viewers.

At Channel 4, a sense of parity, or equality, was communicated clearly from the outset even though there was not a budget to match (see Chapters 3 and 6). I was able to establish through my interviews that this directive for equal treatment filtered through to the technical crews pervasively during production. Interviewing a Camera Supervisor, who had worked at the swimming pool in the Aquatics Centre during both the Olympics and the Paralympics, I asked if there had been any differences for her role. Absolutely not, she said. There was just one technical directive that she remembered as 'different' for her role, apart from extra health and safety issues. This was being asked to widen the shots in the studio 'more than we normally would' (Camera Operator, *Interview*, 2014). The shots were to include crutches and other elements within the frame so that the audience could see they were needed. These wider framings were chosen to emphasise that the guests had disabilities during their studio interviews. The significance of this choice to point cameras at the impairments and supporting equipment was understood as an explicit attempt, including by other producers who mentioned it, to reveal 'reality' rather than as a gratuitous depiction.

Showing the visible reality of physical disability was seen, by Channel 4, as a kind of equality. It seemed clear that previously the Paralympic stakeholders, the IPC and the BPA, whilst also seeking equality, had been more sensitive to the possible revulsion that audiences might feel if they could see amputations or anatomical difference. This has certainly been the sensitivity in previous Paralympic coverage (Gilbert and Schantz, 2012, p. 229). For 2012, the pressure to de-emphasise disability as much as possible came from sports producers and also from the outside stakeholders, even though their organisations' roles are to represent the disabled athletes. Instead, Channel 4 utilised the 'normal' sports tropes, by adopting a realistic stance to provide representations during the coverage. The new visibility was intended to portray reality, equal to other sports depictions.

In an informal corridor conversation with a senior executive I asked if the 'up close and personal' coverage was perhaps an extension of the alternative public service broadcaster's *Embarrassing Bodies* 'in-your-face' type of programming, and he was very quick to jump on that premise. He clearly believed the ethos and aim of their camerawork was for natural visibility, expecting that emphasising imagery would gradually help normalise the impairment experience for viewers as they got used to it. Getting used to it involves a retraining of accepted norms within the media frame, and Gitlin (1980) explains the way the media frame tells us how to interpret what we see onscreen. He describes the 'frame' as, 'persistent patterns of cognition, interpretation, and presentation, of selection, emphasis, and exclusion, by which symbol-handlers routinely organise discourse, whether verbal or visual' (p. 7). In 2012 the Channel 4 symbol-handlers intentionally set out to change the discourse for Paralympic athletes using media frames to do so.

Aesthetic parity

I asked the Video Editor for the powerful *Meet the Superhumans* trailer, Tim Hardy, how he had selected his footage and he explained that he picked startling images intending 'to almost normalise it [the impairment]'. He said:

> We weren't going to shy away from anything...but we didn't want to focus on it in a freakish way or anything like that.
>
> (Video Editor, *Interview*, 2014)

Not shying away from anything was a professionalism of his, giving parity to this project alongside any other. As an ex-video editor myself we were able to discuss the routine search for the best images and how to juxtapose them for best effect. This is a normal part of any video-editing role and Hardy clarified his not shying away approach to mean 'the balance we're always looking for, and to make things beautiful as well' (ibid.). Looking for beautiful images is a central element to Hardy's work, whatever he is editing, and he made no exception here. Disability was treated the same as any other imagery, with parity, at this point, from the Video Editor's perspective.

Seeing the body as visually beautiful, regardless of taboo or difference, was a noticeable characteristic of Hardy's work and work ethic more generally. There was artwork on the walls of his office, showing off his style, which was in keeping with the *Meet the Superhumans* trailer he edited for Channel 4. He also, through his creative choices, contested the visual imagery associated with 'repulsive' disability and did not resolve this by hiding it. Hall (2012) describes 'contesting the stereotype from within' (p. 264) as a 'representational strategy' (p. 265) useful for subverting existing stigmas or attitudes towards anomaly. By taking the body as the principal site of the stereotype and making it beautiful rather than bad, odd, or wrong, Hall says 'stereotypes work against themselves' (ibid.). Hardy undid the 'wrong' stereotype for disability in pursuit of his normal professional goals. Just as the sense that 'black is wrong' could be restated as 'black is beautiful' (Hall, p. 262) with racial imagery, Hardy was able to do the same for disability, restating it as beautiful, visually, in this commercial.

Visual communication scholars (e.g. Aiello and Parry, 2019; Domke et al., 2002; Petersen, 2005; Arpan et al., 2006) have discussed how inclusion of particular angles and gestures affect critical or positive evaluations of a depicted group. In practice, editors make evaluations, by sifting through all the available footage, that then affect other evaluations of what or whom they are depicting. The 4Creative Video Editor was therefore the potential author of a considerable level of the framing and attitude that prevailed towards the disabled elite athletes, particularly as the marketing campaign was to set up the momentum for interest in the Games. Methodologically, Domke et al. (2002) have said, of news analysis, that:

> While scholars in recent years have begun to devote increasing attention to people's use of core values and mental categories to sift through [...] messages, the role of visual images is virtually unexamined.
>
> (ibid., p. 133)

Textual analysts do examine these images, but less enquiry is made into the producer's understanding of the role they play at the time of production, or what mental categories are used by them to sift through the visual material. Hardy often, he told me, prioritises beauty as an aesthetic to tell stories when looking for powerful and striking images. He simply looks for what he considers to be outstanding images, whatever form they take. Notwithstanding this, Parry (2010) points out that framings created by visual imagery do, however, produce an 'outlook' or a 'point of view' (p. 70). Hardy's core values, therefore, of promoting beauty and startling imagery, in this case, may have provided parity with his other work, but also delivered a particularly sympathetic perspective on physical deformity.

Historically, for sport, the body beautiful has already been defined as a form of perfection, famously on film by Reifenstahl (1938). Theoretical notions of the Olympian Spirit were visually embodied by her through dramatic imagery elevating the Arian physique. In the last few decades, visual representations of Olympic athletes have continued to resonate the focus on attractive bodies (see Horne et al., 2013, pp. 105–111) without applying any focus on the bodily imperfect Paralympic athletes. Hardy's search for beauty within the hours and hours of footage he had at his disposal, even for his minute-long trailer, took him to what he regarded visually as the perfect *image*, rather than the perfect body. This is a departure from previous Paralympic portrayals which have not been given this equal treatment; these have instead glossed over and away from the anatomies of its elite sportspeople (Howe and Jones, 2006; Brittain, 2010), leaving legitimate athleticism uncelebrated.

Visually, Claydon (2015) suggests that 'representations of disability sport can disavow the framing of the athlete in terms of the body beautiful to reject the primacy of the body in favour of the primacy of the sport' (p. 89). My interviewees have articulated that this was not the case in the edit suites of 4Creative for London 2012. Before the Editor got to the sport, he chose the best imagery for its own sake, which is a normal practice for many television advertisements, especially high-performance sports ads. What this means is that part of what changed the representations of disabled athletes with the 2012 coverage, was the selection of impactful imagery; it was chosen purely on merit, for its aesthetic value.

Across other media, Hilgemberg et al. (2019), when comparing Australian and Brazilian newspaper coverage of the London 2012 Paralympics, observed that images were distinctly 'spectacular' within the Brazilian print media, perhaps to help engage the audience in readiness for their own Rio Games and also to sell tickets. Noticeably, the Australian camera angles were less spectacular with their having no imminent commercial interest in making them so. By contrast I got the sense, from Hardy, that his visual selections were not driven by commercial imperatives at all, instead they were consistently purely cinematic ones.

The Film Director, Tom Tagholm, also played a role, in that he steered Hardy away from cutting narrative sequences, which he had begun to do, in order to emphasise 'the startling yet beautiful imagery in an exciting way' (Video Editor, *Interview*, 2014). These kinds of decisions and choices were made in a collaboration of what scholars call above-the-line and below-the-line production roles (Hesmondhalgh, 2013; Banks, 2009). The disruption suggested by Tagholm, of the natural instinct to make sense of what we see, was deliberate and the Editor had to recut his material to achieve this anti-narrative form of engagement instead. Meanings were made and a point of view constructed that went against normal disability conventions in order to introduce the Paralympians in a new way. Usually, only the strongest and the most able are celebrated in mainstream competitive sport (Whannel, 1992) which makes the connection between disability and elite sport something of a representational paradox (see DePauw, 1997; Silva and Howe, 2012). However, by treating the subjects of the project as if they were any other in a high-performance sports ad, he was able to combine his art with the athletes' reality. Both were embedded in the visual representations where he revealed the stumps *and* redefined elite parasport. The emphasis on reality therefore provided a real parity on many levels, including skilful treatment of subjects and crafted representations of them.

Emphasise to minimise

Producer perspectives on whether to 'show the stumps', or not, shaped many key decisions made by Channel 4 and the creative emphasis produced images that were more striking than any previously used in disability sport. The production teams across the different output types were all advised to:

> Linger on the athlete's body, like you'd linger on an Olympic athlete's body, however warped and cracked.
>
> (C4TVC, 2011)

This directive, to make it like the Olympics, filtered through into actual footage and the form of engagement, using the close-up medium of television, was a typical Channel 4 strategy. According to my participants it was well thought out but had attendant risks.

There had been a repeating mantra at the trainings:

> Don't focus on the impairment? Do, if it engages the audience.
>
> (ibid.)

Engaging the audience is not necessarily the fairest way of treating disability on television, as other Paralympic scholars have pointed out:

> Representational media secure our attention as readers and viewers in the double bind of our fascination/repulsion with physical difference.
>
> (Mitchell and Snyder, 1997, p. 15)

It may have been in order to protect against this wrong kind of fascination, therefore, that there was resolute resistance by the BPA and IPC to risk-taking visuals. This resistance was referred to by personnel with roles in marketing, commissioning, sports production, and presentation. The outside organisations suggested a de-emphasising mode of depiction, in contrast to the parity-treatment coverage, using the highlights packaging style previously used in order to gloss over difference. It was a general consensus amongst all my contributors that the typical television trope for disabled sport using 'slow-motion with music' was both cheesy and patronising and they refused to tone the imagery down.

The Commercial Lawyer involved from the beginning, and also part of the top-level wrangling throughout, said he overheard many of the confrontational conversations. He referred to the minimise/emphasise battle against the patronising tropes by saying:

> We definitely didn't go that way [slo-mo music sequences] and I think some of the people in the BPA had some initial reservations about how that might go, because they felt...[exposing disabilities]...might be a turn off to some sections of the audience. They felt that some of our plans about showing, for example, instances of disability right up close – so people jumping into the pool, being lowered into the pool which is

something you would not have seen so clearly in the past... might be a turnoff to some people, and almost to the athletes, focusing on the wrong thing rather than focusing on their extraordinary achievements.

(Commercial Lawyer, *Interview*, 2015)

The conscious decision to emphasise disability came clearly from a position of understanding both sides and Baker went on to say that there had been a mixture of feelings about it. In spite of these misgivings voiced by others, the decision was upheld to emphasise visual disabilities even though some considered it 'the wrong thing'. It was explained by several people that these close-ups were 'giving parity' to the Paralympians, and not intended to make a separate spectacle of them. I discuss this spectacle in the next section.

Whilst it is commonly understood that defining 'difference' is intended to create a sense of otherness (Hall, 2012, Ch. 4), in this case, according to the producers, it was to create a sense of similarity. Not shying away from shot types and sizes that would have been used at the Olympics meant showing 'stumps' and other potentially shocking physical impairments, such as absent limbs, in a way that had not been done before so overtly. Otherwise the coverage would not have had the look and feel of an Olympics, or any other sort of mega-event. The BPA initially feared the reveal-all approach would detract from the value and performance of the athletes whom they represented. As will become clear later in this chapter, these stakeholders later found that in practice the Channel 4 creative choices enhanced the standing of the athletes as elite sportsmen and women, and gave them greater parity with their Olympic counterparts, which was the outcome that all parties wanted.

Several of the Channel 4 creatives explained why they had adopted their emphasising approach. As well as giving parity, it was felt that 'letting people notice' a difference, in both appearance and function, helped the normal group, without the stigma, to 'stop noticing'. This is an effect that those with a stigma know well, and was theorised many decades ago by Goffman. He called it 'disclosure etiquette' (1963, p. 172) saying that giving the 'normal' person a chance to adjust to the stigma helped overcome the feeling of 'otherness'. For some at Channel 4, 'showing the stumps' was a clearly planned winning strategy. For others involved in the media production, I sensed, the success of this may have been accepted as a hindsight observation. Showing the sport first, by itself, instead would have involved masking disability, and was an approach that was consistently overruled by the in-house editorial team. They steadfastly held to their remit to 'take risks' and justified the undisguised portrayals as part of providing equal treatment.

An example of how the emphasise-first strategy may have been central to the 'shift in perceptions' that was attributed to the coverage later (C4, 2013; Hodges et al., 2015; Spence, 2018), was noted by one of the TV presenters of the *Tea-time and Evening* programme. Parity with non-disabled sport-speople apparently removed the issue of disability for some of the younger audience. She pointed out, as one of her key memories, how she and Ade Adepitan had been surprised by their trips out into the Olympic Park when they went out with a camera to film the 'Ask Ade' segment (*Tea-time and Evening Show*, 2012). Children were canvassed for questions, and the presenter particularly remembers still that, unexpectedly for her, they 'did not mention disability until about day four or five'. She went on to say that if they did mention wheelchairs it was about 'the kit' not the disability. When I asked her why she imagined this was so, her thoughts were that because the disability 'had been visible from the outset' it was no longer an issue, helping the viewers 'focus purely on the sport'. The camera crews had also, as I have discussed, been asked to reveal the 'kit' using wider shots. This helped the children, that the presenters interviewed, accept impairment predicaments alongside technical solutions as normal, for these new sporting heroes. Goffman's (1963) disclosure effect can be seen to be at work here, with people relaxing about the stigma after noticing it, because it was out in the open. The trait, or obtrusion, was no longer in the way. Having pieces of anatomy missing, for example, is something that is regularly played down in media representations of disability, unless being examined in particular within a disability programming segment.

Channel 4 subverted this norm by paying passing close attention to disability but en route to the other attributes. Paralympic stakeholders wanted their television event to be 'received easily' but tried to skip this step. They were clearly not aware of the benefits of disclosure (Goffman, 1963) to help overcome a sense of stigma. Instead all the other stakeholders (the BPA, IPC, and LOCOG) suggested and tried to insist upon a minimising only strategy. This view was communicated as well by one of the heads of the television sport production (who wanted to remain anonymous). In an interview with me he simply said that, 'with extraordinary sporting performance it is immaterial that there is a disability' (Sports Executive, *Interview*, 2015).

The Channel 4 team did not consider it to be immaterial though, feeling it had to be addressed, at least initially. In particular with the Paralympics, the stigma has to be revealed and noticed, as the disability is in itself a qualifying hallmark for the competition, and needs to be considered as part of understanding the rules of individual events. However, the sentiment that other attributes are the important ones to highlight ties in with the rest of Goffman's thesis that an 'obtruding stigma' has the effect of 'breaking the claim any other attributes may have on us' (p. 76). At this point the one with the stigma has lost any chance of equal treatment, or parity. In other words the disability, or stigma, whilst not immaterial in the sporting context, is *in the way* until it has been observed and adjusted to. There was a way of preventing this blinding to normal human characteristics, and sporting prowess, other than by avoidance, and that, the producers felt, was by showing it.

For the 2012 coverage, emphasising *in order to* minimise was achieved by using the cameras to reveal difference, and changing the meanings of the representations to evoke normal humanity and elite athleticism. Drawing again on Hall's (2012) argument about the transcoding of meanings (pp. 260–262) to think through this phenomenon, it became clear how meanings were changed. As noted earlier, a shift historically occurred with the transformation of racial difference in certain media representations, from meaning 'black is wrong' to 'black is beautiful' (ibid., p. 262) by applying normal conventions. Likewise here, beyond beautiful imagery, disability is imbued with new and positive elite meanings by the combination of unashamed 'stump' disclosure but also high-performance sport camera angles, thus bringing another marginalised and 'different' attribute into the mainstream. 'Elite disability' had not previously been considered or framed, in the way that it was for 2012.

'Show the sport!'

Having shown that it was visual parity with the Olympians that prevailed, to support showing 'the stumps', I now explore the two reasons that were given for the opposite perspective. Seeking to claim attention for the athletes' performance achievements, by providing parity with other sports programmes, was the intention of some groups. When it came to what to actually focus on it was the outsourced sports producers and the Paralympic associations who just wanted to 'show the sport'. Two reasons surfaced for apparently wanting to do this.

The first was expressed at Sunset+Vine, one of the sports producers to whom the coverage was outsourced (the other was IMG), where their remit was to deliver high-quality sports coverage and achieve good ratings, as they are well known for doing. The strategy of avoiding showing physical impairments would have helped to achieve those ratings as it could have appealed to their 'normal' viewers. Editorial leanings in this direction by the Head of Television Sport did, according to other contributors, beneficially affect the overall television output in what became a collaborative effort. He was called 'a safe pair of hands' by a senior colleague; however, his stance also created 'a battleground', according to the Disability Executive at Channel 4.

The second reason others wanted to focus on the sport was to conceal the impairments. For some stakeholders this was so that the Paralympians 'could be taken seriously as athletes' (BPA Press Officer, *Interview*, 2015). Their concern for parity was not in terms of visual treatment, but in terms of being accepted as if they were other athletes, who are normally taken seriously. At the time it seemed very important for the BPA (British Paralympic Association) to make sure sport was exclusively the focus. In the chapter on marketing it is made clear that in fact, once the disability element had been flagged up, the schedules and trailers did then go on to focus on the sport, literally switching from one emphasis to the other. However, at the production stage the IPC, as well, were apparently upset by, and distanced themselves from, the more direct representations of the *Meet the Superhumans* campaign. Letters of objection were written, but not taken into account.

The BPA, who represent the group of athletes, were not able to affect the editorial decisions with the fiercely independent Channel 4 in the way that they had apparently been able to do with the BBC (who mainly ran edited highlights packages). It was over this point, of what to show, that they fell out. However, after the event I went to visit the BPA offices where it was clear from the artwork over all their walls that the Paralympics coverage had in fact been a fantastic success for them, fulfilling their true focus of, perhaps, sport for sports' sake. The unexpected outcome and benefit to them was that by focusing, against their better judgement, on disability, the result was then a desired focus on sport and sporting performance. The Communications Officer for the BPA told me that their sportsmen and women just wanted to be regarded as elite athletes. It was clear, though, that the organisation had initially resisted the risky approach that the Channel 4 network felt was required to get them there. One of the Paralympians themselves had understood the 'disclosure etiquette' better, when he told a Sports Editor for Channel 4:

> Yeah, we understand people want to know why I've only got one arm, but once you've done it once can you talk about how far I'm jumping?
> (Commissioning Editor for Sport, *Interview*, 2015)

The Paralympic athlete recounted by the Editor here understood that first you need to 'come out' as other stigmatised groups do, then be celebrated in all your normality or, in the case of elite sport, extraordinariness. Negrine and Cumberbatch (1992) in their comprehensive study of disability on television surmised that:

> Given [...] people with disabilities wish to be treated first and foremost as people, and only secondarily as people who happen to have disabilities, they should be so treated on television.
> (ibid., p. 141)

In practice, though, the difference needs to be addressed first, so that, setting the anomaly aside, the person can then be viewed as they normally would, if they were 'normal'. This was the firm view, at least, of the in-house editorial teams who commissioned the programmes for 2012.

A measurable and key success of the visually shocking media coverage, as it transpired, is that journalists and magazine writers now ring up the Press Office at the BPA to ask if their gold medallists would like to feature in fashion magazines. Previously, I was advised, they were rung up by medical magazines who would say 'can I speak to the one who had cancer?' (BPA Press Officer, *Interview*, 2015). It appears the strategy to 'show the stumps' and then 'show the sport', whilst perhaps not a 'hegemonic manipulation' (Dayan and Katz, 1994, p. 5) that the Olympics can achieve on a global scale, was at least a visual manipulation of 'dramatic character' and 'tone' (Roche, 2000, p. 1).

Reversing old stereotypes, as discussed, worked in a similar way for the normalisation of racial difference. Also, Hall observes that once people of colour had been made central within certain media genres this made them 'essential to what we may call [the] mystical life and culture of American Cinema' (2012, p. 261). Now that the Paralympic athletes have joined the elites at the centre of international televised sport, this same phenomenon has occurred, to some extent, for them. They can now sell fashion items based on the shift of their personas from margin to mainstream. The ghoulish focus on, for example, cancer, has been transposed into 'normal' human celebrity, parity even, as regards magazine interest and articles, with their non-disabled celebrity peers.

The role sport plays in creating celebrity, and specifically through artificial rivalry narratives, is explored in the next chapter. However, this strategy of noticing, in order to stop noticing, worked here in the 2012 media representations of disabled athletes with curiosity possibly amplified in this context by heightened viewer interest that year in athletic performances. This interest was probably enhanced by the known sense of collective national identity derived from hosting an Olympic Home Games (Tomlinson and Young, 2006), against which the Paralympics was deliberately compared. Equal treatment, visually, was a risky strategy and was justified, by my participants, on the grounds of giving parity to help normalise disability. The demystifying process, achieved here by emphasising *in order to* minimise, did seem to some degree to remove the stigma (recognised by Jackson et al., 2015), making the athletes appear more 'normal' and 'human', at least in the visual representations. According to my contributors, it was clearly a producer intention, therefore, to achieve normalisation by 'showing the stumps' first, within the sports context, then go on to celebrate the unfettered focus of 'showing the sport'.

Which stereotype to use?

One of the other ways that the producers sought to bring the Paralympics into the mainstream was by redefining the identities of the Paralympic athletes. To give the disabled athletes parity with the Olympians they needed to reject the existing negative stereotype associated with disability sport, and create new meanings. In this section I explore the theme of the selection process, showing that the producers first chose to not use the 'victim of circumstance' stereotype, with its connotations of brave and courageous. They did then begin to construct the Paralympians as fictional 'superheroes', with technological cyborg references, but finally, with an intervention from the Director of Brand, Marketing and Culture at LOCOG, settled for a disability/Olympian hybrid of 'superhumans'. They felt this last one was more grounded in reality and made them more like Olympians. I will show how the seeming nuance, of what still seems to be the exceptional trope, created a stereotype onto which they were then able to superimpose a new type of extraordinariness. This new meaning was a combination of 'extraordinarily different', 'extraordinarily good at sport', and also 'extraordinarily human'.

Stereotypes, as already noted, give one group a dominant power over the 'other'. In the field of communication theory, building on Silverstone's (2005) and Livingstone's (2009) discussion about 'mediation' in the meaning-making process, Thumim (2015) suggests that 'specific instances' (p. 57) of media production should be analysed as part of the process of understanding more fully how meanings are constructed. Thumim reinforces the point that it is the 'power relations' (ibid.) that should be acknowledged, as these continue through the whole mediation process, beginning with production. Examining the construction of the superhuman stereotype, at the production stage, can therefore reveal those power relations because, as Hall (2012) has established, power is made apparent when one group make representations about another. This power is revealed in the micro details, in this case, of how one stereotype was rejected and another powerful one adapted to mean something potentially new.

The mediation process is particularly transparent with the Olympic and Paralympic Games. As part of the media sports complex (see Jhally, 1989) televised sport is understood to be a highly mediated environment, with powerful constructions of apparently 'live', neutral-sounding 'coverage'. The coverage does not actually 'cover' the sport, rather it articulates constructed narratives (Horne et al., 2013) which are developed using the actions and stories of stereotyped athletes. In this setting, then, how meanings are negotiated and constructed, in specific instances, reveals more about the power relations that operate within the production process.

For example, recent semiotic analysis of the 'superhumans' trope, as used by Channel 4 for London 2012, has revealed resonances with other cultural influences (see Alexander, 2015) such as Nietzsche, X-men, and a superhuman race. Strong connections are made to these historic references derived from an analysis of the content. My discussions with those who actually encoded the stereotype tell a slightly different, but overlapping story to the one derived from scrutinising the texts.

For London 2012, the producers met the 'superhumans' in real life before they represented them onscreen which affected how they sought to portray them. As well as some athletes coming into the studios (Commissioning

Editor for Sport, *Interview*, 2015), in particular the 'normal' TV producers encountered the 'other' athletes at an international swimming gala and also at a wheelchair basketball match. The reality of those meetings imbued everyone I spoke to with the desire to no longer sanitise depictions of this group of sportspeople, and instead represent the raw reality of their high-performing athleticism in a more tangible way. They also watched the documentary *Murderball* about wheelchair rugby, and that had its own aggressive and masculine style which several contributors referenced.

Disability scholars have noted that wheelchairs are the most commonly accepted trope to symbolise disability on television (e.g. Hardin and Hardin, 2004; Barnes and Mercer, 2010) and heightened masculinity is still the prevalent representation for Olympic sport (Morris, 1991, p. 93; Horne et al., 2013; Howe, 2008). *Murderball* and the competitive basketball had both. Close encounters with the 'crashes and the clashes', which I discuss below, changed their attitudes towards disability sport and the Paralympic athletes. The swimming gala, for other reasons, shifted their paradigms too. Between these two events it was collectively decided that they were 'not victims', they were 'nearly superheroes' but actually 'superhuman', in every sense of the word that the range of producers understood it, as I will now show.

Not 'victims'

The first moment that changed attitudes within the production teams, and triggered the determination to give the Paralympics parity with the Olympics, was a swimming gala in Sheffield. This was one of several pre-events attended by many of the production staff (another included the World Championships in Eindhoven, 2010). Unsolicited, the occasion came up in many of my interviews because it had clearly left an impact for some that never really left them. This swimming event is where many contributors had their own perspective on disability changed. The shock of the spectacle of 'torsos, stumps and stuff' (Film Director, *Interview*, 2014) was laid bare and an extraordinary contrast between the athletes either being helped, or crawling to the poolside, and then achieving record-breaking swimming speeds, challenged notions of their pre-existing stereotypes. A recurrent observation from my interviews was voiced by the Video Editor, who said:

> The interesting thing was that you could see all they were thinking about was qualifying [as] fully focused athletes.
>
> (Video Editor, *Interview*, 2014)

That their sporting performance was 'all they were thinking about' was a dramatic realisation for Hardy and many others. They no longer saw the Paralympians as tragic victims, with their own 'special sports' event. The tragic victim is the most prevalent or 'normal' way of perceiving people with disabilities (see, for example, Hevey, 1992; Clogston, 1990; Brittain, 2010) and this shift away from that normality to a different one happened at an early pre-production stage. Most of my participants had something to say about the personal paradigm shift the first-hand exposure to the swimming events had on them. There was also a striking line in the film they all watched, at one of the team away days, that summarised this perspective of not being a victim. One of the athletes says, 'I don't want a hug, I want a medal' (*Murderball*, 2005). The Channel 4 output reflected this perspective, with a distinctive point of view. They also rejected any hint of victimhood in the programme tonality throughout, and this was a perspective change for the producers that took place, notably, before the representations were constructed. As such these constructions were genuine reflections of the attitudes held by the programme creators.

By contrast to this more positive perspective, a senior executive told me that a Paralympian had come in and said that she'd just done a piece with a national news outlet and the tonality of it was just so awful she'd never want to do anything for them ever again:

> Because it was all that kind of 'oh, aren't they brave' thing. She went on to say that this was the 'kind of crap that we desperately wanted to get rid of'.
>
> (anon.)

With the issue of tone it was clear the Channel 4 teams were aware of what to do and what not to do. The tone of voice delivered in vision, or with the voice-overs and commentaries, was also carefully managed and trained to avoid the 'victim of circumstance' trope. In their trainings one of the slides read as follows:

> For the Paralympics, with emphasis on elite sport, if we're not careful with tone and balance across all our programming we'll be right back in 'exceptionally brave and talented' mode.
>
> (C4TVC, 2011)

The 'brave and talented mode' stems from a well-used media representation suggesting that as a disabled person 'anyone living a normal life must be extraordinary' (Charlton, 2000, p. 52). The separation they were trying to make was between being 'extraordinary at sport', which would normalise them as Olympians, as distinct from the old victim trope for the weak sub-human disabled person.

It was as if the effect of those personal encounters with extreme and challenging difference somehow shocked the production teams into looking more closely at what they were seeing, finding a more compelling meaning beyond the appearance and the classic victim stigma. Exposure to the realities of the athletes' differences, whilst living, training, and competing, forced the production teams to pay attention to their other attributes. My first interviews were conducted 18 months after the event and the details were recounted with clear and vivid insight with each contributor demonstrating that the moments had made an impact on them. This is important because there was a clear transmission of the personal and collective experience of the production personnel into the creative production process. Exposing the producers to those they were to create representations of, prior to the creation of that content, played a significant part in shaping their rejection of the tragic victim stereotype.

I observed that the experience of the producers almost exactly replicates what made it to the screens. The most well-known television presenter, brought in by Channel 4 for the 2012 and 2016 coverage from the BBC, had an insight that is particularly significant as she was uniquely positioned to notice the details, having personally presented the television coverage of the Paralympics since 2000 for the BBC and then, from 2012, for Channel 4. She had not attended the pre-events, but she told me how she suddenly realised what was different, for her, about the London 2012 coverage. It was the swimming:

> I remember the first time I went to a swimming event at the Paralympic Games, and I – you cannot not be shocked because there's no prosthetic limbs; there's no clothing either, so you are seeing everything and, you know, you will see an amputee – a double-arm amputee, for example, helping a double-leg amputee to get dressed, or you'll see somebody clothing themselves on their own with their feet or eating breakfast with their feet. I mean, it is amazing. But when the BBC covered the swimming, they would join it as the athletes were – as the gun was about to go, so you'd only briefly see the swimmers on the podium. And they would leave it before they got out of the pool.
>
> (BBC and C4 TV Presenter, *Interview*, 2016)

The impact of the exposure to physical difference was the same for this TV presenter as it had been for the producers previously. However, she noticed that these differences were being displayed on camera for the first time:

> Channel 4, because it was live, live, live [...] joined as you would join for an Olympics, as the athletes were coming out of the changing room. Now some of them were coming out in chairs; some of them were coming out with prosthetic limbs that they then removed. You then would see them either get on the start block or get into the water and they would stay with the pictures for them getting out of the water. Now that does something in your – you know, to a viewer – that is showing you an awful lot more of the human body than you would ever have seen before.
>
> (ibid.)

It was clear to someone who presented both the BBC and the Channel 4 coverage, that what we were seeing onscreen, although stark, was visual parity with the Olympic coverage. Schantz and Gilbert (2012) summarise the media portrayals within disability sport in the decades immediately prior to London 2012 as either 'glamorous hagiography' transforming the athletes into tragic overcoming 'heroes' or nothing much, as overlooked 'zeros' (p. 14). In my interviews there was no evidence of intended portrayals as either tragic or overlooked. In fact the tragic or brave portrayals were studiously avoided.

There were also, as well as visual and tone-of-voice considerations, issues of storytelling. Whilst framing the narrative for disability is part of the next chapter, it needs a mention here because the 'exceptionally brave and talented' mode is also commonly associated with the use of back-stories which have constructed narratives. Very often disability back-stories are used to evoke sympathy (Barnes, 1992; Garland-Thomson, 2002), and this was something Channel 4 were trying to change. The sporting context of back-story usage has been briefly addressed in some of the recent academic articles relating to media representations of the Paralympics (Gilbert and Schantz, 2012; Silva and Howe, 2012) and more specifically following Rio 2016 (Pullen et al., 2019). However, very few Paralympic researchers examine television in particular (Howe, 2008, p. 4). I found a range of views towards these back-stories amongst my interviewees, particularly relating to the perpetuation of tragedy and victimhood:

> The back stories were clearly a very powerful tool and a slightly controversial one, because I think some people felt that an old-fashioned approach, that is potentially overly sentimental, actually takes away from them as sports people.
>
> (Commercial Lawyer, *Interview*, 2015)

Whilst it is an old-fashioned approach to documentary, and current affairs pre-interview profiles, the televisual treatment is still newer to sport and not necessarily sentimental. This comment by the Head of Marketing gives an indication of why it was used at all:

> It is a tool in every sport and I would say that the only sport that probably get away with it, without doing it, is something like football because it's so popular. The footballers can be the most boring people in the world and it doesn't really matter, they are forgiven. But in a lot of Olympic sports they don't actually get much coverage outside the Olympics, aside from athletics and the hundred metres. Most of them are sports that only really get interest every few years.
>
> (Head of Marketing, *Interview*, 2014)

The point here is that the backgrounder packages are made so that the audience can relate to and identify with the characters. When the back-stories were used, they were being utilised as they would for other sport and not to exacerbate the victim stereotype. In this way then, the production personnel consciously steered away from the 'brave and courageous' disabled trope, during the 12 days of the event, only utilising that televisual treatment when it served the sporting context.

No to 'superheroes'

Having refuted the victim trope, the team then started to design another one on paper. Glorifying high achievement is central to the drama of televised sport, and was therefore a necessary device for the Paralympic Games, if it were to be viewed on a par with other international sports competitions. Creating superheroes, though, as a media representation, unfortunately falls directly into the category of the much-denounced disempowering supercrip framing (Barnes, 1992; Haller, 1995; Howe, 2011; Gilbert and Schantz, 2012). This depiction was originally identified by Barnes, and specifically refers to the need for 'super' or 'magical powers' to achieve acceptance if you are different (1992, p. 12). The racial equivalent stereotype he cites (ibid.) is that they be 'good at rhythm or exceptional athletes' (p. 12). He goes on to say that if a disabled person is, for example, blind, he/she needs to have super sensitive hearing, or some other extraordinary compensating facility that makes them an exception that we can allow, whilst keeping, as Hall (2012) would say, a safe distance.

Depicting these 'elite' others as superheroes was an intuitive reflex for the Creative Network Director, who also directed the film called *Meet the Superhumans*. Tom Tagholm told me how he had been affected by watching wheelchair basketball players, as he sensed their competitiveness and raw energy, even just 'racing to barge through a door first' after their practice. He went on to say that:

> Their rage and their fuel and their way of turning that into a positive energy, you know, seemed like quite an interesting way to build up a way of seeing Paralympians.
>
> (Film Director, *Interview*, 2014)

Tagholm's initial idea, he told me, had been for the 'superhero' frame rather than 'superhuman' which was the later change made by Greg Nugent, Brand, Marketing and Culture Director at LOCOG. The feel for how to create the personas of the Paralympians was based initially on thoughts of the X-Men triggered by the sportsmen and women that Tagholm had met. This concept was underpinned by other connotations, which he described as, 'the way that a lot of these superheroes have some kind of a society-perceived flaw that becomes their strength'. He personally experienced their 'flaws' as *part of* their strength and it was this that he was trying to convey.

Whilst disability is often depicted as something that needs fixing (Barnes, 1992; Shakespeare, 2013), or sometimes seen as incidental (Ellis and Goggin, 2015, p. 81), Müller et al. (2012) assert that this is not always the case. They say it may be *part of* the disabled person's identity that should be accepted, rather than overlooked or overcome (ibid.). It was Tagholm's experience that disability could not be separated from his sense of who the athletes were. He felt it was partly what gave them their extraordinary athleticism and this was what *he* meant by superhero, as he felt 'who they were' gave them powers. His genuine assimilation of the athletes' energy and emotional drivers was communicated clearly to me and he spoke of his desire to catch this essence on film.

The Film Director's depictions were not destined or designed, by him, to separate the viewer or create a safe distance as a cognitive act. It was my observation that he intended there to be nothing safe about his directing or filmic style at all and that the essence of raw reality was essential to his depictions. It appeared to me that Tagholm's own absorption of the Marvel comics, as personally assimilated childhood texts, helped him construct his conceptualisation of the Superhero trope. He remembered and understood the cyborgian undertones. Hall speaks of the 'intertextuality' (2012) between cultural forms where one existing cultural product can affect the creation of others. Tagholm's childhood affinity with the Marvel comics and the film is an example of this intertextuality as his previous experience clearly touched his adult creative imagination when concocting the superheroes concept.

The film, *Murderball*, watched by all the team, may have affected him too, as he particularly mentioned it. It starts with a close-up of a spanner as part of the getting-out-of-bed routine for a disabled athlete, in a sequence reminiscent of a fantasy cyborg future. It is significant that Tagholm's take on the meaning of superheroes as a frame for the athletes was 'where biology meets technology'. This did also come from his self-confessed passion for watching technology in other sport. He said:

> The geekiest side of my sport viewing is that I like Formula One as well. And you look at these things [Paralympic wheelchairs] and think, 'Okay, it's quite incredible, the lightness of the chairs and the engineering that goes into them' and that's kind of visual, very visual actually, you know, if you watch X-Men or you watch any of these Marvel or DC Comics franchises, how that is very filmic. And like the sprint chair, or a carbon fibre blade, is straight out of moviemaking. And it just seemed like that way of seeing humans...yeah, there was a lot of that DNA in it.
>
> (Film Director, *Interview*, 2014)

As another dimension to textual analysis and decoding research, such as that undertaken by Alexander (2015, pp. 107–111), of the *Meet the*

Superhumans trailer (2012), this producer insight demonstrates a slightly different creative perspective shaping the 'encoding' (Hall, 1973; 1980) stage. Scholars are seeking to 'understand their ideas regarding the delivery of Paralympic sports to the public' (see Schantz and Gilbert, 2012a, p. 237) and this interview excerpt demonstrates the influence of both phenomenology and intertextuality in the concept of the superheroes. Tagholm was affected by the direct experience of those he was seeking to create representations of, as well as by fictional texts he had enjoyed in his non-professional life. It was mainly the filmic nature of the Marvel and DC Comics franchises that Tagholm sought to emulate, he told me, to emphasise the athletes' differences. In this case it was filmic parity he was wanting to achieve whilst engaging with, and wanting to borrow from, the fictitious but real, struggle-against-society connotations.

In the real-world sporting context, away from fiction, Howe (2011) questions the 'cyborgification of Paralympic bodies' (p. 868) by suggesting that this particular framing disempowers disabled athletes. In my interview with Adepitan, a technology-dependent ex-Paralympian, his view of his own empowerment, as seen on and offscreen, was far more positive. He said:

> Wearing blades or having technology – it was always going to go that way, but I think people didn't realise that, when you have a disability, technology is a really big part of your life....it helps us to go where we want to go.
>
> (Ex-Paralympian TV presenter, *Interview*, 2015)

The relationship of a Paralympian to his or her technology, sporting or otherwise, recalls what Coutant (2012) describes as a prototype for future forms of human being. She argues that, in this sense of predicting the future, the Paralympics has not yet fulfilled its potential or full reach. This makes it important to choose a stereotype conveying the right nuances. She sees the technology fusion within the sporting arena as a laboratory for future interventions that many of us might need or want (p. 168). Less positively, Haraway (1991) calls the cyborg the 'awful apocalyptic telos' (p. 150) suggesting a future that none of us want, where humanity ultimately loses its independence. Adepitan, however, put it another way saying that:

> Everything [is] happening at the right time when we're going through a technological revolution and also maybe a cultural revolution in the way that people look at disability and disability sport.
>
> (Ex-Paralympian TV presenter, *Interview*, 2015)

Amongst others, Shakespeare (2006) has pointed out that disability is uncomfortable because, even if we don't have a sudden accident, it points to a future version of ourselves, if we live until we are handicapped by old age.

The cyborg element of the Paralympics may be more watchable now because we realise that technology can make up for our deficits and therefore disability is not necessarily as threatening as it once was. I would also assert that because ableist society is becoming more and more dependent on technology too, as indeed I was in locating the rendezvous for my interview with Adepitan, there should, therefore, be less stigma attached to the disabled 'other' group also using it. However, for London 2012, it was felt that the 'freaky cyborg' connotation, within the superhero stereotype, carried unwanted science fiction references. Therefore, resonating too much with fictional characters, on these grounds, the stereotype of the 'superheroes' was dropped.

One of the 4Creative Business Managers, Kuba Wieczorek, described their thinking in more detail:

> If you position them as sort of superheroes, almost it's never going to work, so the big, big, strategic creative flip that happened, when we went back to the drawing board was, rather than 'Meet the Superheroes' let's change it to 'Meet the Superhumans'. And that was a big flip – they turned from superheroes to superhumans so we rooted them in reality and we rooted it in real sport and that was a huge turning point for us – it goes from you positioning them as bionic men that are almost fictitious to real sports people – it's a huge shift: a campaign rooted in reality rather than in a conception.
>
> (Business Manager, *Interview*, 2015)

By changing the language, initially by eliminating 'disability' from their own vocabulary, and now by changing a single word, they repositioned the Paralympians so that they could treat them equally and normalise them as 'real sports people'.

Yes to 'superhumans'

The word they finally chose has never been a neutral one for representation scholars, as it carries other meanings relating to the extraordinary, specifically, with disability, the 'having to over achieve to be accepted' trope (e.g. Barnes, 1992; Garland-Thomson, 2002; Haller, 2010; Clogston, 1990; Purdue and Howe 2012). However, for some of my contributors this was not the focus.

Whilst considering the framings for his subjects, in his role as Film Director, Tagholm had another defining experience. This was a profound 'lightbulb moment' for him about realising their need to purposefully focus on the sport:

> These little windows open in your creative brain and you think, 'Oh, that's what this is about'. This is about people busting themselves to succeed and to win. There's a backdrop of a fuck load of adversity [sic.]

as there is with all elite sportsmen and women, and that was a sort of...
that was a sort of important gear change for us in our thinking and the
way we saw this.

(Tagholm, Creative Network Director, *Interview*)

This shift, or gear change, was a shift in representation of 'others' to try to
capture 'the essence' of the athletes that these creatives had met. It is one
of those specific instances of mediation (see Thumim, 2015) that shows the
power lies not only in the representation, but even more with the producers
who create it. The producers here were powerful agents who changed the
athletes' personas from a fictional to factual stereotype. In turn this decision
changed the trajectory of the Paralympians as they were propelled into the
public domain. Silva and Howe (2012) suggest that disability is essentially
misrepresented in disability sport (p. 175) by exacerbating the 'supercrip'
representation as an 'othering' spectacle. However, in this case, the Channel 4
team were aiming for a closer to 'us' kind of human reality when they dropped
the superheroes concept and finally adopted the 'superhuman' idea, as the
defining frame for the Paralympians.

Although it may seem a fine nuance between supercrip and superhuman,
the lexicon of sports descriptions, that includes this word, does not carry the
same stigma with it for sports high achievers. Also, for the team, the step
from *hero to *human was meant to bring the raw reality they had experienced, in the presence of the training athletes, constructively into the media
frame. For the *Meet the Superhumans* trailer, the athletes were depicted
preparing for their events, with a high-performance sports build-up, that
is briefly interrupted, then their energy is unleashed in the stadium, on the
track, and in the pool as if the Olympics was back on TV. Hall calls this way
of reversing a known stereotype the 'revenge film' (2012, p. 260) to bring
the weaker 'other' group into its own, and into the arena, literally in this
case, to inhabit the space of the 'normals'. It was an interesting extra detail
that the crowds and full stadium were faked using CGI so that the Paralympic athletes really did look like Olympians, transforming their previous
stereotype. The full stadium depiction may also have helped sell tickets to
the real event.

One of the benefits of a media production study is to be able to establish
what meanings were intended at the encoding stages. Whilst the producers
here had a collective intention, they did however have individual understandings of what the superhuman trope might convey. From the outset,
within the team who made and promoted the *Meet the Superhumans* television trailer, there were a variety of opinions about what 'superhuman' might
mean. An Executive Producer for 4Creative, the in-house marketing team,
felt 'superhuman' was the right word, 'because they are pushing against
more than other people are pushing against. It's harder for them'. Also he
pointed out that they run into people not wanting to help or support them,

who resist them and 'as athletes it is unlikely they will ever get parity in funding'. He felt that this made them superhuman, training with less financial support. The extra effort required for their achievements did in that sense make them 'super' human beyond, rather than equal to, the Olympic athletes.

Superhuman, as a concept seems to conflict with human vulnerability. Yet, the Head of Communication at the International Paralympic Committee felt the Superhuman ad helped to give the disabled athletes 'equal status' to the Olympians whilst also providing insight into their pasts. He explained:

> So it comes back to London 2012, LOCOG, saying, 'We're going to try and aim for parity between the Olympics and the Paralympics'. Fine [...], how are we going to position the Paralympics? Well if we can achieve that, we need to position Paralympic sport as high-performance sport. But we still need to tell people a little bit about the back-stories. We need to show – we need to focus on – a certain number of athletes and their training regimes and how they get to high-performance sport. And if you encapsulate all of that, that's the Superhumans advert.
>
> (IPC Head of Communication, *Interview*, 2015)

The declared purpose, then, was not to patronise but to help us get to know the personalities, for the purposes of enjoying the rivalries and the sport. Schantz and Gilbert (2012b) ask what the Paralympic media producers' intentions are (p. 237). In this case, 'humanising' people who had previously been objectified and caricatured was felt to be a necessary route to bridging the gap, to make something of no interest into watchable mainstream TV.

In addition to surviving dramatic life events, there were still other interpretations of the 'superhuman' term that my participants articulated. One of the sports producers felt that it was their elite training which made them 'superhuman' especially combined with the effort, with or without limbs, of 'just getting out of bed in the morning, let alone to the trackside'. There was considerable debate amongst various stakeholders as to how the group of superhuman characteristics should be represented. The Disability Executive at Channel 4, according to others, doggedly pursued a particular line which eventually prevailed. Her recollections of this experience she described as follows:

> There was some degree of suspicion because they didn't know us and they were slightly worried I think that because our pitch had been so much about bringing disability to the fore, and if I use the word 'confronting', I mean, 'making people realise' that disability was being overcome as well as [presenting] the delivery of an extraordinary sporting performance.
>
> (Disability Executive, *Interview*, 2015)

It seems to be the case that creating distance was not a direct intention and that personal engagement with the elite team inspired and informed their decisions to give the Paralympians parity with other athletes. The Film Director explained:

> There's a texture to it and a really compelling and tough back story to these guys' lives. But, it all comes into focus when you realise that one of the massive tragedies is being 0.5 of a second over the time they wanted to get.
>
> (Film Director, *Interview*, 2015)

The Paralympians were seen by the creative team, who concocted the *Superhumans* campaign, as an extraordinary group of high-achieving athletes who were being overlooked just because of their physical impairments. Bringing them out into the open was felt by many to be a way they could make a difference using their creative roles in public television. They were not personally trying to disempower the athletes; they wanted to give them a mainstream televisual treatment.

The connecting back-story element they all mentioned was the much contested 'eight second explosion sequence' in the *Meet the Superhumans* trailer, consisting of soldiers stepping onto a land-mine, a pregnant woman receiving bad news, and a car crash causing paraplegic injuries. Arguments raged about whether to include these realities, and the reasons for inclusion are relevant here. The Chief Marketing and Communications Officer said:

> We have got such a job to do to change people's minds that you have to shock people. And if that is what it takes, that is what it takes. But it wasn't a shock for the sake of it, it was shock based in truth! You are just telling a little bit of the back story, and of course you know there was no way we were going to take that out. It goes on the air and that is part of what creates this amazing response that people have to it.
>
> (Chief Marketing and Communications
> Officer, *Interview*, 2015)

By connecting the viewer to the eight second unexpected-life-event sequence, the producers wanted to break the detachment commonly experienced when viewing disability and make us realise that we could also become them. In this case, the Paralympians ceased to be vulnerable, but we became so.

In order to depict disabled athletes as members of the human race rather than extreme outsiders (that we don't want to look at), plenty of other devices were used. These are described within each programme format in the next chapter. What is not included there is the controversial middle section of the aforementioned trailer. The 'eight seconds explosion sequence' cuts across binary representations, where the 'normal' collection of characteristics is implicit from the spectacle of the 'other' characteristics (Hall, 2012). This happens because the visuals and the soundtrack yank the viewer across the threshold of 'them' to 'us'. The producers discussed this at their away day training, using the following slide:

> It's when viewers happen on disability when they least expect it, that we can really open eyes, stretch minds and change attitudes.
>
> (C4TVC, 2011)

Almost all of my contributors described this sequence that they had to defend, as a lynchpin within the coverage. Drawing on previous research it is clear why, as it shifted the power of legitimated exclusion to seeing disability as a life-event for all of 'us' that may have to be faced. Garland-Thomson (1997) articulates that historically 'the extraordinary body is fundamental to the narrative by which we make sense of ourselves and our world' (p. 1). The sense we make of ourselves is that 'they' with extraordinary bodies are so 'other' we can feel ourselves to be safely normal. To show disability suddenly happening to some of us, by stepping on landmines, hearing bad news in the maternity unit, or crashing a car, forces a step-change from 'them' to 'us' in just this one brief televisual moment. The trick was to make the viewer 'just happen on it, when they least expected it'.

The surprise moment disrupts not just audience expectation but also the modern spectacle of freakery, where 'an inextricable yet particular exclusionary system [is] legitimated by bodily variation' (Garland-Thomson, 1997, p. 10). Once bodily differences are noted in the film, we are then, in the eight seconds, forced to associate with the differences, making our viewing of it unsafe. This is presumably why some people objected to it. We were just getting used to the high-performance sport effect, then were forced to identify with unexpected life circumstances, and this jolt was deliberately intended by the producers to make the audience experience and understand the Paralympians' vulnerable humanity.

In this section I have shown that whilst still aiming for parity with the human race in general, and the Olympic athletes in particular, the producers rejected one stereotype, nearly used another, and finally opted for a third. They actively chose to dismiss the 'victim of circumstance' trope with its associated 'brave and courageous' narrative. The 'superhero' was next, with its cyborgian connotations, but this was rejected after a while, because it was derived from fiction and not reality. When, on the grounds of 'reality', the superhero stereotype was adapted, or 'flipped' (Business Manager, *Interview*, 2015), to 'superhuman', I have shown that this frame was chosen to *give the Paralympians parity* with the Olympians, and with normal, not disenfranchised, human beings. Some of the Olympic athletes had already been called 'superhuman' (e.g. Michael Phelps, the US Gold medallist swimmer), and this was part of their justification. My contributors made it clear that they associated the idea of superhuman with 'normal', able-bodied, Olympians. Critical disability scholars recognise the redefined athleticism framing but still contest, from an emancipatory perspective, what sort of parity the extraordinariness achieves (see McGillivray et al., 2019).

The superhuman stereotype is of course extremely close to the supercrip framing that many scholars have analysed in great detail (e.g. Barnes, 1992; Schantz and Gilbert, 2001; Thomas and Smith, 2003; Snyder and Mitchell, 2010; Peers, 2009; Silva and Howe, 2012). In this instance the editorial decisions appeared to be based on a conceptual meaning of superhuman as gold medallist, not superhuman as tragic victim. The quest for joint parity, with 'us' the humans, and 'them' the high-performing elite Olympic athletes, may have moved this 'super' and 'human' portrayal forward, or not. Normalisation would depend on whether a somewhat contradictory meaning could be superimposed, of the disabled athletes somehow being extraordinary but also just like 'us' as well. A concerted effort was made by the producers to normalise the Paralympians and this was partly achieved through the negotiations around the group of athletes being 'extraordinarily human', 'extraordinarily good at sport', as well as being 'extraordinarily different'.

The momentum of the Olympics and the home nation's desire to continue identifying with Team GB will have helped frame these extraordinary disabled athletes, in a superhuman sort of way, but now suddenly they were also framed as agonisingly human – like the rest of 'us'. There was a shift in emphasis from the oddity of difference to recognised outstanding qualities, making the athletes extraordinary, in the same way as the Olympians are. This was to normalise their difference into a more acceptable elite athleticism which we had grown to enjoy in the summer of 2012. Walsh put it this way, 'It finally feels like there are no "no go" areas for disability, and disabled people have joined the human race as depicted on TV' (Disability Executive, *Interview*, 2015).

Inspired by the Paralympics, MP, Mark Harper, afterwards expressed in a government paper a similar thought, 'I want to get the message out that disability is about "us" not "them"' (DWP, 2014, p. 3). He went on to say that with now almost 12 million disabled people in the UK:

> Many of us have disabled people among our friends or family and we are all increasingly likely to live to an age when we may well experience multiple impairments ourselves.... Removing barriers is not just good for disabled people but for all of us.
>
> (ibid.)

Media representations at the London 2012 Paralympic Games were already going some way to reflect this change in our cultural and political thinking. The *Superhumans* campaign, with carefully chosen characteristics to represent that stereotype, was considered by my interviewees to have started that trajectory. Changing audience perceptions of disability was a declared aim through the original bid stage and throughout the production process and I have shown that it was undertaken by deliberately altering and reconstructing existing stereotypes. The type and style of coverage was internally promoted across the teams with the *MENTAL4 the Paralympics* in-house training to all decision-making executives and creatives. It was felt that the intended messaging would be risky, but it was nevertheless gladly embraced by the producers, many afterwards saying it was the best thing they had ever worked on.

It emerges that through the two normalising strategies encapsulated by the directives to 'show the stumps' and 'show the sport' a dual depiction was taking place. One looked at the outside, at the anatomical anomaly, which is very much a point of difference. The other focused on the inside, at the triumph and trials of the human spirit, at the points of our human similarity. The coverage included both and was deliberately set within the superhuman framing for marketing purposes in the run-up to the Games. Whilst the word derives from the lexicon of stigma and difference, the producers borrowed it from what they saw as a mainstream Olympic paradigm.

Conclusion

By exploring exactly *how* the producers arrived at which intentional portrayals in this chapter I have shown that they were attempting parity in order to normalise disability. This equal treatment was expressed and applied as equality with other humans; with elite athletes; with other Channel 4 programmes; other projects; other depictions of art, beauty, and sporting imagery and the Olympics presentational style in particular. Whatever the individual level of focus of each producer's role, there was a distinct recollection amongst my participants that, for them, normalisation equalled treating the athletes on a par.

Normalisation and parity, though, are not the same, just as expectation and equality are not. In this case, one may have led to the other; they certainly seem to be linked during this media coverage. Disability is still normally unexpected on television, and triggers the shock of difference, therefore remaining unequally portrayed. Perhaps what may now be *expected*, or normalised, for depictions of disability has been changed, however, through the course of the Channel 4 producers' actions. For a variety of reasons, they nevertheless treated the project as *equal to* other mainstream high-profile programme output.

So, did anything else change? It is evident that some of the apparently distancing models or frames were still being invoked, such as extraordinariness and super-achievement, although many contributors felt these were appropriate for an 'Olympic'-style Games. However, the patronising, victim frames were essentially broken down during the high-achievement events, based around the discourse of peak performance, talent, and training. The Rio 2016 UK press coverage, it was observed, shifted its focus within a Media Event Arc, focusing on problems before the Games, then switching to sports performances, records, personal bests, and medal tallies, before returning to disability in society and legacy issues afterwards (see McGillivray et al., 2019, pp. 10–12). The athleticism element in the middle is how the media teams wanted the event to be positioned.

Whilst encoding the UK host nation output, the understanding that the represented group had been through 'a fuck load of adversity' (Tagholm, Film Director, *Interview*) was an underlying sense experienced by most of my contributors behind the scenes. However, the disability representation of 'triumphing', where present onscreen, they felt was part of the sporting narrative within the sporting context, as the more acceptable 'triumph of the human spirit' that is a standard media trope for elite sport. Since all sportsmen and women have courageous back-stories of determination which often include physical injuries and pain, the familiar context of this normality for depictions of winning elite athletes was used to modify the inherent disability meanings associated previously with marginalised disability sports.

Following on from the Olympic Games, through careful 'thanks for the warm-up' linking by Channel 4, Paralympic athletes had their personas transformed from victim into victor. They were profiled and celebrated for breaking sporting records and winning medals, notwithstanding their added day-to-day victories in managing their lives or even just getting to training. The association, by framing them as Olympians, was intended to break the tragic mould that Paralympic theorists have highlighted in the past (DePauw, 1997; Smith and Thomas, 2005; Howe, 2008). It was noted by my contributors that the athletes that they met train with Olympians and they do Olympian things. They were perceived as extraordinary athletes, physically different in extraordinary ways but also extraordinarily human. Those that I interviewed felt that this combination of meanings was 'cool' and decided to portray the group of previously uncool and tragic 'others' as such.

It is already the case that the extraordinarily cool vibe, blended with superhuman and heroic connotations, is recognisably normal for some ableist sports teams and personalities. Applying this vibe and media treatment to the disabled athletes gave the Paralympians mainstream positioning, changing the meanings that were made about them, at the encoding stage. As well as attempting to normalise disability in this way, by giving the production and the represented group this positional parity, the producers also reframed meanings using the programme types into which they were set. How this was achieved, by adapting existing formats across three different genres of television, is the subject of the next chapter.

Bibliography

Aiello, G. and Parry, K. 2019. *Visual communication: understanding images in media culture*. SAGE.

Alexander, J. 2015. 'Superhumanity' and the embodiment of enlightenment: the semiotics of disability in the official art and advertising of the 2012 British Paralympics. In: D. Jackson et al. eds. *Reframing disability?: media, (dis)empowerment, and voice in the 2012 Paralympics*. Oxford: Routledge, pp. 105–120.

Arpan, L.M., Baker, K., Lee, Y., Jung, T., Lorusso, L., and Smith, J. 2006. News coverage of social protests and the effects of photographs and prior attitudes. *Mass Communication and Society*, 9(1), pp. 1–20.

Banks, M.J. 2009. Gender below-the-line: defining feminist production studies. In: V. Mayer et al. eds. *Production studies: cultural studies of media industries*. London: Routledge, pp. 87–98.

Barnes, C. 1992. *Disabling imagery and the media: an exploration of the principles for media representations of disabled people: the first in a series of reports*. Halifax: Ryburn Publishing.

Barnes, C. and Mercer, G. 2010. *Exploring disability*. Chichester: Wiley.

Berger, P.L. and Luckmann, T. 1979. *The social construction of reality: a treatise in the sociology of knowledge*. Harmondsworth: Penguin.

Braye, S., Dixon, K., and Gibbons, T. 2013. 'A mockery of equality': an exploratory investigation into disabled activists' views of the Paralympic Games. *Disability & Society*, 28(7), pp. 984–996, DOI: 10.1080/09687599.2012.748648

Brittain, I. 2010. *The Paralympic Games explained*. London: Routledge.

Brittain, I. 2012. British media portrayals of Paralympic and disability sport. In: *Heroes or zeros: the media portrayal of Paralympic sport*. Champaign, IL: Common Ground, pp. 105–113.

C4. 2013. *Born risky: Channel 4*. [online]. [Accessed 15 May 2017]. Available from: www.youtube.com

C4TVC. 2011. *MENTAL4 the Paralympics*. [PowerPoint]. Written and presented by Alison Walsh. London: Channel 4 Television Corporation.

Charlton, J. 2000. Living the normal. In: C. Riley ed. *Disability and the media: prescriptions for change*. UPNE Online, pp. 47–55.

Claydon, A. 2015. Framing the difference(s) analysing the representation of the body of the athlete in the 2012 Olympics' and Paralympics' official programmes. In: D. Jackson et al. eds. *Reframing disability? Media, (dis)empowerment, and voice in the 2012 Paralympics*. Oxford: Routledge, pp. 79–93.

Clogston, J.S. 1990. *Disability coverage in 16 newspapers*. Newcastle: Avocado Press.

Corker, M. and Shakespeare, T. 2002. *Disability/postmodernity: embodying disability theory*. London: Continuum.

Coutant, E. 2012. Post-modern perspectives of the media and disability. In: O.J. Schantz and K. Gilbert eds. *Heroes or zeros? The media's perceptions of Paralympic sport*. Champaign, IL: Common Ground, pp. 165–170.

Davis, L.J. 1995. The construction of normalcy. In: L.J. Davis ed. *The disability studies reader*. 4th ed. New York: Routledge, pp. 3–16.

Dayan, D. and Katz, E. 1994. *Media events: the live broadcasting of history*. Cambridge, MA; London: Harvard University Press.

DePauw, K. 1997. The (In)Visibility of DisAbility: cultural contexts and 'sporting bodies'. *Quest*, 49(4), pp. 416–430.

DePauw, K.G.S. 1995. *Disability and sport*. Champaign, IL: Human Kinetics.

Domke, D., Perlmutter, D., and Spratt, M. 2002. The primes of our times? An examination of the 'power' of visual images. *Journalism*, 3(2), pp. 131–159.

DWP. 2014. *Fulfilling potential: making it happen strategy update*. London: The Stationery Office.

Elias, N. 1978. *The civilizing process: the history of manners*. London: Blackwell.

Ellis, K. and Goggin, G. 2015. *Disability and the media*. London: Palgrave.

French, L. and Le Clair, J.M. 2018. Game changer? Social media, representations of disability and the Paralympic Games. In: I. Brittain and A. Beacom eds. *The Palgrave handbook of Paralympic studies*. London: Palgrave Macmillan, doi. org/10.1057/978-1-137-47901-3_6

Garland-Thomson, R. 1997. *Extraordinary bodies: figuring physical disability in American culture and literature*. New York; Chichester: Columbia University Press.

Garland-Thomson, R. 2002. The politics of staring: visual rhetorics of disability in popular photography. In: *Disability studies: enabling the humanities*, pp. 56–75.

Gilbert, K. and Schantz, O. 2008. *The Paralympic Games: empowerment or side show?* Maidenhead: Meyer and Meyer.

Gilbert, K. and Schantz, O. 2012. An implosion of discontent. *Heroes or zeros*. Champaign, IL: Common Ground, pp. 225–236.

Gitlin, T. 1980. *The whole world is watching: mass media in the making and unmaking of the new left*. Berkeley; London: University of California Press.

Goffman, E. 1963. *Stigma: notes on the management of spoiled identity*. Harmondsworth: Penguin.

Hall, S. 1973. *Encoding and decoding in the television discourse*. Birmingham Centre for Contemporary Cultural Studies, The University of Birmingham.

Hall, S. 1980. Cultural studies: two paradigms. *Media, Culture and Society*, 2(1), pp. 57–72.

Hall, S. 2012. *Representation: cultural representations and signifying practices*. 2nd ed. London: SAGE in association with The Open University.

Haller, B. 1995. Rethinking models of media representations of disability. *Disability Studies Quarterly*, 15(2), pp. 26–30.

Haller, B.A. 2010. *Representing disability in an ableist world: essays on mass media*. Louisville, KY: The Advocado Press.

Haller, B. and Preston, J. 2016. Confirming normalcy: 'inspiration porn' and the construction of the disabled subject? In: *Disability and social media*. Routledge, pp. 63–78.

Haraway, D.J. 1991. *Simians, cyborgs, and women: the reinvention of nature*. Virginia: Free Association Books.

Hesmondhalgh, D. 2013. *The cultural industries*. 3rd ed. London: SAGE.

Hevey, D. 1992. *The creatures time forgot: photography and disability imagery*. London: Routledge.

Hilgemberg, T., Ellis, K., and Magladry, M. 2019. The spectacularization of disability sport: Brazilian and Australian newspaper photographs of 2012 London Paralympic athletes. In: *The Routledge companion to disability and media*. Routledge, pp. 101–112.

Hodges, C.E.M., Jackson, D., and Scullion, R. 2015. Voices from the armchair: the meanings afforded to the Paralympics by UK television audiences. In: D. Jackson et al. eds. *Reframing disability? Media, (dis)empowerment, and voice in the 2012 Paralympics.* Oxford: Routledge, pp. 172–186.

Horne, J., Harvey, J., Safai, P., Darnell, S., and Courchesne-O'Neill, S. 2013. *Sport and social movements: from the local to the global.* A&C Black Online.

Howe, P.D. 2008. From inside the newsroom: Paralympic media and the 'production' of elite disability. *International Review for the Sociology of Sport,* 43(2), pp. 135–150.

Howe, P.D. 2011. Cyborg and supercrip: the Paralympics technology and the (dis) empowerment of disabled athletes. *Sociology,* 45(5), pp. 868–882.

Howe, P.D. and Jones, C. 2006. Classification of disabled athletes: (dis)empowering the Paralympic practice community. *Sociology of Sport Journal,* 23(1), pp. 29–46.

IPC. 2019. *Change starts with sport: brand platform* [Corporate Document].

Jackson, D. 2013. *2012 Paralympics changed people's perceptions of disability and disabled sport, BU study finds.* [Online]. [Accessed 31 October 2016]. Available from: www.bournemouth.ac.uk/

Jackson, D., Hodges, C.E.M., Molesworth, M., and Scullion, R. eds. 2015. *Reframing disability: media, (dis)empowerment, and voice in the 2012 Paralympics.* Oxford: Routledge.

Jhally, S. 1989. Cultural studies and the sports/media complex. In: L.A. Wenner ed. *Media, sports and society.* London: SAGE.

Livingstone, S. 2009. On the mediation of everything: ICA presidential address 2008. *Journal of Communication,* 59(1), pp. 1–18.

McGillivray, D., O'Donnell, H., McPherson, G., and Misener, L. 2019. Repurposing the (super)crip: media representations of disability at the Rio 2016 Paralympic Games. *Communication & Sport.* Online.

Maika, M. and Danylchuk, K. 2016. Representing Paralympians: the 'other' athletes in Canadian print media coverage of London 2012. *The International Journal of the History of Sport,* 33(4), pp. 401–417, DOI: 10.1080/09523367.2016.1160061

Misener, L., McPherson, G., McGillivray, D., and Legg, D. 2019. *Leveraging disability sport events.* London: Routledge, https://doi.org/10.4324/9781315108469

Mitchell, D.T. and Snyder, S.L. 1997. *The body and physical difference: discourses of disability.* University of Michigan Press.

Morris, J. 1991. *Pride against prejudice: a personal politics of disability.* Women's Press.

Müller, F., Klijn, M., and Zoonen, L. 2012. Disability, prejudice and reality TV: disablism through media representations. *Telecommunications Journal of Australia,* 62(2).

Murderball. 2005. Rubin and Shapiro. USA: ThinkFilm.

Negrine, R.M. and Cumberbatch, G. 1992. *Images of disability on television.* New York; London: Routledge.

Oliver, M. 1982. *Social work with disabled people.* London: Macmillan, for the British Association of social Workers.

Olympia. 1938. [film]. Leni Riefenstahl. dir. Berlin: GmbH [de].

Parry, K. 2010. A visual framing analysis of British press photography during the 2006 Israel-Lebanon conflict. *Media, War and Conflict,* 3(1), pp. 67–85.

Peers, D. 2009. (Dis) empowering Paralympic histories: absent athletes and disabling discourses. *Disability and Society*, 24(5), pp. 653–665.

Petersen, T. 2005. Testing visual signals in representative surveys. *International Journal of Public Opinion Research*, 17(4), pp. 456–72.

Philo, G. 2012. *Bad news for disabled people: how the newspapers are reporting disability.* [Online]. Glasgow: University of Glasgow.

Pullen, E., Jackson, D., Silk, M., and Scullion, R. 2019. Re-presenting the Paralympics: (contested) philosophies, production practices and the hypervisibility of disability. *Media, Culture & Society*, 41(4), pp. 465–481.

Purdue, D.E.J. and Howe, P.D. 2012. See the sport, not the disability: exploring the Paralympic paradox. *Qualitative Research in Sport, Exercise and Health*, 4(2), pp. 189–205.

Rees, L., Robinson, P., and Shields, N. 2019. Media portrayal of elite athletes with disability – a systematic review. *Disability and Rehabilitation*, 41(4), pp. 374–381, DOI: 10.1080/09638288.2017.1397775

Riefenstahl, L. 1938. See *Olympia*.

Roche, M. 2000. *Mega-events and modernity: Olympics and expos in the growth of global culture.* London: Routledge.

Rowe, D. 2011. *Global media sport: flows, forms and futures.* A&C Black.

Schantz, O.J. and Gilbert, K. 2001. An ideal misconstrued: newspaper coverage of the Atlanta Paralympic Games in France and Germany. *Sociology of Sport Journal*, 18(1), pp. 69–94.

Schantz, O.J. and Gilbert, K. 2012a. The Paralympic movement: empowerment or disempowerment for people with disabilities? *The Palgrave handbook of Olympic studies.* New York: Springer, pp. 358–380.

Schantz, O. and Gilbert, K. 2012b. Researching the future. In: O.J. Schantz and K. Gilbert ed. *Heroes or zeros? The media's perceptions of Paralympic sport.* Champaign, IL: Common Ground, pp. 1–25.

Schantz, O. and Gilbert, K. 2012c. *Heroes or zeros? The media's perceptions of Paralympic sport.* Champaign, IL: Common Ground.

Shakespeare, T. 1999. Art and lies? Representations of disability on film. In: M. Corker and S. French eds. *Disability discourse.* Buckingham: Open University Press, pp. 164–172.

Shakespeare, T. 2006. *Disability rights and wrongs.* London: Routledge.

Shakespeare, T. 2013. *Disability rights and wrongs revisited.* Taylor & Francis Online.

Silva, C.F. and Howe, P.D. 2012. The (in)validity of supercrip representation of Paralympian athletes. *Journal of Sport and Social Issues*, 36(2), pp. 174–194.

Silverstone, R. 2005. *The sociology of mediation and communication.* SAGE.

Smith, A. and Thomas, N. 2005. The 'inclusion' of elite athletes with disabilities in the 2002 Manchester Commonwealth Games: an exploratory analysis of British newspaper coverage. *Sport, Education and Society*, 10(1), pp. 49–67.

Snyder, S.L. and Mitchell, D.T. 2010. *Cultural locations of disability.* University of Chicago Press.

Spence, C. 2018. *Transforming lives – London 2012 progress and challenges.* [online]. [Accessed 12 January 2019]. Available from: www.paralympic.org/news/transforming-lives-london-2012-progress-and-challenges

Stevenson, A. 2010. *Oxford Dictionary of English*. Oxford: OUP.

Tea-Time & Evening Show. 2012. Channel 4. 30 August – 9 September, 17:30–22:00.

Thumim, N. 2015. *Self-representation and digital culture*. Basingstoke: Palgrave Macmillan.

Thomas, N. and Smith, A. 2003. Preoccupied with able-bodiedness? An analysis of the British media coverage of the 2000 Paralympic Games. *Adapted Physical Activity Quarterly*, 20(2), pp. 166–181.

Tomlinson, A. and Young, C. 2006. Culture, politics, and spectacle in the global sports event: an introduction. In: A. Tomlinson and C. Young eds. *National identity and global sporting events: culture, politics and spectacle in the Olympics and the Football World Cup*. Albany: State University of York, pp. 1–14.

Whannel, G. 1992. *Fields in vision: television sport and cultural transformation*. London: Routledge.

Chapter 5

Reframing meanings

Encoding disability across multiple TV programme formats

I have shown in the previous chapter that the combined meanings of being extraordinarily human, extraordinarily different, and extraordinarily good at sport were overlaid onto existing sports representations in order to normalise disability rather than caricature it as stereotypically 'other'. Now I explore how those same combined meanings about disability were also embedded creatively by the producers within the different genres of the saturation coverage programme schedule. My research material suggests that in each case the familiar formats were adapted for the specific purpose of *reframing* as well as normalising disability.

In this chapter I draw on interviews and internal documents to assess how meanings were made, utilising and adapting the forms and structures of each of these genres. I have divided this chapter into three sections to discuss the different programme outputs separately. In the first section I show how *The Breakfast Show* adapted its current affairs format to give some of the filmed inserts a 'first-person' reality TV-style treatment, reinforcing the athletes as 'extraordinarily human'. The second section shows how the producers chose to deliver daytime sports coverage, for morning, afternoon, and early evening, as normal, but with the intentional use of 'a different voice' whilst depicting the athletes as 'extraordinarily good at sport'. Thirdly, I show how the late-night highlights show, *The Last Leg*, was converted at the last minute into a satire, chat format, breaking taboos about disability with humour and banter and a Twitter hashtag #IsItOk. This programme noticed the characters were 'extraordinarily different' as well as human and very good at sport. (*The Last Leg* was brought into peak-time viewing for the Rio 2016 coverage to bring their relaxed brand of familiarity and humour to a broader family audience.) The production teams treated the Paralympians as equal to the Olympians throughout, and they used each programme type differently to do so, as I will show.

The type and format of a television programme frames what Hall (1973; 1980) has called the dominant or preferred meanings associated with media representations. The meanings are not only contained within the screen frame, they are shaped by where the programme is placed in the schedule and what type of content the audience understands it to be. As Lisus and Ericson (1995) argue, audiences read and make sense of messages differently, depending on their expectations of that genre. Other scholars (e.g. Fiske, 1989; Tulloch, 2000; Kuhn, 2007; Dover and Hill, 2007; Livingstone and Lunt, 1993) have also noted that the genre, or type of programme, creates a kind of contract between the producer and the audience, as to how the content should be read and understood.

Initially, the promised segments set out in the Channel 4 broadcasting bid were, loosely, morning, noon, and night coverage with a possible round-up at around midnight (C4TVC, 2009). According to my interview with Channel 4's Commercial Lawyer these slots were originally 'sketched out on the back of an envelope' and others intimated that they improvised as they went along. As the live sport was occurring in the UK's own time zone, being a Home Games, the early and late slots necessarily morphed into other genres, since there was no live sport to show at these points.

All-day every day coverage was something that Channel 4 had the flexibility to do, switching programmes around on their suite of channels to suit what might appeal to their audiences. This level of coverage, in and of itself, has the power to change meanings as I outlined in Chapter 2 (see also Dayan and Katz, 1994). The identification of the athletes as mainstream, rather than marginalised or ostracised, was facilitated by utilising the unifying dynamic of collectively shared mediated sport. Additionally the newly encoded depictions were reinforced by saturating the media coverage. Media saturation, according to Hepp and Couldry (2010), produces cohesion and commonality as outcomes. They describe these phenomena as:

> Situated, thickened, centring performances of mediated communication that are focused on a specific thematic core, across different media products and reach a wide and diverse multiplicity of audiences and participants.
>
> (ibid., 2010, p. 16)

The following sections will show how the sense of collective identity, generated in the mega-events saturated sporting context, was used to overcome the gulf between disabled athletes and able-bodied viewers. Mediated Olympic representations of extraordinary athletes have always been conducive to 'social integration of the highest order' (Dayan and Katz, 1994, p. 15). By contrast, historically, the 'supercripisation' (Howe, 2008b) elements of the Paralympic spectacles of 'otherness' have been considered to be negative (see, for example, Schantz and Gilbert, 2001; Smith and Thomas, 2005; Britain, 2012; Purdue and Howe, 2012; Hodges et al., 2015; McGillivray et al., 2019). The producers for London 2012 intentionally sought to change perceptions in the whole of society, and they used the mega-event occasion as a reason for including the Paralympians in all their scheduled programme formats.

By carefully changing meanings about disabled identities through the representations they used within those programmes, and the sheer volume of content, the Paralympics was given centre stage on the channel. In the sections below I show how they filled the schedule with newly minted representations, slightly adapted, within each of the following programme formats. The purpose within each of the genres utilised was to bring a marginalised group into the mainstream and this was largely achieved by disrupting expected patterns, or adding to familiar formats, to reframe disability as follows.

Magazine format

The first programme in the morning was *The Breakfast Show* and it particularly added the 'extraordinarily human' meaning to the recently reconstructed superhuman stereotype. In this section I argue that the format for this genre of programme was adapted creatively to help reframe disability, and make audiences want to watch the Paralympics. A theoretical issue with this intention is that by portraying some characteristics as extreme, or extraordinary, 'they', with those characteristics, are not like 'us' and are consequently depicted as 'other' rather than normal (Hall, 1997). Usually there is no parity between 'them' and 'us', as 'we' hold all the power to say they are not normal. This happens because extraordinary stereotypes are cameos or caricatures, and are achieved by choosing a small selection of extreme characteristics, whilst overlooking, or not portraying, other humanising traits. Since production decisions about what to include or exclude are based on needing to create a trope that we can easily and safely identify as 'other', being normally human is more difficult to portray than other traits. In this case, though, the producers used the genre and certain studio and filmic formats to close the gap between them and us and so begin to normalise and reframe the disabled athletes.

The Breakfast Show

This morning programme, with two studio presenters, followed a familiar format including chat, filmed inserts, and studio guests. Whilst the genre might not seem to have a direct bearing on the Paralympics event coverage it nevertheless set the agenda for each day. Why agenda setting is important, even in this case for a light-weight current affairs programme, is that, as Coleman (2008) explains:

> Media contribute to the creation of a public mood towards particular individuals, issues and themes, which leads to them being thought about in terms of respect, derision or suspicion.
>
> (ibid., 2008, p. 199)

Being handed a programme slot to discuss disability carried with it the potential risk of losing viewers. The stigma of revulsion and the television history of invisibility within the mainstream schedules made popularising the topic difficult for the Programme Editor, Luke Gawin. He was very aware of his power to induce respect, derision, or suspicion and told me, during his interview, how he had wondered how to fill the hours each day. Klein (2011), in her exploration of unconventional representations of social issues (p. 911), assesses producer perspectives and the power that they can wield. Of those who wanted to 'make a difference' she found a tension between two roles, of creative and of instructor (ibid., p. 918). Gawin was both. Whilst he called his programme current affairs it was in fact a form of edutainment. It included elements that were both entertaining and instructional; a form he was able to shape to promote interest in disability and the upcoming sports coverage each day.

The overall role of the programme was a strategic one. It was used to involve and interest audiences using multiple perspectives. Horne and Manzenreiter (2006) note that modern spectacles have become multifocal 'bridging the gap between frontstage and backstage' (p. 155) in order to communicate to multiple audiences. They say that people need to see behind the scenes, especially those who are not taken in by the commercialism and the hype (ibid.). The standard format for the magazine programme was adapted to some degree to get behind the lives of the Paralympic athletes, as well as connect with the audiences who were going to watch them. Gawin, the Programme Editor who was responsible for the whole series as well as the programme each day, said that he was first approached by Sunset+Vine, the sports producers, who were not actually keen on all his ideas, but gave way in the end. Then he communicated with the Project Leader, Deborah Poulton, who knew him in other contexts, and he felt he had her trust to operate with his normal level of autonomy.

He also spoke extensively, on multiple occasions, with the Disability Executive, Alison Walsh, who was clearly able to shape elements of the show. She told me:

> My thing was always, show them as human; don't show them as sort of two-dimensional, you know, automatons who are so media-trained that we, the audience, will never engage with them. Because I think that's really important… if we stick to this line where they're elite athletes and they've got to be treated as, you know, elite human beings we won't have moved the portrayal of disability on really.
>
> (Disability Executive, *Interview*, 2015)

The extent to which the Disability Executive was able to shape the culture of the programme, and its relationship to the audience, was evident in one of the encounters Gawin recounted to me:

> Alison is very good because we had a meeting, more than ten actually, at the Channel at various stages and the run up to it where there was

[sic.] various amounts of kind of 'Oh Shit, what are we doing? And how are we going to do this, what do we do about saying the wrong thing?' and the answer from Alison and everybody else was, 'just say the wrong thing and then correct yourself and stand corrected live on TV because that way we are the audience and the audience will identify with us making a mistake'.

(Programme Editor, *Interview*, 2014)

The query about getting things wrong, with the taboo of even discussing how to talk about disability, and what would be 'ok' if we treated them the same as everyone else, later became a centrepiece of the topical satire programme, as I discuss in the final section. The dynamic step-change, of making mistakes on-air, was understood, by the production team of this morning programme, to be a construction designed to create the sense of 'we [the presenters] *are* the audience'. This construction, to say the wrong thing and let the audience identify with the team, was designed to *pull the audience towards disability*. It was significant that the production staff creatively used the informal morning format in this way, to encode this identification connecting 'us' to 'them'.

Handling the stigma of disability was a challenge for almost everyone I encountered in the production team. As discussed in Chapter 2, Goffman (1963) says that stigma occurs where the normal and the different actually meet. There were many occasions during my research where the presence of disability amongst the team and onscreen with presenters and guests was mentioned as a catalysing factor in how perceptions within the team were changed. Now the magazine programme had to deal with disability on location and within the studio on both sides of the camera. It was clear from my interviews that these interactions created a new culture. When Gitlin (2005) interviewed individuals at every level within his busy network, he discovered that the creatives and executives were shaped by their political and cultural climate too, as well as whilst crafting shared meanings for their mass audience. These conditions and dynamics developed similarly at Channel 4.

The climate set by Gawin, to cope with stigma, was one of informative creativity. Klein (2011) has highlighted that some educational entertainment programming 'does not function as mere amusement for viewers, but a site through which contemporary social issues may be considered and negotiated' (p. 905). In Gawin's pursuit of the renegotiation of the *social* issue of disability, he adapted the 'roving reporter' format into a mini form of 'reality TV'. If not reality TV per se (see Skeggs and Wood, 2008a; 2008b), it was certainly 'first-person programming' relying on actors, as I show below, to create drama 'from contrived situations' (Wood and Skeggs, 2004, p. 178). Gawin set up instances for the 'different' and the 'normal' to meet in planned ways that he could film so that their interactions could then be negotiated and discussed in the studio, as well as revealed in situ.

A key example of this was when he sent out three disabled people to a busy shopping mall. Going shopping was not a conventional media framing of disability since it is usually the 'medical model' (Barnes and Mercer, 2003), with a focus on individual impairments, that is represented and focused upon. Instead the Programme Editor chose to take the disabled 'actors' out into the normal public domain and film them there to explore and highlight the disabling barriers. These 'social model' (Finkelstein, 1980; Oliver, 1983) barriers might include, for example, having nowhere to sit down in the changing cubicle when you have a prosthetic leg to take off. He described what happened as follows:

> So I got the three girls to go shopping in the West End to see how they coped and how people reacted to disability in shops. And it was great. I mean, it was just such a lovely, lovely piece. They did exactly what they were supposed to do. They sat in changing rooms. They tried dresses on. They had to take legs off to try things on. There's nowhere to properly sit. There's no, you know, the air-conditioning was not always right. John Lewis let us in, which was very sweet, and, good for them. A couple of the others, like Topshop said 'no', and somebody else said, 'no, we don't have time for that, it's Saturday, it's busy'.
>
> (Programme Editor, *Interview*, 2014)

He spoke at length to me about how difficult it is in society for people with particular impairments and it was my observation that this personal belief shaped his creativity and decision-making. Gawin employed the normalised caricature 'girly' trope of 'shopping on a Saturday' to highlight this difficulty, and by employing the familiar to depict the strange he used one trope to attempt to redefine another. In this instance it strengthened his intentions to show normality by only having one variable of difference – legs that come off. In every other sense they were 'normal, girly' girls. The film was designed to tell a story, and he used a standard narrative form to do so. Narrative structures very often have a single particular 'anomaly' that disrupts the norm creating a story about how this anomaly will be handled (see Walsh, 2007). The leg issue served as that anomaly.

Rather than attempting to explain the 'social model' of disability, Gawin decided that the shopping expedition would be able to *show* the disabling barriers, and thereby create a depth of understanding that is not normal for depictions of disability (see Darke, 2004; Shakespeare, 2006). By sending the girls to try on clothes, their bodily difference created a logistical dilemma in this setting. The adaptation here was to use the swap feature of, for example, *Faking It*, or *Wife Swap* to put the disabled athlete in the normal person's shoes. There being no seat to use to take off a prosthetic leg in the changing cubicle was an educative moment for the viewer, whilst remaining entertaining within the 'reality' genre.

Demonstrating the 'social model' within a 'reality' style entertainment segment does nevertheless have an apparent limitation. As many have established (see Fiske, 1989; Livingstone and Lunt, 1993; Kuhn, 2007; Dover and Hill, 2007), utilising recognised television formats helps steer the audience's reading, and acts as a container for specific ideas and values. A particular limitation is that 'television formats offer only contained emotional experiences and limited theoretical explanations' (Lisus and Ericson, 1995, p. 2). This simplifies the role for the communicator, although the inherent structure can then restrict the understandings that can be communicated. A key point, however, noted in previous format research, has been that the format privileges *emotional* experience over detailed *understanding* (Ericson et al., 1991). This lighter touch, than say a documentary on the subject, does mean, however, that a broader audience is likely to watch it, and this was vital for bringing disability into the mainstream. It is also key for sports television coverage as well as for entertainment generally in all its forms.

Gawin had a specific strategy for connecting the viewer to previously overlooked or negatively considered disability sport, through the construction of various programme elements. He explained:

So every day I had commissioned, I think, four films to do with the sport of that day. Off the back of those, we could build guests in the studio. So we'd have the British Equestrian Association there. We'd have someone from, you know, swimming and things like this, all tied into the sport. But the film would set off the issue about what the sport is going to be.

(Programme Editor, *Interview*, 2014)

The Breakfast Show is a classic magazine format often used at breakfast time, as well as later in the schedules, and is a familiar one he could use as a solid foundation. He then played with it a little. By buddying up 'one of them', a Paralympian, and 'one of us', a normal celebrity, the audience were able to explore the context of difference within the proximity of respect and friendship rather than purely observationally or as a report looking 'over there'. Gawin described 'a meeting of the minds' between two selected characters on one of his set-up films. Again he is using other 'feminine' tropes to make his point:

So, when the equestrian thing started, we had filmed with unbelievably, Katie Price, who likes horses…and one of the Paralympic dressage competitors, I can't remember her name now, lovely girl, so, we got the two to meet, the dressage rider and her hero, because she always loved Katie Price who thought [she] was great, so it was a really perfect meeting of minds. And it was, you know, it was a three and a half minute film, but it made the point. And it also gave you box office kudos to have Katie

Price sitting there because then obviously, we'd invite her in to talk about dressage and Paralympians off the back of the film.

(Programme Editor, Interview, 2014)

Just as the *Meet the Superhumans* campaign had done (see previous chapter) the production team used a jolting mechanism to attempt to break the existing views on disability:

> I explained how we're going to jump from sport to the tragedy of Melanie Reid and the bravery of her trying to get on with the rest of her life, but also her saying things like, you know, I felt like ending it all because it was so bad. And I just didn't – it's such a difficult thing to deal with. And it was heart-rending. But, so to go from glory of sport to that is a hell of a gear change, which Rick [presenter] found uncomfortable to start with, but then got it. He just switched into it, and I said, this is current affairs broadcasting, it's not a sports program. It's about current affairs and it's about the issues that make a difference, that make you realise why the Paralympics is important as an event. Because it tells you the human story behind these things...Obviously, each and every sportsman has, and woman has, a back story. You just got to be careful about this.

(ibid.)

Gawin communicated to his team that it was not a sports programme, but was a current affairs programme, reminding them of the genre. Yet, before it could become a disability programme, in the minds of the production team, he reminded them that every sportsperson has a human story that might be heart-rending. This brought the focus, therefore, back to sport as the wider context. In this adapted format there was an active dynamic between representations of sport and representations of disability, particularly on a visual level. As discussed in the previous chapter, the issue had been whether to 'show the sport' or 'show the stumps'. My interviews suggest there was also an internal wrangling over the narrative storytelling – of whether to focus on the showmanship of the sport or the humanity of the athletes. The former was the overarching initial idea, expressed to me by Julian Bellamy, who was the Head of Programming in 2009, handling the bid and the early stages of the coverage planning. His perspective remained prevalent even after he had handed the baton to his successor. He explained:

> First and foremost all these guys were sportsmen. That is the beginning and the end of the story. You know they are amazing sportsmen and [you] tell the story through that prism.

(Head of Programming, Interview, 2015)

A year later, in 2011, at an in-house producer's briefing, another perspective had emerged:

> They are not all heroic and perfect and 'elite'– at least not all the time. Some are arrogant bastards, divas, or hard drinking party animals – ALL of whom make great telly.
>
> (C4TVC, 2011)

Entertainment, or what would 'make great telly' was still the overriding concern for each of these viewpoints and struggling to achieve both was felt, at least with hindsight by my contributors, to enrich the coverage and bring the representations of disability to life. As one of the producers put it:

> There was a frankness, you know, that honesty – it somehow captured the mood – captured the imagination of people in a way that I didn't expect would happen. I thought we'd do a good job and make it really different.
>
> (anon.)

The adaptation of current affairs roving reports to include, for example, bringing disability into the shopping mall as a 'girly' shared shopping trip, and using celebrity endorsement for the Katie Price dressage experience, *was* really different to what had gone before. Researchers of infotainment scholarship, who have considered reality television, suggest that the format holds 'distinct opportunities for delivering messages' (Klein, 2011, p. 184). Klein asserts that viewers are more likely to believe and attend to advice and information when 'real people propel the narratives' (ibid.). In this sense, of also including advice and information, the film inserts were a form of hybrid, or at the very least an adaptation of the current affairs roving report. They also showcased the 'social model' of disabling barriers rather than medicalising people's predicaments.

Skeggs (2009) has argued that the genre of 'reality' television, whilst offering a clearly constructed reality, also includes the encouragement of voyeurism, something that disability scholars have highlighted as a common situation with media representations of disability across other genres (e.g. Garland-Thomson, 1997). Taken together, my interviewees suggest that voyeurism would not necessarily be a bad thing in this case, because of the inclusive framings they were trying to portray. Reality TV as a particular format is popular, according to Klein (2011), because it attracts an audience to 'real relatable characters' (p. 183). Swapping roles, environments, and temporary status were all creative production decisions that made these characters more relatable. They also made the coverage very different. The disabled actors were treated as subjects rather than objectified and distanced, as they normally are using reductive stereotypes. Thumim

(2015) has noted that both talk shows and reality TV use their formats to frame people as 'ordinary' (p. 78). These formats were used similarly here to reinforce the everyday, common, aspects of the Paralympians, not so much as extraordinary but as real ordinary human beings.

Members of the Paralympic production teams were well aware that they needed to create relatable characters in order to draw audiences to the media coverage. In this section I have shown that they extended representations, utilising the informal magazine format, with allowable presenter mistakes, and first-person reality-style inserts, to construct an 'extraordinarily human' identification of them, as the same as 'us'. The collective identity, according to my interviewees, was designed to connect Paralympians, in the non-professional segments of their lives, with 'us' learning about handling disability in the studio, alongside the rest of the viewing public being informed and entertained on the sofas at home.

Sports coverage

After the breakfast magazine programme, the next segment of the television schedule needed to demonstrate that Paralympians are 'extraordinarily good at sport' rather than tragic or brave. In this section I demonstrate that the change in meaning was achieved by utilising the tropes of Olympic and mega-event live sports coverage, whilst using what they called 'a different voice' (see below). Interview data from the producers suggests the intention was to provide a change in tone for disability coverage, by adapting some of the normal techniques used for television sports. Within the genre of sports coverage, the main formats are live action, edited highlights, often including a studio discussion with presenter and pundits, results round-ups including interviews and features, and short backgrounder films profiling individual personalities or teams (BBC Sport, 2011). These all featured during the sports coverage of the London Paralympics, but using a different voice, as I shall explore.

Within Channel 4 the focus on high-performance sport began when, as I have previously shown, the in-house creative and editorial team collectively decided to remove 'disability' from their thinking *and* their vocabulary. There was a cultural shift within the organisation away from the Head of Channel 4 TV's initial thought, in 2009, that 'I didn't think anyone would be interested in the races' (Head of Television, *Interview*, 2015). Realisations came, for later decision-makers, that the worst pain for any particular athlete was not his/her disability but that s/he was defeated because they had failed to beat their own personal best. It was encounters with the disabled group themselves, as I have noted in other chapters, that stirred the sense of a 'not disabled' reality amongst the key communicators and changed attitudes within the organisation. Throughout this book I argue that the changes in attitude that were encoded onscreen and picked up by the audience, happened in-house first.

Even within that culture, there were naturally many individual approaches and outlooks within the teams, at Channel 4 and within the sports production houses, as to how to present the live footage of the London 2012 Paralympics. These needed to be managed and steered in roughly the same direction and the role fell to the Commissioning Editor for Sport, who explained this to me:

> One of the biggest challenges was taking a load of sports producers, who are used to making cricket, football etc. and saying to them, 'Here's a sports event but it's not a sports event, it's something much bigger than that and you're going to do this in a completely different voice to how you've done any of your other programmes before'. So it was putting together a team – trying to put together a team of people producing it, who – their, sort of, default settings had to be changed for the period of the Paralympics.
>
> (Commissioning Editor for Sport, *Interview*, 2015)

Clearly, then, this sports editor wanted to 'change their default settings', particular as Channel 4's remit is to show things differently and provide programmes that are not available elsewhere (*Digital Economy Act*, 2010, v). They had changed the programme treatment for the cricket previously, and what they wanted to achieve with the Paralympics was different again. It was to borrow the Olympics style of live sports coverage but also adapt it.

Walsh explained the adaptation when I asked her whom she felt the target audience was for this project. With her agenda for the promotion of disability rather than sport particularly, she replied:

> Well people who might not be sports fans, who would be more – who would be interested in the drama and the fact that it's a Home Games – and the excitement of it all, and maybe dip in and out. So I wanted us to do a lot more weaving in the disability information and the back story into the commentary. It was quite successful with some commentators; they really got it. Others didn't.
>
> (Disability Executive, *Interview*, 2015)

Weaving disability into the live commentary was something that was practiced, as they trained up new talent, including disabled presenters and reporters, to do that. Elsewhere, weaving disability together with sport wasn't all plain sailing. The 'different voice' was not so well understood by those outsourced producers who worked outside the Channel 4 culture. Two sports production companies, Sunset+Vine and IMG, were picked by Channel 4 'because they've done big global events like this and we wanted to show that we were serious by employing the best' (Commercial Lawyer, *Interview*, 2015). However, having 'the best' did bring challenges when they tried programme treatments outside the norms. An example of this was described to me as follows:

> There was a VT that went out which I was very annoyed about and tried to stop them – but, you know what a live production is like – you don't see everything before it goes out, particularly if the production company doesn't like you to see everything before it goes out. They just want it to – it was a piece about how the Paralympics would change things for children who have disabilities and there's this able-bodied reporter wandering around interviewing parents, over the heads of their disabled children who are sitting in their chairs, not really – you know, talking about them as though slightly they weren't there. And it just felt – it had the wrong tone. It had this sort of plinky-plonk music going on in the background. They should have known better by that stage, you know.
>
> (Disability Executive, *Interview*, 2015)

Having 'the wrong tone' was something that the Disability Executive had tried to train the crews and the producers out of. Disability had been consensually removed from the thinking of the in-house teams, but it seems not from the outsourced organisations. The opening of the Rio Paralympics on 8 September 2016 also carried a video of a very similar ilk, with an able-bodied actor using a heavily theatrical tone of voice over sadly determined music underneath (C4, 2016). Perhaps, rather than being a retrograde step into 'othering' representations by Channel 4, this second piece was also made by an outside company who did not identify with the cultural perspective, expressed by some of my contributors. The internal shift in perspective towards disability, in 2012, seemed tangible within the teams that I encountered. However, only being a publisher-broadcaster, a non-production commissioning structure I discuss in Chapter 3, would seem to limit the sphere of editorial influence, especially when commissioning 'the best' experts in their own field, as these other sports producers clearly considered themselves to be.

By adding, as the ex-Paralympian TV Presenter had also called it, 'plinky-plonk' music, and using able-bodied actors to observe or discuss the 'otherness' predicament, boundaries between 'us' and 'them' could have been heavily reinstated. Born (2004), in her study of the BBC, noted that producers she encountered felt they held a neutral standpoint when constructing framings, and the sports producers I spoke to, outside of Channel 4, were certain of it. However, the confidence they had in their own production skills did mean that the request for nuanced 'weaving in' of disability was rather lost. The pre-existing tropes that patronise disability (see Barnes, 1992; Haller, 1995; Garland-Thomson, 1997; Shakespeare, 2006) were clearly something that Channel 4 were aware of and wanted to avoid. However, the outsourced producers did not actively dismantle the 'othering' process (see Hall, 1997) and therefore continued to use their power to potentially infer that others are not normal.

Aside from inconsistencies of this sort, the Channel 4 team were mostly able to capitalise on the 'live sports' trope, to move representations of disability forward in line with their intentions. They sought to connect us with the Paralympians, by encoding their television coverage in a sympathetic but equitable way, providing parity with the Olympians in the televisual treatment of their sporting regimes, achievements, and abilities. Hall (2012) states that once meanings have been transcoded, or superimposed, onto existing stereotypes, they do not go fully back (p. 267). So, using live sports coverage and adapting it to weave in stories about disability was a very successful way of normalising them, and I would argue this for the following reason.

Drawing on Bakhtin's (1968) theory of the carnival, Horne and Manzenreiter (2006) observe that, in addition to strengthening communal bonds, ritualised masquerades and exceptional events enable the inversion of everyday hierarchies (p. 154). They consider the modern sporting spectacle an extension of the historic carnival, with nationally branded sports 'uniforms' acting as masquerades for the athletes, thereby providing a temporary removal of social constraints. What they call the 'festival of status inversion' (ibid.), based on everyone sharing the experience together, is clearly an opportunity, I would argue, to place new meanings about disability successfully into this context. Cultural differences of race, for example, are accepted far more within athletics than they are down at the job centre (UK employment and welfare payments office). With normal judgements about hierarchy and power suspended, therefore, for the duration of the carnival, and with everyday power relations inverted, the distinction between 'able' and 'disabled' surely can also be temporarily removed. What would remain, usefully, is a type of televisual representation that audiences then come to expect.

Encoding the spectacle as high-performance athletics rather than, as the BBC had done, a special but 'sad third cousin' (Head of Marketing, *Interview*, 2014) was a powerful way, therefore, of changing meanings about the Paralympic athletes. Even though the extraordinary anatomical differences were given onscreen visibility, by 'showing the stumps' (see also Smith et al.'s [2017] fascinating study on priming), when the focus was on Olympic feats of superhuman achievement, the dynamic of 'them' and 'us' was changed in that setting. Because the *athletes represent 'us'*, rather than act as representations to us of 'others', as disability representations do, we are able to feel their winning and losing as passive members of the team, in spite of any obvious differences. Further, at mega-events, our own national identity is also reinforced by the athletes, even though we are spectators and they are actors (Dayan and Katz, 1994; Roche, 2000), because the distinction between us and them dissolves (Abercrombie and Longhurst, 1998,

p. 78) in this televised sporting context. The decoding stage has therefore some default settings built into it with international sport, and the spectacle of live sports coverage provides a different resonance with our identities and experience. This opens up possibilities for reframing representations at the encoding stage.

Disability sport has never previously had any parity with the way marketable sport is treated on television. The audience-pulling power of international sport had not been associated, until London 2012, with the Paralympic Games (Gilbert and Schantz, 2012), because meanings about normal elite athletes are constructed as positive and engaging (Whannel, 1992), whilst disability causes revulsion or an unwanted kind of fascination (Barnes and Mercer, 2003). What changed for the London 2012 coverage was that the producers realised there was actual parity between the two groups of Paralympians and Olympians, so they tried to depict them in a similar way. The Commissioning Editor had wanted to utilise the live television sports genre, but also chose to adapt the format slightly.

When it came to how they might produce the key elements of the sports event with 'a different voice', there was still some doubt and a range of views were expressed amongst the other decision-makers that I interviewed. The Head of Channel 4 Programmes, Julian Bellamy, had expressed the decisive moment for him, as being when he told his team to 'just produce a bloody great bit of sport'. This could not actually be achieved just by itself, though, because there was no previous interest in the Paralympics (Brittain, 2010), largely, some of the producers believed, because the characters were unknown.

The strength of the project lay, according to Poulton who led the televising element, in being able to solve that lack of recognition, with the treatment, voice, and framing of the live sports coverage:

> We believed in the narrative, not just showing isolated sport. We believed that if you're going to show Jonnie Peacock running the hundred metre final on a Thursday night from the stadium – [because] the general British audience really had no engagement with Paralympic sport – we had to work a lot harder to tell the story of Jonnie Peacock at the beginning so that people would engage with the fella. And that's where the nervousness was. We had to work a lot harder because the Paralympics athletes do not get the coverage the Olympic athletes get. They are not household names so we had to really go for it.
>
> (Project Leader, *Interview*, 2016)

They had to make some of the characters household names, and the producers also had to get across that the athletes were 'extraordinarily good at sport', in order for the live sports segment to work.

How vitally important the elevation of sporting achievement was, to the television coverage, became clear for the Director of Communications for the IPC (International Paralympic Committee), who worked closely with Channel 4. He explained to me how his own perceptions were changed after he joined the Paralympic movement and discovered how hard the Paralympians actually train. He was surprised to learn that some are so close in standard to their Olympian counterparts that they train alongside them (e.g. Jonnie Peacock, the Paralympic 100m sprinter, and Greg Rutherford, 'Super Saturday' long-jumper; both these men are London 2012 gold medallists). Being personally affected by this understanding affected his communications with, and suggested directives to, Channel 4 executives.

The spur to promote elite sportsmanship thus seems to have come from the Director's own experience but also from pressure from other stakeholders who wanted their Paralympians to be recognised as international high-performance sporting athletes. In terms of disseminating the message he spoke of the challenge in this way:

> I get journalists who come to me going, 'Oh I love covering the Paralympics; the back-stories are amazing'. And I'm like, 'yeah they are, but their athletic performance is absolutely amazing because there's a guy there with no arms who can swim 50 metres free-style in less than 30 seconds'. We can't do that and we've got two arms and two legs and it's just like they are incredible superhuman athletes – and you've got to really hammer that home.
>
> (IPC Director of Communications, *Interview*, 2015)

These views and feelings successfully filtered through into the programme treatments, and, within the live sports coverage, particularly with the commentators. For example, one commentator, on day three, at the end of a track and field event, declared 'on-air', in an excited tone, 'This is not about disability, this is pure sport!' (*Afternoon Show*, 2012). There was a sense of the audience growing into this new idea *with* the commentator. It was a spontaneous onscreen remark but it reflected the shift in focus away from 'disability sport' to elite high-performance and it involved all of 'us' who were watching. When there is media saturation for spectacular events, which comes with mega-event status, Abercrombie and Longhurst (1998) have observed that the strict separation between actors and spectators/audiences dissolves (p. 78). Joining actors and audience in this context, I would argue, also acts as a way of breaking down the 'othering' process by familiarity and immersion. The programme treatment for round-the-clock mega-events coverage is constructed so that we share the commentator's viewpoint, especially when events are transmitted live.

According to Rowe (2003), the role of the commentator, within live sports coverage, is to get the audience 'on the team'. The manufactured style of delivery, with its friendly camaraderie, is delivered in order to attract, secure, and retain the target audience (ibid., p. 118). Sports commentators, therefore, play a unifying role to keep audiences but this also closes the gap between 'us' and 'them' in a way that is specially designed for televised sport. Unifying moments are achieved for commercial reasons, in order to secure audience engagement, and to that end promote the sense of a shared experience. Significantly, and by design, in 2012, this existing element of the sports coverage programme type, the unifying tone of voice, was utilised to also integrate the delivery of messages about disability. This was a key way of adapting the format and resetting a familiar trope to keep the audience onside, as 'part of the team' of the nation's Paralympians.

In reality, adding depth to the commentary, my interviewees suggest, was in fact difficult to achieve with the outsourced seasoned reporters and also because they were using so much new talent. An easily flowing narrative was still something that they hadn't got quite right according to the advisor on disability, Walsh. Her criticism of some of them, was:

> You haven't told them [the audience] the story, so all you've told us is the sun's shining, and, you know, the stand is packed and all your, kind of, standard commentary.
>
> (Disability Executive, *Interview*, 2015)

This was in spite of the training they had been given by her, as she recalled:

> I went big on that in my presentations to all of them; the [...] things I did with the *MENTAL4 the Paralympics*. I just said, you know, 'It's really patronising to make assumptions about disability and about disabled people, and what I want you to do is, you know, always go in wanting to be frank and honest and get under the skin of these athletes'.
>
> (ibid.)

There was a temptation then to either patronise or talk about the weather and, as the Commissioning Editor of Live Sport, had pointed out, 'default settings' needed to be reset, or in the case of the new presenters created from scratch. The existing commentary tropes acted as a structure, dictating behaviours/agencies, and were difficult to overcome – even for the creatives with the vision for a different kind of representation. However, as Rowe (2003) has argued, the role of the sports commentators to engage the audience is an important one. I would argue that feeling 'part of the team' affects how one does or does not objectify difference. If the commentator is not doing so, or the studio team, then neither do we, as the audience.

With this adaptation, the athletes were not high achievers *in spite* of, or to *overcome* their disability, as Paralympic scholars have noted in the past (e.g. Brittain, 2010; Silva and Howe, 2012). They were high achievers because peak performance is what is expected of *all* elite athletes, as reiterated by the commentators and live reporting teams. Changing this expectation, that the disabled athletes needed to be different to be accepted, is how their sporting profiles were normalised, as I have shown in the previous chapter. Now they needed to be extraordinary to qualify for the final. This is a shift in meaning. Adapting the live sports format to include the rivalry and drama, but with disability information woven in, is one of the ways Channel 4 were able to make this shift. The meanings associated with the elite group of Olympians were transcoded (see Hall, 2012, p. 267) onto the old supercrip one, by the particular way that they were represented.

Being 'extraordinarily good at sport' used to be a key *overcoming* framing for black males too, along with their having an 'extraordinary sense of rhythm' (Hall, 2012, p. 254; see also Barnes, 1992b). This was true within programmes about race, or where the diverse actors were bit-parts or accessories to the lead white roles (see Hooks, 2006; Hall, 2000). Similarly programmes about embarrassing or fascinating bodies, or where disabled characters are used as plot devices (Barnes, 1992a; Garland-Thomson, 1997) carry the same *overcoming* meaning. By reconfiguring the Paralympics as live international elite sport, during the daytime (in 2012) sports coverage segment, this decision changed the references for reading onscreen depictions.

Using the live sports format to embed differently decodable meanings altered the old stereotype of the victim 'trying his best' (BBC, 2008) at sport, reversing the stereotype (see Hall, 2012, p. 262) to show athletes as elite. In terms of power, the elevated status, and mega-event all-day coverage, produced a shift in position from the viewer looking down, with more power, at overachieving 'supercrips', to looking up at them, now with the greater power and status of Olympic athletes. These athletes, according to the favourable and respectful commentaries, could master their bodies and, for example, swim 50 metres faster than most people in the world. They were overcoming what all elite athletes do, rather than just their physical differences, and were not therefore overcoming tragedy with bravery (see Barnes, 1992a; Garland-Thomson, 2002a).

Walsh, the Disability Executive with overall editorial control over the disability agenda, saw the event not only as another Olympics, in terms of achievement, but also as raw entertainment. She wanted emotions and tears onscreen, as part of the Olympic narrative, and not because they were 'crips' (Haller, 1995; Philo, 2012):

> Prior to *Big Brother*, we were at that stage where disabled people only appeared on screen if they were sort of tragic or brave or exceptional in some way and I wanted to get us to the sort of human side and embrace the sort of tantrums and tears and… I mean I don't know if you remember after the Olympics, or watching the Olympics, it was just

tears, tears, tears. I remember doing a montage of all the tears at the Olympics and showing it to the production teams just before we went into the Paralympics and saying, 'That's what I want on the Paralympics. I want it all – I want the audience you know, absolutely wrapped up in all that drama'.

(Walsh, Disability Executive, *Interview*)

Her reference to *Big Brother* was not to a gap in the schedules that needed filling, as it had been for the Head of Channel 4. Nor was it a reference to the consequently tarnished brand image, as it was for the 4Creative Business Director. According to these two interviewees, the Paralympics was used to compensate for both deficiencies left by the show. For Walsh, however, *Big Brother* gave her confidence to adapt the live sports format. When 'Pete', with Tourette Syndrome, won the public vote and the seventh series (*Big Brother*, 2006) she explained that he was centre stage, in the mainstream, *with* his disability but not only because of it. He won a prize that normal people always win, in a normal person's arena, and she considered this a milestone for disability. She now wanted to utilise the ableist Olympics arena too, without belittling the realities that having a disability may present.

Within television sport, argues Whannel (1992), the tears of frustration, grief, and joy experienced by elite athletes, are all part of the able-bodied spectacle. Those able-bodied tears reflect the drama of winning and losing rather than the 'poor me this is really difficult' adversity inference (Schantz and Gilbert, 2001) which had hitherto been the default framing for representations of disability (see Philo, 2012). The transposition of the Olympic narrative onto disability sport meant that familiar meanings could be reworked within the adapted format. As I noted in Chapter 3, sponsorship money was used to pay for extra cameras so that the production could visually emulate other elite sporting competitions. A key one of these cameras was deployed at the trackside specifically to capture raw emotions.

Wheatley (2016) questions whether inequalities are reproduced or subverted through moments of mediated emotional excess. In this case I argue that inequalities were *not* reproduced because more equal meanings, inherent within the genre, were transposed onto the disabled athletes. Tragedy, suffering, loss, and redemption are key components of television drama in general, and as Horne (2007) and Wenner (2009) have argued, sport has evolved as commercialised entertainment, such that these elements have been gradually included into this genre too. Modern coverage no longer simply reports on the action of a mere match or track and field event without employing dramatic narrative. The high drama, as the *MENTAL4 the Paralympics* montage demonstrated, needs to include 'tears, tears, tears' just as it does for the Olympics.

Grindstaff (2002) establishes that developing emotional involvement with the main characters, in her case with talk show participants, creates an important connection between the audience and the television content. She points out that it is the need to generate audiences that leads to the manufacture of emotional displays. With the 2012 Paralympic coverage, the 'money shot' (ibid.) moments of open emotional displays did not need to be manufactured but they did have to be styled to emulate the trackside dramas of other international elite sports events. Depleted, exhausted athletes are now caught on camera so that we can feel their triumphs and their pain. In sport there are winners and losers, and the spectacle is emotional, but loss in this context is represented not necessarily as disempowering, as it is for those with a disability, but as part of the sporting rivalry narrative.

Channel 4 producers adapted the sporting rivalries trope by adding more depth and detail to their coverage. Historically, analysis of television sport has highlighted that the televisual framing of rivalries used in sports programmes creates personalities for us to identify with (Whannel and Tomlinson, 1984) but that other things disappear with the personified rivalry framing (Daney, 1978). Historic and social contexts are lost from the frame (ibid.) as well as the losers who mysteriously disappear (Whannel, 1992, p. 96). The consequence of this process is that the focus just on winning forces correlated onscreen absences. In this way, the selective construction is far from objective and Kinkema (1998) say that 'although institutions claim to present athletic events objectively, they engage in considerable selective construction and interpretation in the production phase before their programs reach an audience' (p. 32). Channel 4 mediated their athletics event in a particular way, by weaving in disability and using a different voice to show that the event was 'bigger than just sport' as the Commissioning Editor had said.

In the case of the London 2012 Paralympics, adding the social context is something they did differently to previous packages that only included events round-ups. Whilst it was important that Team GB did win medals to keep the ratings up, lack of funding for disability sport was mentioned, as was access to facilities and the need for improved talent spotting at schools. As the Disability Executive had said in her interview, 'we did not want them [the athletes] to be two-dimensional'. Contextualising with back-stories was a deliberate construction to play a different and better role than the purely emotional encapsulations of the sob-story trope. These social contexts were woven into the commentaries and conversations of the onscreen reporters and presenters and were still based around being 'extraordinarily good at sport'.

One of the other programme treatments adapted to consciously stop patronising the athletes was to inject the coverage with humour. The style and content of commentary was reconstructed for their desired frame:

> It's the triumph of the human spirit and you can be funny with it. You can put comedians on the boccia [wheelchair bowls] commentary, so

long as they have admiration for the athletes – we had one lovely commentator on the rugby who said something like, 'Oh I would have said he got that by his fingertips, but he hasn't got any so I won't'. You know those sort of throw-away lines that come out naturally. Giles Long, the LEXI creator is full of those. He talks about, you know, 'she lost because she finished on her stump arm instead of her good arm'.

(Disability Executive, *Interview*, 2015)

Other suggestions from Channel 4's Commissioning Editor for Sport, included:

'elevate the talent, so you're treating them as you would an Olympic athlete in terms of what you show, and how glossy your VT is and everything' and 'don't try and tip-toe around things'.

(ibid.)

Live coverage matters because it draws the audience in, according to Dayan and Katz (1994). The inclusion of so many hours of live footage was a huge adaptation from previous disability sports coverage. Packaged highlights had been the main treatment that the BBC had used on its primary channels and was something that they would perhaps be unlikely to go back to, if they were to regain the broadcasting rights for Paris 2024 or beyond. The social media interactions, of course, also work best with live sports coverage, and London was really the first to benefit from the Twitter momentum alongside the Home Games excitement (IPC Digital Marketing Manager, *Interview*, 2015). So now that the expected type of programming has been changed and developed, live coverage of the Paralympics, subject to compatible time zones for viewing, has also become the norm, at least within the UK. After-the-event highlights might still run the risk of the commentary sounding patronising, as it has done so often in the past, but the positioning and the tone of voice has changed.

In this section I have shown that Channel 4's treatment of live sports coverage included 'pure sport', outsourced to purist sports producers, but also a change to 'default' producer settings to ensure, for example, that the commentators would weave in disability information as an adaptation of the format. The blending together of two types of representations, of elite and also disabled athletes, seems to have worked because it was dropped into the powerful commercial framing of mega-event live sports coverage.

Topical satire/review programme

Finally in this last section on formats I show how one format has endured, and I argue that this unconventional hybrid has delivered the most change for disability representations. Since the London 2012 Paralympic Games coverage, there has been one specific programme legacy. It was created at the last minute and it encapsulated what the Business Director called 'the magic' of the Paralympics. The programme was innovative and has been recommissioned for other uses since, including general elections, where disability has nothing to do with the show at all. The three presenters are apparently all disabled, except one of them isn't and he is the odd one out. They laugh at each other and introduce guests providing a post-mortem on the day's proceedings. Within this hastily reinvented format the satire show genre allows disability into the mainstream by confounding the existing boundaries, as I will now show.

The Last Leg

The top executive, who inherited the Paralympics from a predecessor, told me that her main challenge with the media coverage of 2012 had been persuading the production company to take a chance on disabled talent. It had been, she said, 'quite a battle'. She then went on to say that getting *The Last Leg* to work was the other huge challenge:

> We were keen to have a show that had a different approach to disability and an irreverent tone but it had never been done before. The host, Adam Hills was completely unknown in the British market. Alex Brooker was cast after he stood in, in a rehearsal. Josh Widdecombe was also unknown. There is also a long and noble tradition of sports entertainment shows struggling and this one was particularly problematic. Landing it successfully was one of the real high points of the Games.
> (Head of Channel 4, *Personal Communication*, 2016)

It came about after the Disability Executive, who has never worked on sport, but was a rower herself before contracting rheumatoid arthritis, noticed what she felt to be a gap in the types of programming. She recalled the thinking behind her actions, as follows:

> Why isn't there any entertainment element here in these programmes – in this line-up? Who do we know? I went down to Comedy, spoke to [a colleague] who was the Head of Comedy then, and I said, 'I need a presenter who's funny, and happens to be disabled – who've you got?' 'Adam Hills'. So, [I] went back to [another colleague] – he found this clip of him doing this hilarious routine and we just – we just said, 'Right, he's in. He's got to do it'. And then, of course, we had to get him past Sunset+Vine.
> (Disability Executive, *Interview*, 2015)

Humour was clearly going to have a part to play in this formatted slot, as the selected Australian presenter was a former stand-up comedian.

As a performer, he emphasised that although they put the sport first every single day:

> Once you've covered the sport, and you've given it the respect it deserves and, you know, the coverage it deserves as a sports event, you then buy yourself, almost, the kind of, the leeway to then go and kind of have a little bit of fun with it.
>
> (Hills, 2015)

It needed to be fun as the Chief Sports Editor said, when I asked him about the challenges they faced, 'No one would want to watch highlights of disability sport so we had to do something else with it'. He also pointed out that Sunset+Vine 'hated it'. Presumably because it didn't fit their idea of an appropriate sports format. It was new, and, according to every producer who mentioned it to me, Channel 4 made it up as they went along.

Nobody was sure what to do with the slot until the Entertainment Commissioner turned up on set and took over. The chaos was recalled by one of the team:

> Rehearsals were hilarious, all the script meetings, where we were all tossing ideas around, but she brought in the rigour of building the show, you know, coming up with ideas; having a writer attached to each presenter; you know, going out and shooting VTs – and bringing in, you know, the athletes, and as many funny guests on the sofa as you could...there was also this hash-tag segment, yeah...even when they got to the Olympic Park, we weren't quite sure how we were going to use Alex [Brooker]. It was still undecided whether he was going to be a reporter, out doing little pieces, and then come in and do studio pieces – but after the first night, Syeda [Irtizaali] the Entertainment Commissioning Editor, was asked to go down and she spent the whole time down with us then and she – she basically shaped the show.
>
> (Disability Executive, *Interview*, 2015)

So this sporting format, originally intended as a highlights show, morphed into entertainment by much agency, and more than a little denting of the structure. With lots of comings and goings on the set, disabled athletes, celebrities, and comedians reported, discussed, and joked about the day and also just joked about. 'They' got muddled in with 'us' and Josh Widdicombe, who does not have a prosthetic limb or a deformity, was constantly teased onscreen by the 'others' for not being disabled. This turning around of the trope that ordinary people are normal confused the public enough, says Widdicombe, for him to be offered the disabled toilet offscreen when appearing in public elsewhere. Shaking up the format, and messing about with the stereotypical behaviours acted as a disruptor, in the way that Hall (2012) noted for representations of race when they similarly changed (p. 216). Drawing on Goffman's (1967) theory of the Wise and Own (pp. 30–33), I would argue here that there was also another phenomenon at work to bring disability into the mainstream.

Goffman suggests that where the token 'normal' is accepted into the 'other' group and allowed to be one of them a change in understanding takes place. The role of Wise One (ibid., p. 31) is allowed by virtue, normally, of that person having some connection with the stigmatised oddity, 'whilst not actually possessing it' (p. 31). This tacit permission at play in *The Last Leg* is a nuanced dynamic utilised to advantage to create a new programme format, arguably a new genre. Embedding Widdicombe into the team of *The Last Leg* made him the 'wise' outsider on topics of disability. He has said himself that he is allowed to make disabled jokes 'for some reason' and this, according to Goffman's theory, is because the main 'other' presenters accept him as one of their 'own'. Of course, in practice, they were thrown together by the producers, but their camaraderie onscreen was, initially, rehearsed to make inclusion of each other, whether disabled or non-disabled, a two-way shared experience.

The audience are linked to the 'wise' one who is actually one of 'us' (not disabled) and also to the others who, in this context as show hosts, explainers, and joke-makers, also feel like they are one of 'us'. This close relationship with the viewer is an extension to the contrivance cultured on *The Breakfast Show*, that 'we *are* the audience', as the presenters said. It works because we are all trying to make sense of the Paralympics together on live TV. There are no 'others' in this setting. Hereby Hall's (2012) spectacle of the other evaporates. Confounding the 'we' and 'you' audience dimension with the 'us' and 'them' onscreen mash-up creates changes in how difference and commonality are perceived. By making everybody acceptable, the blurred boundaries curiously normalise everyone, including in relation to the viewers at home.

This adaptation of an existing format is standing the test of time. By extending the commissioning of the programme, since 2012, to other broader topics, such as the UK's General Election, an even more extraordinary 'us' and 'them' role reversal has taken place. Placed in the mainstream programming slot, Hills and Brooker, both with a prosthetic limb, are back to being two 'other' presenters, but now they are acting as 'wise' ones to the 'normal' populous on matters of general interest away from disability. Their continued presence in the programme has been protected by the format, allowing the bonding and chemistry of the able-bodied and disabled trio to continue their agency, laughing and joking about serious matters, with live input from the viewing public. The cheeky trio format is similar to the *Top Gear* style of presenting but includes a dynamic continuous swapping of who is normal, which appears to be a new dynamic with disability.

The new hybrid format, which has morphed into topical satire, was born out of necessity because the producers in 2012 knew nobody wanted to watch a highlights programme. All players have an equal voice, albeit an irreverent one, and seeing their stumps, in the case of Brooker, or having no disability at all, like Widdecombe, are seen as the same, without one being the 'other'. Hills' prosthetic limb is under the desk, but we know it is there. It is no longer visible, but it is alluded to in the title of the show. Disability is not invisible or repulsive but has a raised profile, deliberately, within as normal a context as the genre allows.

The safe distance between the audience and the actors was also crossed by the use of social media. Reading out tweets on-air is not new, but actively incorporating them into a segment to tackle tacitly held taboos specifically might be. It was considered by my participants to break new ground, and came about accidentally on the first day of the Paralympics. Alex Brooker, the sports journalist who became one of the stars of the show by accident, told me how the Twitter hashtag segment happened:

> Afterwards [the first programme] we got a tweet asking 'is it ok to ask why some of the people are competing because they don't look disabled?' And there might have been another one that night saying 'is it ok to find some of the para Olympians quite fit?' [Laughs] we talked about it ourselves and we thought 'yes of course it's ok' why shouldn't you? And I remember the next day in the meeting saying ok we've got to cover these and someone said we should call it '#IsItOk' and that should be the segment. So it kind of came organically out of what people were actually tweeting us.
>
> (TV Presenter, *Interview*, 2015)

This viewer and producer agency created a structure within the programme format that others may want to copy. Widdicombe, the able-bodied presenter on *The Last Leg*, who feels he now has a licence to tell disabled jokes on his own show, said:

> We will get away with jokes on *The Last Leg* that you can't do on other shows and then you go on other shows and make these jokes and then people tense up and you go 'oh wait a minute maybe that's not appropriate on other shows'.
>
> (Widdicombe, 2014)

The shows that Widdicombe appears on tend to be of a similar late-night entertainment genre, with ingredients of chat, comedy, and observational satire. However, having forged a format of their own, his remarks show that the delicately nuanced meanings are dependent on the format in which they are framed. Inadvertently Channel 4 had created one with a new dynamic.

Conclusion

With each of the formats discussed in this chapter it is clear that representations of disability are still finely balanced in terms of what they mean. I have shown that the media frames for each genre necessarily continue to adhere to at least some unwritten rules, and are undergirded by their own particular templates. Utilising these, specific efforts were made by Channel 4 to appeal to wider audiences through the use and adaptation of these well-known programme formats. By placing a marginalised group inside the televisual sporting machine, and including them right through the daily domestic television schedule, disability was to some extent normalised. By treating the coverage as pure sport (at least during the 'live' action segments) the athletes were celebrated whilst embracing their disabilities, rather than in spite of them. This coverage was flanked by the other familiar formats to fill out a rounder picture of who this group really were. Previously, disability was still framed with the challenging back-story, and sporting prowess as a form of redemption. Notably, the culture within the organisation changed and new riskier representations were embedded into the formats that they consequently felt confident to adapt, or reinvent.

The marginalised group were lauded and applauded across a series of programme formats, and no longer were they contained purely in programmes about their differences. The breakfast show, the sport, and the topical satire show set out to normalise these disabled athletes by utilising familiar programme treatments. These treatments made 'us' feel normal about watching 'them' precisely because the tropes and media frames were already familiar. The magazine show paired up celebrities and athletes, and interviewed kids and people-in-the-street to relax the setting. The sport was given the full 'live' sport spectacle and rivalry treatment, which was followed on social media. A Twitter stream also ran alongside *The Last Leg* and was allowed to interrupt the programme, asking those 'others' directly if 'it was ok' to think and feel in ways 'we' were previously uncertain of. This process restructured and redefined acceptable behaviours crossing the divide between 'us' and 'them' because they could reply directly. It was not *about* disability, it included disability. Even the satirical highlights replacement programme was live and therefore more engaging for normal audiences. My research demonstrates that all of these things were creative adaptations of familiar television formats and tropes.

In this chapter I have shown that the unifying effect of this suite of programmes, which temporarily monopolised and saturated the Channel 4 TV schedules, reframed meanings about disability, adapting the mainstream formats throughout the day. The role of marketing was also an influential one, building momentum for the Games, and their strategy, along with how brands were used, borrowed, and repaired, is the subject of the next chapter.

Bibliography

Abercrombie, N. and Longhurst, B.J. 1998. *Audiences: a sociological theory of performance and imagination.* London: SAGE.

Afternoon Show. 2012. Channel 4. Tx: 15 September 2012.

Bakhtin, M.M. 1968. *The dialogic imagination: four essays.* University of Texas Press.

Barnes, C. 1992. *Disabling imagery and the media: an exploration of the principles for media representations of disabled people.* Halifax: Ryburn Publishing.

Barnes, C. 1992d. Images of disability on television. *Disability, Handicap and Society*, 7(4), pp. 385–387.

Barnes, C. and Mercer, G. 2003. *Disability policy and practice: applying the 'social model'.* Leeds: Disability Press.

BBC Sport. 2011. *Programme formats.* [online]. [Accessed 4 May 2016]. Available from: www.bbc.co.uk/programmes/genres/sport

Beacom, A., French, L., and Kendall, S. 2016. Impairment re-interpreted? Continuity and change in media representations of disability through the Paralympic Games. *International Journal of Sport Communication*, 9, 42–62.

Big Brother. 2006. Series Seven. Endemol.

Born, G. 2004. *Uncertain vision: Birt, Dyke and the reinvention of the BBC.* London: Secker and Warburg. Bournemouth University/Creative Enterprise Bureau. 2013. See under Jackson, D. 2013. [Online].

Breakfast Show. 2012. Channel 4. 30 August – 9 September, 07:00–09:15.

Brittain, I. 2010. *The Paralympic Games explained.* London: Routledge.

Brittain, I. 2012. British media portrayals of Paralympic and disability sport. In: *Heroes or zeros: the media portrayal of Paralympic sport.* Champaign, IL: Common Ground, pp. 105–113.

C4. 2016. *James Corden's Ode to the Rio Paralympics.* [online]. [Accessed 11 May 2017]. Available from: www.youtube.com/watch

C4TVC. 2009. *Proposal for UK Broadcast Rights.* [Document] London: Channel 4 Television Corporation.

C4TVC. 2011. *MENTAL4 the Paralympics.* [PowerPoint]. London: Channel 4 Television Corporation.

C4TVC. 2013. *Annual Report 2012.* [Report]. London: Channel 4 Television Corporation.

Caldwell, J.T. 2008. *Production culture: industrial reflexivity and critical practice in film and television.* Durham, NC: Duke University Press.

Chouliaraki, L. 2013. *The ironic spectator: solidarity in the age of post-humanitarianism.* London: John Wiley and Sons.

Clogston, J.S. 1990. *Disability coverage in 16 newspapers.* Newcastle: Avocado Press.

Coleman, S. 2008. The depiction of politicians and politics in British soaps. *Television and New Media*, 9(3), pp. 197–219.

Corner, J. 2004. Mediated persona and political culture. In: *Media and the restyling of politics*, pp. 67–84.

Couldry, N. and Hepp, A. 2016. *The mediated construction of reality.* Wiley.

Daney, 1978. Cited in Whannel, G. 1992. *Fields in vision: television sport and cultural transformation.* London: Routledge.

Darke, P.A. 2004. The changing face of representations of disability in the media. In: J. Swain et al. eds. *Disabling barriers – enabling environments*. 2nd ed. London: SAGE, pp. 100–105.

Davis, L.J. 1995. The construction of normalcy. In: L.J. Davis ed. *The disability studies reader*. 4th ed. New York: Routledge, pp. 3–16.

Dayan, D. and Katz, E. 1994. *Media events: the live broadcasting of history*. Cambridge, MA; London: Harvard University Press.

Digital Economy Act. 2010. (section 22). London: The Stationery Office.

Dover, C. and Hill, A. 2007. *Mapping genres: broadcaster and audience perceptions of makeover television*. Luton: I.B. Tauris.

Elias, N. 1978. *The civilizing process: the history of manners*. London: Blackwell.

Faking It. 2010. Series One. First Tx: 18 September 2000. RDF Media.

Farey-Jones, D. 2012. *Paralympics coverage changed people's perceptions*. [Online]. [Accessed 31 October]. Available from: www.mediaweek.co.uk

Finkelstein, V. 1980. *Attitudes and disabled people: issues for discussion*. New York: International Exchange of Information in Rehabilitation.

Fiske, J. 1989. Moments of television: neither the text nor the audience. In: *Remote control: television, audiences, and cultural power*, pp. 56–78.

Garland-Thomson, R. 1997. *Extraordinary bodies: figuring physical disability in American culture and literature*. New York; Chichester: Columbia University Press.

Garland-Thomson, R. 2002a. The politics of staring: visual rhetorics of disability in popular photography. In: *Disability studies: enabling the humanities*, pp. 56–75.

Gilbert, K. and Schantz, O. 2012. An implosion of discontent. *Heroes or zeros*. Champaign, IL: Common Ground, pp. 225–236.

Goffman, E. 1963. *Stigma: notes on the management of spoiled identity*. Harmondsworth: Penguin.

Goffman, E. 1967. *Interaction ritual: essays on face-to-face behaviour*. New York: Doubleday.

Goffman, E. 1969. *The presentation of self in everyday life*. London: Allen Lane.

Goggin, G. and Newell, C. 2000. Crippling Paralympics? Media, disability and Olympism. *Media International Australia incorporating Culture and Policy*, 97(1), pp. 71–83.

Grindstaff, L. 2002. *The money shot: trash, class, and the making of TV talk shows*. Chicago, IL: University of Chicago Press.

Hall, S. 1973. *Encoding and decoding in the television discourse*. Birmingham Centre for Contemporary Cultural Studies, The University of Birmingham.

Hall, S. 1980. Cultural studies: two paradigms. *Media, Culture and Society*, 2(1), pp. 57–72.

Hall, S. 1997. *Representation: cultural representations and signifying practices*. London: SAGE in association with The Open University.

Hall, S. 2012. *Representation: cultural representations and signifying practices*. 2nd ed. London: SAGE in association with The Open University.

Haller, B. 1995. Rethinking models of media representations of disability. *Disability Studies Quarterly*, 15(2), pp. 26–30.

Hayes, G. and Karamichas, J. 2012. *Olympic Games, mega-events and civil societies: globalization, environment, resistance*. Basingstoke: Palgrave Macmillan.

Hepp, A. and Couldry, N. 2010. Introduction: media events in globalized media cultures. In: N. Couldry, A. Hepp, and F. Krotz eds. *Media events in a global age*. Abingdon: Routledge, pp. 1–20.

Hesmondhalgh, D. 2013. *The cultural industries*. 3rd ed. London: SAGE.

Hills, A. 2015. *Interview*. [unpaginated].

Hooks, B. 2006. *Black looks: race and representation*. Academic Internet Pub Inc.

Horne, J. 2007. The four 'knowns' of sports mega-events. *Leisure Studies*, 26(1), pp. 81–96.

Horne, J. and Manzenreiter, W. 2006. Sports mega-events: social scientific analyses of a global phenomenon. *Sociological Review*, 54(Suppl. 2), pp. 1–187.

Howe, P.D. 2008b. From inside the newsroom: Paralympic media and the 'production' of elite disability. *International Review for the Sociology of Sport*, 43(2), pp. 135–150.

Howe, P.D. 2011. Cyborg and supercrip: the Paralympics technology and the (dis) empowerment of disabled athletes. *Sociology*, 45(5), pp. 868–882.

Inside incredible athletes. [Film]. Mike Christie. TX: Dir. London: C4/4OD. TX date: 29 August 2010.

IPSOS. 2012. *Superhuman Paralympians change view on disabled people*. [online]. [Accessed 12 February 2015]. Available from: www.ipsos.com

Jackson, D. 2013. *2012 Paralympics changed people's perceptions of disability and disabled sport, BU study finds*. [Online]. [Accessed 31 October 2016]. Available from: www.bournemouth.ac.uk/

Kinkema, K. and Harris, J. 1998. Mediasport studies: key research and emerging issues. In: L.A. Wenner ed. *MediaSport*. London; New York: Routledge, pp. 27–54.

Klein, B. 2011. Entertaining ideas: social issues in entertainment television. *Media, Culture and Society*, 33(6), pp. 905–921.

Kuhn, A. 2007. Women's genres: melodrama, soap opera, and theory. In: *Feminist television criticism: a reader*, pp. 145–154.

Lisus, N.A. and Ericson, R.V. 1995. Misplacing memory: the effect of television format on Holocaust remembrance. *British Journal of Sociology*, 46(1), pp. 1–19.

Livingstone, S.M. and Lunt, P.K. 1993. *Talk on television: audience participation and public debate*. London; New York: Routledge.

McGillivray, D., O'Donnell, H., McPherson, G., and Misener, L. 2019. Repurposing the (super)crip: media representations of disability at the Rio 2016 Paralympic Games. *Communication & Sport*. Online.

Oliver, M. 1983. *Social work with disabled people*. London: Macmillan, for the British Association of Social Workers.

Philo, G. 2012. *Bad news for disabled people: how the newspapers are reporting disability*. [Online]. Glasgow: University of Glasgow.

Purdue, D.E.J. and Howe, P.D. 2012. See the sport, not the disability: exploring the Paralympic paradox. *Qualitative Research in Sport, Exercise and Health*, 4(2), pp. 189–205.

Roche, M. 2000. *Mega-events and modernity: Olympics and expos in the growth of global culture*. London: Routledge.

Rowe, D. 2003. *Sport, culture and media*. McGraw-Hill Education.

Schantz, O.J. and Gilbert, K. 2001. An ideal misconstrued: newspaper coverage of the Atlanta Paralympic Games in France and Germany. *Sociology of Sport Journal*, 18(1), pp. 69–94.

Shakespeare, T. 2006. *Disability rights and wrongs*. London: Routledge.

Silva, C.F. and Howe, P.D. 2012. The (in)validity of supercrip representation of Paralympian athletes. *Journal of Sport and Social Issues*, 36(2), pp. 174–194.

Skeggs, B. 2009. The moral economy of person production: the class relations of self-performance on 'reality' television. *The Sociological Review*, 57(4), pp. 626–644.

Skeggs, B. and Wood, H. 2008a. The labour of transformation and circuits of value 'around' reality television. *Continuum*, 22(4), pp. 559–572.

Skeggs, B. and Wood, H. 2008b. Spectacular morality: 'Reality' television, individualisation and the re-making of the working class. [unpaginated].

Smith, A. and Thomas, N. 2005. The 'inclusion' of elite athletes with disabilities in the 2002 Manchester Commonwealth Games: an exploratory analysis of British newspaper coverage. *Sport, Education and Society*, 10(1), pp. 49–67.

Smith, N.L., Zhou, Y., and Green, C.B. 2017. Framing Paralympic sport to build audience interest: the effects of priming on visual attention, attitudes, and interest. In J.J. Zhang and B.G. Pitts eds. *Contemporary sport marketing: global perspectives*. London: Routledge, pp. 179–195.

The Breakfast Show. (see *Breakfast Show*).

Tea-Time & Evening Show. 2012. Channel 4. 30 August – 9 September, 17:30–22:00.

The Last Leg. 2012. *Series One*. Channel 4. 30 August – 8 September, 22:30–23:15.

Thumim, N. 2015. *Self-representation and digital culture*. Basingstoke: Palgrave Macmillan.

Tulloch, J. 2000. *Watching television audiences: cultural theories and methods*. New York: Taylor & Francis.

Walsh, R. 2007. *The rhetoric of fictionality: narrative theory and the idea of fiction*. The Ohio State University Press.

Wenner, L.A. 2009. *Sport, beer, and gender: promotional culture and contemporary social life*. Southampton: Peter Lang.

Whannel, G. 1992. *Fields in vision: television sport and cultural transformation*. London: Routledge.

Whannel, G. and Tomlinson, A. 1984. *Five ring circus: money, power and politics at the Olympic Games*. London: Pluto.

Wheatley, H. 2016. *Spectacular television: exploring televisual pleasure*. I.B. Tauris. Wiley Online Library.

Widdicombe, J. 2014. *Interview*. [Unpaginated].

Wife Swap. 2003. Series One. First Tx: 1 January 2003. RDF Media.

Wood, H. and Skeggs, B. 2004. Notes on ethical scenarios of self on British reality TV. *Feminist Media Studies*, 4(2), pp. 171–182.

Chapter 6

Marketing parasports

Media, cultural production, and branded authenticity

In the same year that the London 2012 Games took place, but before the event itself, an important compilation of the latest Paralympic research was published, from a range of international scholars connecting various types of media, disability, and the Paralympic movement. The editors, Gilbert and Schantz (2012), conclude with a widely accepted perspective at that time:

> In the field of hyper-commercialised sports the Paralympics are becoming increasingly irrelevant and the media's fear of being irrelevant when reporting about it has given their irrelevance an air of self-prophecy. [...] However, this scenario can only lead to [a] relationship downfall and finish in a disaster for both Paralympians and the media.
>
> (p. 235)

This was written, seemingly, after the Beijing 2008 Games, which was the first to benefit from the new agreement that obliges the host Olympic Committee to organise the Paralympics too, and host them shortly after the Olympics using the same facilities. However, these scholars assert that it is how the media connect or disconnect with the Paralympics that gives the athletes their due status, or makes them irrelevant. For Beijing, ABC Australia broadcast more coverage than ever before, as did SPS in Germany (Newlands, 2012, p. 218). The BBC have historically produced some live sports from recent Games too, but mainly for streaming on their digital Red Button channel with not much as primetime viewing.

The pivotal moment, then, for reframing and defining the Games as a sports mega-event, came after the spikes of interest and other success stories enjoyed by, for example, Barcelona, Sydney, and Beijing (see IPC, 2018). Sports narratives were beginning to prevail over the disability stories but not apparently enough to fill stadiums and change attitudes towards physical impairments in society more generally. Wardle et al. (2009) assert that the impact of an increasingly competitive television market is the strongest argument against there being more representation of onscreen disfigurement, and they found that 'without evidence that audiences won't switch off, producers don't want to experiment' (p. 67). Nevertheless, as the previous chapters have shown, the UK's Channel 4 understood that commercial and creative risks *had* to be taken, if they were to achieve a transformational shift with any kind of perceptions.

Within the UK bid for their host nation broadcasting rights, Channel 4 included coinciding their documentary schedule dates with the launch of the ticket sales and also suggested other ways that they could increase audience engagement, amongst both spectators and digital consumers. For London 2012, a new record was set for ticket sales at around 2.75 million, which made it almost a sell-out (Hodges et al., 2014), and around 40 million people, making up 70 per cent of the UK population, watched some of the Games on television (p. 6). How meanings about the previously marginalised group were encoded for the mainstream audience really matters, therefore, since the powerful mediation at this point provided the host nation an opportunity for authentic inclusion of a diversity within their society.

The success of the London 2012 Paralympic Games media coverage has been attributed in huge part to the marketing campaign that created a build-up of interest. The Paralympians and the coverage were carefully branded by the marketing team, creating new meanings for disability sport and its sub-set of elite athletes, whilst reassuring the public at the same time. In this chapter I will show how these new meanings were embedded into the mainstream television culture through a carefully designed marketing strategy, and by *collaborating* with particular brands, *borrowing* from other brands, and *creating* a new brand, whilst simultaneously managing and *repairing* their own channel brand.

It is perhaps common to assume that artistic creatives create content and that commercial advertisers and marketing teams promote that content, but a key finding of my research is that these roles and relationships were much more complex and not as clearly defined. Well-known brands were needed to support, shape, and stabilise televisual meanings about disability, and it appears that these brand associations especially facilitated the pioneering journey from the margins into the mainstream for the previously ignored parasport athletes. Significantly, in this case-study, the marketing influence extended from the inception of the project through to the end of its creation, and contributed to what ended up onscreen, as I will show.

Meanings were framed, representations clearly defined, and depictions of disability were shaped in a form of cultural production that relied upon a well-defined marketing strategy and also, perhaps more definitively, brand identities, brand associations, and branded meanings. I need to address these constructs here because television audiences associate values, attitudes, identities, and emotions with particular brands, and certain messages are more acceptable when delivered by some brands rather than by others. The sections below analyse the intangible as well as the tangible branding influences that affected how representations of disabled athletes were created for the London 2012 Paralympic Games coverage. The discussion on brands, how they were used, borrowed, and repaired, follows a brief description of the marketing strategy and its focus on the promotion of plainly commercial objectives that were established before the project began.

This chapter seeks to contribute to a wider debate on the role of commercial objectives within the creation of apparently non-commercial cultural media products. The context for my analysis derives from Davis' (2013) notion that a promotional *culture* exists and has been formed by the marketing of *ideas* as well as the marketing of products and services. He suggests that the subtle promotion of ideas and people and the diktats of related corporate strategy form a promotional culture that influences huge swathes of cultural and civic life. In addition to shaping representational meanings, this culture, he says, shapes and influences society's perceptions about itself and 'others'. As such, the pervasive promotional culture is an important dynamic to consider within the creative-commercial debate, and also within this case-study here.

In order to investigate some further impinging factors upon the construction of disability representations, beyond those in the previous chapters, I draw on Klein's (2009) insights into the role of branding. Particularly useful is her understanding of what a brand association can achieve, as a short-cut to authenticity, promoting social significance, and also, potentially, as a mask for other commercial objectives. Banet-Weiser's (2012) similar focus on authenticity hints that creativity is now used in the service of brand cultures (ibid.) and is at the very least 'reconfigured' (Banet-Weiser and Sturken, 2010, p. 268) within a promotional commercial context. In this study, on meaning-making, it is necessary to include a final chapter, therefore, on the role of marketing and the configuration of brand influences that were used to promote the Paralympic athletes and shape meanings about them onscreen.

It became clear to me, as my interviews progressed, that some producers involved with London 2012 were talking about changing perceptions of *their brand*, not changing perceptions of disability. Certain framings of disability and sport were not only marketed directly to attract viewers but were also developed for commercial objectives connected to the reinforcement of brands and corporate branding. For Channel 4's London 2012 media coverage there was specifically a brand reputational issue (see Chapter 3) that had a pervasive effect and informed the creativity at the very early stages of idea development and throughout the production and marketing processes. In theory, amongst scholars (e.g. Banet-Weiser and Sturken, 2010; Davis, 2013), and in practice, with my participant producers, discussions about audience perceptions and encoded meanings point towards the power of a permeating and overarching promotional culture. This culture is understood from both sides to shape content and creative ideas (see also Moor, 2007, pp. 71–73).

Drawing on my own interviews, in the sections below, I highlight the blurring of commercial and creative objectives within the production of this important one-time cultural product. Multiple purposes, encompassing both creative and commercial goals, were fulfilled alongside standard promotion of the coverage, and I discuss what net effect the dynamic of those differing purposes had on disability representations both at the time and afterwards. I also draw on contributor donated internal documentation, in order to avoid the methodological weakness of relying too heavily on personal interviews.

In the first half of this chapter I evaluate Channel 4's stated objectives and draw on my material to argue the persuasiveness of the marketing influence over key creative decisions right from the very beginning of the project. In the second section, I discuss the role of brands and branding and their effect on the shaping of meanings about disability. I will show how significant the issue of channel brand management was to the whole process, and explore how the producers borrowed and utilised the power of other brands, including Nike, Public Enemy, Sainsbury's, BT, and the Olympic Games, to develop a new branded identity for the disabled elite athletes whilst also repairing their own. I argue *why* and *how* the emphasis and focus morphed from 'otherness' and 'difference' to 'normality' and 'inclusion' through an analysis of the marketing strategy and the use of brands and branding below.

The marketing strategy

This section examines the role of the outline marketing strategy drawn up at the initial bid stage of the London 2012 Paralympics project. Hesmondhalgh (2013) has flagged up the need for academics to acknowledge the increasing role that marketing is playing, whether positively or negatively, in the creation of media texts, not simply towards the end of projects to promote them, or during the production process, but also at the inception of ideas (p. 234). With that in mind I looked back at the original documentation that was presented to the London Organising Committee (LOCOG) and was also able to ask some of my participants, many of whose roles were linked to marketing and brand management, about the inception stage of the Rio 2016 Paralympics coverage. Decisions were being made about this coverage during the initial interview period in 2014/2015 and this provided a chance to examine the influence of key individuals at the earliest stage of the production cycle.

The documents I was given that clarify the role of marketing and branding in the shaping of disability representations are primarily the 2009 proposal bid, provided by the Commercial Lawyer, Martin Baker, and a major presentation, *MENTAL4 the Paralympics* which was written and delivered by the Disability Executive, Alison Walsh. Changing onscreen representations and corporate attitudes towards disability was so important that a Brand Manager, outsourced from Insight, was asked to organise an Away Day for Marketing, Press, and executive producers from Sunset+Vine and

IMG. The Disability Executive was a keynote speaker at this event and was then tasked to write and deliver her bespoke *MENTAL4 the Paralympics* presentation four times, between 2011 and May 2012, to groups including all Channel 4 Paralympic presenters, reporters, and commentators; senior execs (executive producers, programme editors, directors, producers) from Sunset+Vine and IMG; Channel 4 News teams and, for online, Twofour and DeltaTre Media.

Scholars have highlighted how few people with disabilities work in the media generally (Barnes, 1992) and at the Paralympic Games 'in the important positions within the media' (Schantz and Gilbert, 2012, p. 239). What was significant here was that the Disability Executive at Channel 4 had a disability of her own, and was enabled to share her ideas and potentially shape the internal culture through the presentation of her perspectives to so many of the media creators. Ideas about disability were promoted and marketed to them under the umbrella of Channel 4 but organised by a Brand Manager from an outside agency. For London 2012, everybody was briefed about how disability ought to be portrayed, in all the organisations listed above.

In this section I argue that there was an underlying strategy, even before the programme making stage, to promote meanings through the use of their own brand across the creative content that was to follow. This is in addition to the discussions in previous chapters that show marketing and branding executives were key decision-makers in programme meaning-making. They were also, crucially, involved from the outset.

In order to understand the location of editorial control in the designing of the marketing strategy I first need to explain that the organisational structure of Channel 4 includes a Marketing Department with a Head of Marketing, as well as 4Creative, their in-house advertising agency. These separate departments reflect the differing functions of marketing and advertising, with 4Creative creating tools for, and receiving their briefs from, the Marketing Department. The advertising agency were at pains to tell me they also retained a degree of autonomy outside the politics of the company. Overseeing both groups was the Chief Marketing and Communications Officer, who was also on the Board of Directors. This is an increasingly common strategic practice, to have a marketing representative on the board, blending creative-commercial agendas, and both Hesmondhalgh (2013) and Born (2004) have noted that this is the practice in other organisations. Based on my interviews with these teams, and the Board Director, I shall be discussing the relevance of the marketing strategy that was put in place before the development of the television advertising used to promote the media coverage.

A key factor in driving audiences to watch the television coverage was the commitment to utilising the biggest marketing budget ever allocated by Channel 4. This budget was locked into the bid contract by the Commercial Lawyer, Martin Baker, which meant that when successive executives came to it at a later date they were unable to downgrade it, even though they wanted to. I explained in Chapter 3 that the decision to buy the Paralympics coverage was a controversial one made by the team headed by Kevin Lygo, who then moved on, with other members of his team, to ITV Studios before the Paralympics began. Tying funding to the marketing budget was an important part of what they left behind and directly affected the power that the new representations would have over viewers.

This outgoing team's initial enthusiasm for the Paralympics idea was not shared by all of the incoming team, and Lygo's replacement conjectured it would be a 'financial disaster', according to the Project Leader. The marketing dynamic was clearly significant in shaping framings around disability, and was intrinsic to the part marketing played in steering relationships between television programme content and the consumers of that content. As well as driving an audience to engage with the coverage across a multitude of platforms, a push to develop intended meanings ran alongside this process. The marginalised group, in this case of disabled elite athletes, was thrown into the public consciousness over a period of time, and then given the super cool 'Nike'-style treatment. Across the programming normalisation was marketed, and not simply by the series of advertising campaigns.

In order to promote the Channel 4 brand and affect perceptions of disability, a route to market for the actual product was needed. The marketing strategy was planned over time to gradually funnel an audience towards an undesirable subject. As I have already mentioned, the Paralympics TV coverage was purchased as an opportunity for audience growth and there needed to be a plan to drive new viewers to engage with the Paralympians and watch the programmes. Briefly, the plan was to introduce selected characters in advance, not shy away from 'showing the stumps' and physical differences, then shift the focus to the sport, giving it an Olympic televisual style treatment. The purpose was to reach a bigger audience, bolster ratings, enhance channel brand reputation, and justify the public service remit. To change perceptions in society, their published purpose, they had to change depictions of disability, create new meanings about those depictions and then drive an audience to watch them. Throughout this chapter, I show how they used brands and branding, as well as a marketing strategy, to do that.

Brands have to be taken into account because they have values and emotions attached to them which affect meaning-making (see Keller, 2009; Klein, 2009; Banet-Weiser and Sturken, 2010), and the producers at Channel 4 had a clear understanding of this association. Other production researchers have highlighted that marketing is now inevitably playing a key role in programme making and the promotion of ideas (including, for example, Grindstaff, 2002; Born, 2004; Klein, 2009; Mann, 2009) and it became obvious that no part of the production process was free of a relationship to branding of some kind. When I finally received a copy of the bid proposal I saw that utilising the 'golden brand' of Channel 4 was also written into the contract in at least two places.

The usefulness of that brand, the document says, was to be better able to promote diversity and also to benefit the other 'inventory' of the London Organising Committee of the Olympics and Paralympic Games (LOCOG). The bid also infers potential beneficial outcomes for its own inventory confirming brand enhancement as a goal for both organisations. These seemingly small details within their strategy to bring the Paralympics to a bigger audience confirm the analysis I also derived from my contributor interviews, that marketing was central to the whole project from beginning to end.

Blatantly commercial objectives, including management of their own brand, were fundamental to the London 2012 Paralympic Games media coverage. But there were other commercial objectives too, not related to the television audience. Davis (2013) acknowledges that promotional culture now extends beyond production into corporate strategies, yet the direct connection between actual television programmes and corporate strategies may not always be as clear cut as it was here. In the UK Broadcast Rights proposal document, written by the Channel 4 Television Corporation (C4TVC, 2009) to bid for the Games coverage, the corporation states that 'we will schedule our key programming around the key moments for ticket sales' (p. 20). The bid was argued on the basis of promoting and adding value to LOCOG's inventory, as I have noted above, and to provide additional revenue opportunities for both parties. One of the ways the enhancement was achieved was by actively promoting ticket sales to 'fill the stadiums' through the use of support programming.

Examples of what they described as 'support programming' were some carefully timed documentaries, including *Inside Incredible Athletes* which was transmitted over a year before the Games. It would seem then that Zoellner's (2009a) observations about the commercialisation of the TV documentary commissioning process also extends to assisting the sales of related event tickets. She explains how digitalised production is now taking place in a new environment of distribution and consumption and that programmes are being decided upon under substantially 'altered conditions' (ibid., p. 508). Coinciding the timing of certain programmes, and presumably the content too, to increase sales of tickets, is potentially yet another altered condition of commissioning. The creep of promotional culture appears to be affecting decisions about programme production in ever increasing ways including, as discussed in the bid document, like this.

What follows the promise of additional revenue for LOCOG in the bid proposal is a list of four benefits to the Channel 4 Corporation (C4TVC, 2009). Each of these benefits refers to either brand management or corporate strategy, suggesting that commercial objectives were pervasive within this creative media production alliance. The marketing strategy generally, in the bid document and later retrospectively, was described as an 'up close and personal' and 'phased approach' to programming. Specifically, the four strategic benefits to Channel 4 for broadcasting the Paralympic Games coverage were set out, in the bid, as a summary sheet, as follows.

The first relied on the 'remarkable crossover' between Channel 4's public service remit and LOCOG's cultural and social objectives to say, 'Being selected as the UK broadcast partner for the Games will strongly reinforce and differentiate our brand and help underline our public service credentials to our key stakeholders'. Notwithstanding a concern for social objectives then, brand management is the key consideration here.

The second benefit also provided a strategic solution for a known corporate challenge. Because of the complete enmeshment and juxtaposition of public service goals with business considerations, I feel the summary should be included here in full:

> Distinctiveness is at the core of the Channel 4 brand. Giving the Games pride of place in our peak-time schedule and positioning them as one of the world's greatest celebrations of diversity, will speak to Channel 4's core values and priorities and help underline our distinctiveness for viewers and opinion-formers at a time when it is increasingly difficult for broadcasters to stand out in the media marketplace.
>
> (C4TVC, 2009)

It is clear from this documentary evidence that the power to 'position' diversity within the mainstream television schedule, mediating a new frame of 'celebration' for erstwhile repulsive or invisible disability, is firmly rooted in the need to fix a deficit in their distinctiveness. This is a brand identity issue with what Davis (2013) calls a 'social-shaping influence' (p. 4). The pressing need to manage a marketplace 'difficulty' apparently triggered this decision to celebrate diversity. It was at least an argument for it. This is a very powerful social-shaping role, for meaning, or framing, about diversity and is driven by something that has nothing to do with it.

The third benefit argued in the bid proposal is simply that the extensive television and multi-format coverage will broaden audiences to provide 'a valuable commercial opportunity for Channel 4 and its partners'. This is perhaps to be expected as Channel 4 relies on advertising revenues to fund its future programming. The reason is not one that was mooted in the press releases, however.

The mutually beneficial collaborative vein extends to the fourth benefit too, based on a need to cohere the rapidly fragmenting audience. The summary concludes, 'The Games represent a rare example of genuine "event" television', which they considered an advantageous opportunity in the current digital media world. The corporate strategy for engaging the fragmented on-demand audience and providing a focus onto its own inventory was to increase coverage by 400 per cent on the previous Paralympics, and, as it says elsewhere in the document, match the BBC Olympics 2008 live broadcasting levels to elevate the coverage status to that kind of high-profile international televisual mega-event. This is another example of the tailored commissioning that is explicitly designed, as Zoellner (2009a) has pointed out, to capture the fragmented digital platform market.

In heavy type, after this list of benefits, the summary concludes, 'we will relish being entrusted with the Games, and our audience will share, develop and enhance our enthusiasm'. Their 'enthusiasm', according to the list I have cited above, is based on differentiating their brand, needing to stand out in the media marketplace, offering a valuable commercial opportunity and attracting an increasingly difficult to reach, rapidly fragmenting audience. The promotional culture therefore is clearly prevalent in this corporate strategy, seeking to protect and enhance the television channel brand and finding a way of capitalising on the Paralympic Games to do that. This is not to say that the executives did not have public service aspirations too, but simply to clarify that their argument for gaining the broadcasting rights was set within these commercial contexts and this brand identity logic.

The brand is described as 'risky' and 'innovative' with references to its parliamentary remit to include diversity both onscreen and off. It can be seen, then, that the remit has been subsumed into the brand as part of its identity, or DNA, in the thinking behind this document. There was also a promise that, during 2012, the Games would be 'the single biggest priority for Channel 4's 40-strong marketing team' and that marketing plays 'a key role in creating a genuine sense of event'. According to Natalia Dannenberg-Spreier, Head of Brand Management for the International Paralympics Committee, they now anticipate similar levels of commitment from the other domestic broadcasters for Tokyo 2020, Paris 2024, and Los Angeles 2028. Hesmondhalgh (2013) makes clear that all parts of the cultural production process are now subject to commercial pressures and other scholars have alerted the need to subject every stage of the production process to scrutiny (see, for example, Corner, 2004; Klein, 2009; Mann, 2009; Banet-Weiser and Sturken, 2010). Here the commercial objectives are set out before the inception of ideas for the media coverage itself. Additionally, the channel brand's role is supported by the full weight of the marketing workforce.

Scrutinising the process for commercial pressure does not negate the other perspectives that are true at the same time. My contributors recalled their genuine sense of purpose in changing perceptions about disability in society. In this case the bid writers also assured LOCOG that 'Channel 4 believes it has a responsibility beyond the Games, and will continue to develop ideas that contribute to a legacy of permanent value'. Underlying a subtly developed promotional culture, Davis (2013) has shown that a social-shaping influence happens, not just on the targets of promotion, but also on those who adopt its strategies. This legacy, within the bid, included creating 'a significant new pool of disabled media production talent for whom we will aim to provide further employment and training opportunities so that they can continue to develop their skills' (p. 27). Leaving a legacy of disabled production talent to carry on working for Channel 4 afterwards has the potential for the shaping of future content far beyond what the 12-day changing of televisual representations in 2012 would be able to do. Additionally, increased representation of diversity within the workforce after the Paralympics could potentially affect more than just attitudes depicted onscreen, but attitudes within the workplace as well.

In the bid description it was stated that historically their sports coverage 'is driven by inspirational stories and our passion to encourage audiences to get involved, get fit and have fun' (p. 26). This was coupled with their bold statement, again in bold type, that 'never again will disabled athletes be treated differently' (p. 4). The bid document articulated that brand management was linked to all these decisions and outcomes, and the outcomes were threaded together and woven into what later became a fully-fledged marketing strategy. To summarise then, brands, enhanced programme inventory, and changes in perception were all included in the mix for this pitch to broadcast the Paralympic Games.

According to Hesmondhalgh and Baker (2011), in other spheres, such as music and magazines, there has been a prevalent shift away from individuals assigned for marketing and advertising to a 'self-directing Marketing Department which has its own priorities' (p. 104). Here too, at Channel 4, the priorities of the Marketing Department shaped the representational content as well as the context and settings for the suite of programmes and advertisements that made up the Paralympics media coverage. Audience engagement was going to be a challenge and the marketing team, according to the Disability Executive, were on hand to remind staff about the need for engagement starting at the first away day in 2010 and restated in 2012. The staff training events, that were organised by the Brand Manager at Insight (the outsourced creative problem-solvers), had this text on one of the Disability Executive's first slides:

> Paralympics is a difficult sell. But it can be done. Audiences are curious about disability; we just need to be clever about how we pique that curiosity and play with their expectations.
>
> (C4TVC, 2011)

That it would be 'a difficult sell' is not just commercial language, it implies that intervention was required, beyond artistically or creatively making high-quality programmes. Playing with expectations was necessary to pique audience curiosity and the technique was cultivated and embedded in the run-up programmes to make the sport 'sell'. It can be seen that editorial freedom was ostensibly governed, here, by the need to satisfy marketing objectives.

These objectives were invisible structures affecting creative agency in ways that may, or may not necessarily, have benefited those being represented.

Given the key role of the marketing strategy for the London 2012 Paralympics from 2009 bid to 2012 broadcast, it made sense during my research, which extended into 2015, to establish if there would be a similar pattern for the following Paralympics. The scope of the response, even from the member of the board who was also the Chief Marketing and Communications Officer, was more surprising than I anticipated. I was told:

> We have already decided how we are going to present the Rio Paralympics – not just in the marketing – the whole thing. And that actually did come out of the Marketing Department.
> (Chief Marketing and Communications Officer, *Interview*)

So, building on its influence over aspects of the 2012 production, how to present *all of the coverage* for 2016 apparently emanated from the Marketing Department. Brooke went on to say that the creativity doesn't have to come from marketing, because they are a small organisation and very porous. He said, 'Literally if somebody suggests [something] someone else says "oh that's a good idea" and the creative process just builds and builds and builds and builds on it'. I asked him to clarify the role of the Marketing Department, as he is the Chief Marketing and Communications Officer as well as a member of the Board of Channel 4 Directors. Did he mean 'the whole thing' conceptually, or in more practical detail? Brooke made it clear the level of involvement of the Marketing Department, for Rio 2016, was significant:

> Well we have just decided, well we, not for how the Games are going to be presented – obviously the sport is the sport and you are given the feed that you are given – but whatever percentage of the coverage, and I don't know what it is, that you control which is in the studio or on the track side, you know, there are umpteen different ways that you can handle that. And you know we have kind of decided now how we are going to do Rio.
>
> (ibid.)

The Marketing Department, in this case, decided how they were going to go about producing the Rio 2016 Paralympics, including the trackside and studio presenting, not just the advertising campaigns associated with the coverage. For both the Olympic Games and the Paralympic Games an outside broadcasting company (OBS) provides the sports feed, with each individual country supplementing the pictures with their own additional camerawork and commentaries. The plans for this particular tailored coverage were, here, decided within the marketing team. Hesmondhalgh (2013) notes that some marketing influences are 'less obvious' (see p. 234) and this is a case in point. He also points out that the importance of the commercially oriented department is often reflected structurally by the inclusion of these decision-makers on corporate executive boards (ibid.). At Channel 4, at board level, the 40-strong marketing team has Brooke's voice heading up their perspectives and needs at the top of the organisation. It was never that clear in his interview whether 'we' meant his department or the organisation as a whole. What was clear was that he wore both 'hats', as he put it, comfortably, and brought his brand objectives to the executive table.

Commercial objectives

Building on Klein's (2009) critical analysis of the restructuring of meaning through the *merging* of commercial and cultural objectives, my research shows that certain decisions about meanings were indecipherably blended at source. The above interview with the Chief Marketing and Communications Officer does suggest that the coverage may not necessarily have arisen through commercial exploitation per se, but certainly did derive, at least, from commercial exploits. Klein (2009), considering exploitation, and particularly the 'asymmetrical relationship' (2009, p. 118) between musicians and advertisers, observes that the creative and commercial relationship is an unequal one. The creatives and in-house advertising company at Channel 4, at least in the case of the Paralympics, appear to have had a more equal, symbiotic, relationship. Both the marketing team and the other in-house decision-makers apparently collaborate in the following way, as Brooke, in 2015, went on to explain:

> We are not going to tell anybody about it [the Rio 2016 coverage] but it will be different from London and that is, it is not a sort of production line type of process. You know, it is a creative everyone-muck-in-together type of process.

> (ibid.)

So, within Channel 4, at least whilst it continues with its current funding structure, anyone with a creative spark can apparently initiate their ideas for production. Brooke reiterated this twice.

Davis (2013) has identified, in the spheres of politics and also civic life more generally, that there are 'promotional intermediaries' (ibid.) operating with decision-making powers within social structures where they do not apparently appear as such. I would argue, therefore, that the power to initiate an idea is not the same as the power to consequently influence and shape the framing, the representations, the timings in the programme schedule and meanings that are then produced from that collaboration. In Chapters 3, 4, and 5, I have included Business Managers, Marketing Executives, and a

Communications Director as key contributors to the shaping of onscreen representations. It seems that all the creative processes from beginning to end had joint objectives assisted by actors whom Davis might term promotional intermediaries.

I interrogated this collaborative practice, for the creation of 2012 Paralympic coverage, to assess its pervasiveness. Klein (2009) and Hesmondhalgh (2013), amongst others, have both asserted that in other fields of cultural and media production the 'collaborative' relationship is intrinsic to production. Klein (2009) found this to be true in cases of popular music used in advertising, where commercial processes can work against the interests of musicians. Hesmondhalgh (2013), too, has found that, within the magazine industry, a particular company, for example, has replaced the marketing person with 'a self-directing' (p. 235) marketing department which has 'its own priorities' (ibid.). Whether or not these priorities match the creative purpose may possibly vary from case to case. What does not seem to vary is that, in both these fields of cultural production, the cultural and commercial processes are inextricably linked.

I have argued throughout this book that, in the case of the 2012 Paralympic production, the commercial goals did not only permeate, but were also connected to their creative and societal ambitions for change. Since then, as the Board Director and Chief Marketing and Communications Officer states, the way to 'do' the Rio coverage actually *originated* within the Marketing Department. This power to design entire productions extends beyond the shaping and promotion of content, or even the commissioning of documentaries, referred to in the bid document. Such powerful influence may be all-pervading, then, within the public service broadcasting sector as well as within the music and magazine industries, at least it seems to be so with Channel 4. 4Creative is the in-house advertising agency, owned by the Channel 4 Television Corporation, whose website asserts that they do the advertising and produce the marketing campaigns. They also, evidently, influence a lot more of the programme content than that.

Clearly, as Klein (2009) has already pointed out, changing media alliances now routinely blur creative ambitions with commercial objectives and this issue, as she asserts, is a critical one. At the end of the Birt era, which involved a radical transformation of the BBC corporation, Born (2004) felt that a team of market analysts and strategists (p. 132) were playing an increasingly influential role over the creatives there. In that case, the influence was with respect to the shaping of programme content to reinforce their separate channel brands (ibid.). In the case of the 2012 Paralympics and the bringing of a marginalised group into the mainstream, the messages were marketed through the 'golden brand' (C4TVC, 2009) of Channel 4, which also sees itself as the public service challenger channel (Commercial Lawyer, *Interview*, 2015). The alliance between in-house ad agency 4Creative and Channel 4 has worked out well. It is still apparently porous and collaborative. There are no guarantees, however, that future influences, or some might say 'interferences', with the creative production process will have such beneficial outcomes. Negative onscreen representations could potentially also be decided upon if it suited the market conditions and other agendas that in this case brought about a championing of diversity. These media alliances need, therefore, to remain under scrutiny.

In this section I have shown that the creators and executors of the marketing strategies for both the London 2012 and Rio 2016 media coverage should also be recognised as key decision-makers in the creative process. They do not just write the marketing strategy, they implement it, affecting programme content, tone, and style. In addition to creating advertising campaigns and advertorial content, they also shape the programme schedule and, for example, are able to decide on production messaging for the trackside and studio inserts for apparently neutral 'live' sports coverage too. Whilst being involved in 'the whole thing', in particular these producers utilised the power of brands to carry messages, and I discuss this method of shaping meanings in the section below.

How brands were shared, borrowed, repaired, and created

Having initially offered up their own brand to win the London 2012 bid, it became clear from my interviews that links with other brands were vital to the project. In this section I show that Channel 4 first needed to *share* brand associations by collaborating strategically with particular corporate sponsors. Two household names, Sainsbury's and BT, were chosen for this purpose as part of a deliberate branding strategy. The next step was to *borrow* brands for their tropes, associations, and values. Nearly all of my contributors mentioned 'Nike' and 'Public Enemy' at some point in their recollections, suggesting a considerable influence by both brands on the producers themselves. The inspirational influence of Nike was indirect, whereas Public Enemy's soundtrack directly influenced the creative process and the practitioners making the content. Collaborating with and borrowing from other brands was also used to *repair* their own brand. According to both the Business Manager and the overall Project Leader, the media coverage was purposed for brand reputational rather than directly financial reasons (alongside what they could do for disability perceptions). Finally, the outcome, of what turned out to be a highly successful project, was to *create* another brand of Olympian/Paralympian hybrids, the 'superhumans' (as distinct from the stereotypes of superheroes, or supercrips, as discussed in previous chapters). This brand, with its specified characteristics and attached meanings, could then be reused and revamped, as they chose to do (Head of Marketing, *Interview*, 2014), to sell the coverage for the Rio 2016 Paralympic Games and attract the earlier audience back.

The significance of branding for 'normalising' representations of disability lies in the attachment of social meanings that Banet-Weiser (2012) says provide specific personal resonances for consumers. She explains that 'the process of branding impacts the way we understand who we are, how we organise ourselves in the world, and what stories we tell ourselves about ourselves' (p. 5). In other words, brands can define who 'we' are in relation to 'others'. Branding, therefore, is more than just a tool of marketing. Both Klein (2009) and Banet-Weiser (2012) have established that sometimes the cultures surrounding specific brands compete and overlap with each other. Amongst the Channel 4 producers, I noticed different relationships with brands were used as shortcuts to create, enhance, and distribute particular messaging about disability. These meaningful messages were embedded in the content, taking advantage of pre-trained audience responses to particular brands, as I outline below.

Brand collaborations

It was not just Channel 4's 'golden brand', as written into the bid, that was used to shape representations. The first action taken, after being awarded the broadcasting rights, was to join forces with two well-known corporate brands and *share* the benefits of their brand associations. At first glance the need for collaboration with sponsors would seem to be simply a financial one, but they also relied on meanings associated with two other brands, in their capacity as corporate partners. Huge sums of money worldwide are invested to amplify the commercial gains afforded by the dynamics of international mega-events (see Whannel, 1992; Dayan and Katz, 1994; Howe, 2008b), but these have not naturally been proffered to the previously low-profile, poor relation, Olympic 'side-show' (Gilbert and Schantz, 2008). Corporate sponsors therefore needed to be approached, but they were approached with meanings, associated with their brands, in mind.

The two sponsors, BT and Sainsbury's, who subsidised Channel 4 (rather than being sponsors of the Paralympic Games itself), were essential for their associated brand values. The Project Leader, Deborah Poulton, as a key decision-maker and responsible for all the media coverage, turned down other companies in order to get them. In earlier chapters I have explained how sponsorship deals provided funding to supply, for example, extra cameras and equipment, so that the coverage could look more like the Olympics. This was an indirect way of positively affecting the visual representations and the 'feel' of the Games. Independently, two Executive Producers made it clear to me that without the financial help of the sponsorship money none of the branding ideals, especially the attempt at parity, which I explored in Chapter 4, could have been achieved. The Project Leader told me she had other reasons for bringing these two particular corporate sponsors on board. She selected them to shape meanings about disability sport and also for their ability to distribute the messaging.

The two brands were, for her, 'what made the Paralympics coverage possible'. As discussed in Chapter 4, Poulton described the merger of a niche broadcaster (Channel 4) with a huge supermarket chain (Sainsbury's) and a high-profile telecommunications team (British Telecom) as the 'perfect mix'. They needed the income and the exposure provided by the separate campaigns and infrastructures of the corporate sponsors to promote the Games but also to make the Paralympics more palatable. Poulton, as Project Leader, felt that to affect long-term perceptions, had it been a 'purely commercial' business venture to yield a definite income stream, rather than a brand alliance, then they would not have achieved what they had done. The Project Leader did not make it clear whether the backing of familiar brands may therefore be a necessary ingredient needed for bringing marginalised diverse 'others' into the mainstream, but she certainly felt it to be necessary for their project.

In their own Paralympic marketing campaigns and short documentaries, aired on Channel 4 and YouTube, Sainsbury's went for the 'wholesome' feel, aligned with their brand, and BT were 'edgy', as Poulton put it. She felt that this helped 'balance the output for the broader audience' as they were reaching, with a niche programme, beyond the niche audience. Adding the 'wholesome' sense of Sainsbury's' family depictions made the inclusion of a wider television audience more likely, and their brand was chosen for that 'warm glow'. This helped allay the 'revulsion' towards disability (Elias, 1978; Davis, 1995; Garland-Thomson, 1997; Gilbert and Schantz, 2008; 2012) that stand-alone programming has suffered from in the past (e.g. Barnes, 1992). Logistically, Poulton explained that she was under contract to deliver their own editorial frame but had to handle the other two frames alongside without compromising Channel 4's. (The Channel 4 logo appeared on their material, as well as vice versa.) The mix was reassuring, she felt, to the public, as it blended meanings in a palatable way, mixing edginess and risk with family cohesion and wholesomeness. Placing disability inside that mix acted as a familiar interpretive cushion against old unwanted interpretations and was a conscious act of design on her part.

I would argue that these 'editorial frames' she describes in media producer language are in fact 'brand identities' in marketing jargon, containing brand values and brand associations. These types of association have to be consistently cultivated over time (Kellner, 2003; Kapferer, 2008) and were utilised to prepare and reassure audiences prior to the Paralympics media coverage. It is clear that the two companies were chosen as collaborators for the inherent feelings and perceptions connected to the brands by their broader base of carefully cultivated and monitored customers.

In the sense that brands have personalities, this group constituted a family of voices. They were necessary to overcome the revulsion or disinterest normally associated with disability on TV. Poulton told me she felt this combination of company identities was more acceptable as a package of reassurances and meanings than if they had broadcast the coverage on their own. One of the Executive Producers at 4Creative felt that their combined efforts would all blend into one and be seen as one campaign, making it safer to bring the disabled athletes into the public eye. It would be safer because more than one familiar point of reference would be giving the new messages. The combination was apparently needed to overcome the qualms that portraying disability on mainstream television was predicted to create, since they were well-known and signalled familiar, safe, ordinariness, even with their different brand images.

The media producers' predictions naturally did not come from reading the work of disability scholars, but from their own audience research (C4TVC, 2012). They were aware there was a stigma to overcome nevertheless. Sainsbury's recognised that their own inherent brand identity, with associated values, was distinctly different to Channel 4's, as they were unable to take risks with their supermarket chain. A marketing person from 4Creative said, 'For the record, when we first presented *Meet the Superhumans*, Sainsbury's loved it. They said "We could never do that and we take our hats off [to you]" '. The mix of brand reassurances then was needed for all parties to reframe the Paralympics in an acceptable way, but this was as a collaboration rather than a merger. By combining their messaging power, inclusive meanings were blended but the brands nevertheless remained separate.

Bringing together the mix of brands with their collective framings was intended to heighten and enhance the impact that was felt by audiences. The Press Officer for the British Paralympic Association (BPA) told me:

> Without the backing of their commercial partners, as well as people like the Sainsbury's and BTs of this world, and without Channel 4 putting all of their energy and effort and creative [sic.] into it that they did, there's no way that we would have – and by we, I mean collective we, not just BPA, that we would have had the sort of impact that we did.
>
> (BPA Press Officer, *Interview*, 2015)

Another stakeholder representative, the Digital Marketing Manager for the International Paralympics Committee (IPC), associated this impact more consciously with the marketing infrastructure:

> I think the Sainsbury's campaign [contributed] as well, with David Beckham and football five-a-side [a schools initiative]; that massively elevated the Paralympics as well.
>
> (IPC Digital Marketing Manager, *Interview*, 2015)

Commercial and creative elements throughout can be seen to be intrinsically linked at all levels of ideas and initiatives. The collaborative benefits, as a net effect, also extended and amplified the TV coverage in other ways through, for example, the celebrity and school initiatives. Craig Spence, the IPC Media and Communications Director, explained that they needed the sponsors on board to do that. The relationships between sponsors, stakeholders, and their associated brand meanings were complex, he said, but necessary to create the right mix to create new representations of disability onscreen that would be accepted by the public. My contributors understood that the public needed reassurances from multiple places, not just the TV channel.

Even though amplifying the television coverage was important, the 'bumper ads' at the top and tail of each programme segment struck some of the creatives as an impingement. Suggesting a divide between creative values and the marketing imperatives amongst some of the roles, a poolside camerawoman told me, typically:

> I think people felt happy that somebody like Sainsbury's were involved in it. But the idea of having their logo plastered everywhere was just, ugh, let's not.
>
> (Camerawoman, *Interview*, 2014)

She was briefed by her camera supervisor to exclude at least part of the logo in her camera angles wherever possible during the swimming. A *Breakfast Show* editor also did not want the logo in shot all the time admitting, 'Yes, it gave you a warm glow about Sainsbury's, good for them. Good for them'. However he tried to avoid too much brand placement in his studio discussion shots and did not want to see complete names of other brands onscreen, even though they were the sponsors. Here, internally within the production, the clash between commercial and creative goals was clearly prevalent and personally felt. The visual presence of these 'other brands' in shot, whether in the studio, poolside, or as bumper ads, was extensively resisted by the teams that had to accommodate them. Mostly the crews and post-production teams were irritated by them, even though the visibility of brands in shot were, according to executives, reassuring to the public.

The resistance and irritation came from a sense of 'selling out', where their craft was now being devalued for commercial purposes. For some of the below-the-line technicians and operators their creative value comes from a sense of autonomy over the details of how they carry out their roles (Gitlin, 2005; Banks, 2009). Being made to point at the Sainsbury's logo felt different to the camera person, for example, than having to frame a shot to include wheelchairs or crutches. The latter edict, whilst also taking away her autonomy, had a purpose that the programme was about, whereas the former carries the reminder that their art is being commodified.

Banet-Weiser (2012) makes the distinction between commodification and branding saying that one is for profit and the other about meanings. In the case of the bumper ads, the meanings about Sainsbury's 'wholesome family' brand were not picked up on by the technicians I spoke to. They responded cynically. Other research could establish whether it might have been significant for the audience; it was certainly intended to be so by the executive decision-makers.

TV audiences also experienced other endorsements of this 'different' sporting event in other places, to resonate and reassure them during the coverage itself. Not just through schools and shops but through some BT technology poster campaigns as well. Meanings were forged through the collaboration of these big brands. The 'freaky cyborg' (Brittain, 2010; Garland-Thomson, 2009) trope suited BT's brand image, and was used within their televisual marketing, but Channel 4, with their less technological brand, took a more human reading of man and machine. For the media coverage itself then, the cosy family supermarket, the national telecommunications network, and the 'born risky' niche broadcaster came together with their combined brand equities to forge a new profile for the Paralympic Games normalising disability across each of their respective networks.

These brand equities, in marketing terms, are derived from the value that comes from the unique set of attributes associated with individual brands (see Kapferer, 2012). What was intended, to promote the disability portrayals, was that if the audience felt safe enough with the brand or brands communicating with them, then challenges to existing paradigms about otherness could be taken on board or found more acceptable (Project Leader, *Interview*, 2016). Existing consumer knowledge about a brand is known to affect responses to that brand. As Keller (2009) explains, 'different outcomes result in the marketing of a product or service because of its brand, as compared to if that same product or service was not identified by that brand' (p. 140). He also asserts that because of this inherent value of brand equity it is therefore a management priority to build strong brands. For the purposes of bringing a marginalised group into the mainstream, a sense of social significance for the Paralympians arguably needed a boost from some strong brands.

Keller (2009) says that, in order to build a strong brand:

> The right knowledge structures must exist in the minds of actual or prospective customers so that they respond positively to marketing activities and programmes.
>
> (ibid.)

Amongst the decision-makers at Channel 4 I found this priority for brand strengthening to be the case, in particular through volunteered information which I hadn't asked for, from the Chief Marketing and Communications

Officer. Changing perceptions about Channel 4 was unashamedly part of the mix, for him, when promoting the inclusion of disabled athletes into the elite group of high-performance sportsmen and women that already have acceptance. He cared about the knowledge structures in the minds of his customers because he needed them to respond positively to their channel brand.

To help structure the thinking of the audience, I have shown in the last chapter that it is common practice to consistently show certain types of programmes within particular slots in the TV schedule. Genres are reinforced, developed, and invented in this way (Brown, 1990; Fiske, 1989), but so too are brands built and consolidated (Born, 2004; Mann, 2009). Most producers that I interviewed recognised some sort of channel identity. As one of my participants suggested, for example, if the BBC had played a hip-hop track over a segment of disabled sport it might seem strange and incongruent, whereas if Channel 4 did that the audience might expect it. Audience responses are cultivated by relationships with the previous messaging, as was clearly evidenced by the uproar caused when *Great British Bake Off* (2017) was relinquished by the BBC to be shown on Channel 4. The programme is made by an independent company but experienced through the brand that publishes it.

As Born (2004) noted for the BBC, their Marketing Department defined the channel brands by 'symbolising certain values' and proposing an ideal. Her contributors for 'planning and strategy' laid out the challenges for television, at that time in the 1990s. These were the need to attract niche viewers who were not already viewing the channel; boosting TV audiences; securing sporting rights; and acquiring 'landmark' shows to unify the audience (p. 266). Born (2004) points out that the key influence of marketing on the culture of the BBC channels was the impact of 'brand-thinking' (p. 268), where their values had to be 'consciously formulated and performed' (ibid.). This same process was evidenced in my own research at Channel 4.

The other brand with which all three organisations needed to collaborate was the Paralympics Movement itself. The movement's ethos of inclusion and empowerment is central to the ideology of the Games (Brittain, 2010). Sir Ludwig Guttmann had based his original inspiration for a parallel Olympics on what he called 'the values of hope and rehabilitation' (IPC, 1991). These values were then broadened to include enjoyment and then competitiveness. With the commodification of the Olympics (see Roche, 2000), and televisual sport in general (Whannel, 2008), it may well have also been the financial gains that have driven the movement consciously towards the parity I discuss in Chapter 4. Channel 4 accepted the challenge to modify the Paralympic Brand and offered the 'distinct benefits' in the bid for broadcasting rights that were discussed in the first half of this chapter. They went on to offer enhancements to LOCOG including additional revenue opportunities that would come as a consequence of pairing their brands.

For a while, after the event was broadcast, Channel 4 continued to run the channel ident between programmes calling themselves 'The Paralympic Channel'. They have also used it since, at intervals.

In 2006, Howe and Jones evaluated the impact of combining commercial strategies with the marketing potential of the Paralympic Games, in terms of demand and supply, and profit. The list below would directly affect the televisual style, and hints very much at what did in fact transpire in 2012. They wrote:

> Good Games are profitable ones, good sports are marketable ones, and good athletes are endorsable ones. The IPC are conspiring with the IOC to repackage, remarket, refresh, modernize, and essentially sell the Paralympics. The product, however, needs revising to increase demand. The Paralympics needs to be quicker, slicker, shorter, with fewer events and fewer, but higher profile champions.
>
> (Howe and Jones, 2006, p. 33)

This sports product that was purchased by Channel 4 for 2012 was imbued with these characteristics and the marketing remit given to them was to increase demand for that product. For Channel 4, according to my contributors, this would provide audience growth, and for the IPC, according to Brittain (2010), increase the saleability to future sponsors and media organisations (p. 119). Marketing objectives here directly affected representations, and all the types of decisions that have emerged throughout my interviews were shaped by these objectives, including, for example, editing, sporting tropes, and the production of artificial rivalries to manufacture known personalities.

The new positioning of the sporting event as 'high-performance sport' was a brand development requirement for the Paralympics itself, placed upon Channel 4 as part of the deal. What a brand brings to the product is the *meanings* and *associations* understood by the audience or consumers. So, during the encoding process, the decoding, which Hall (1980; 2012) asserts is interpretive, can at least be guided to some extent, through the power of branding. In the bid, Channel 4 wrote about their audience:

> They have come to expect Channel 4 to do significant and surprising things – we are the 'Channel of Firsts' – and the Paralympics would be one of our biggest firsts to date.
>
> (C4TVC, 2009, p. 23)

It is clear from this document that audience awareness of brands shaped the representations of disability and is a measurable factor in the framing of meanings about disability.

The Head of Communications at the IPC also recognised, during his interview, that brands are able to position the subjects of their representations.

He reflected on how 4Creative's *Meet the Superhuman* campaign had successfully rebranded the Paralympics as follows:

> I just think, for us, that advertising campaign did more to re-position Paralympics sport amongst the British public in 60 seconds than probably the last 25 years put together [...] positioning Paralympics sport as high-performance sport for the first time, that advert just did it. It was amazing. I remember watching it for the first time and just going, 'Oh my God!' – if I'd put together a dream list of what I wanted an advert to have, that's it. Because it focuses very much on the training of the athletes and they just look like day-to-day athletes. They don't look like what had previously been perceived in the British public's mind of people with a disability who can't do things. They could do things and it just – it's a tremendous 60 seconds of work.
>
> (IPC, Head of Communications, *Interview*, 2015)

Repositioning, as he calls it, was also rebranding, in the sense that new meanings were associated with the same athletes, so that they might be perceived differently and in a new light.

Whilst talking to the Video Editor who created the '60 seconds' (and the 90-second version) it was obvious that the innate creativity, which he had used in his cutting room, was influenced by the intertextuality of assimilating brand tropes over a lifetime – rather than borrowing directly from other brands himself. In other words, he had not directly used cookie cutter templates for style, pace, or meaning although others did ask him to create a particular attitude and feel. The best way that the Film Director was able to communicate this with him, though, was to cite other brands to give him pointers. These came to mind to the producers who, as well as operating with 'risk', borrowed other meanings from other brands, as the next section shows.

Other brand relationships and dynamics

The pervasive nature of promotional practices, beyond the concerns of products and services, has been examined in depth by Davis (2013) who also includes brands and brand resonances. He suggests that the subtle promotion of ideas and people is influencing huge swathes of cultural and civic life. My findings agree with others, such as Born (2004), Klein (2009), Mann (2009) and Lieb (2016) that this pervasiveness also reaches into the media production process. It is affecting our commercially and non-commercially funded public service broadcasters, even those we did not previously think of as commercialised or branded.

As cultural artefacts are being produced, Hesmondhalgh (2013) has pointed out that marketing executives reduce meanings sometimes down to a single word, and then build their methods and ideas back up from there (p. 234). In the case of the Paralympic athletes, creativity around their depiction did indeed derive from a single word. That word was 'cool'. As a representation I discussed this in Chapter 4, but here I am recognising the word also as the label, or tag-line, for their marketing strategy. This conversation with Kuba Wieczorek, the Business Manager, shows how the shaping began:

> In all our heads we thought, 'okay this has now turned into a really cool project that went from being a little bit grubby dealing with lots of corporate organisations – God how are we going to make it all fit?' into suddenly we were like, with *Murderball* and the away days and seeing wheelchair rugby, there was something we were like now 'okay this is a cool thing and we just need to say to the public this is going to be really cool'. How would Nike approach it? What would Nike do? They make sport look cool – they make you feel like you want to partake in that sport and not just watch it – we wanted to communicate that and that visceral nature that the sport gives you.
>
> (Business Manager, *Interview*, 2015)

When they considered portraying the sport as 'cool', the brand most associated with that meaning immediately sprang to mind. The essence of cool is built into the brand of Nike, so they *borrowed* that essence, not as a formal brand partnership but as an inspirational style choice. By utilising the camera angles, tropes and high production values for a high-performance sports ad, that the Nike company would also do, 4Creative were able to reference meanings built up by another brand, for consumption within their own. This 'cool' buzzword, that everybody was using, had been successfully introduced and embedded into the global sports shoe brand. It came with associated narratives and visual style, all of which the production team copied. Whether creativity was inhibited by this reduction or channelled by it can be argued either way. However, it was clear, from virtually all of my participants' recollections, that the identification and intention to share an association was there.

How these actions came to improve perceptions about disability may well have been through the mobilising of existing cultural myths. As Hearn (2012) point outs, 'goods come to be designed less for their direct usefulness and more for the meanings and myths they are able to mobilise and represent' (p. 204). Hearn (2012) also suggests that with some brands, 'the sign comes to displace the material object to which it refers and in this way acquires a kind of agency' (ibid.). In this case, by styling the televisual representations to look like a Nike advert would also look, the positive 'vibe', trained by that company's previous advertising, helped displace the negative perceptions of disability. I would argue that the mobilisation of invisible devices, in the form of these branded cultural myths, assists consumers in buying into meanings rather than products. For 2012, with the Paralympics as 'a difficult sell', audiences were not expected to buy into disability per se. By overlaying branded meanings, old entrenched meanings of disability were instead simply displaced.

The Head of Marketing, James Walker, explained how and why the high-performance televisual style would give weight to Channel 4's own audio-visual treatment:

> They are clichés of sports marketing, but when people do them brilliantly – as Nike does it brilliantly – there's a sort of energy and a kind of grittiness and a reality to it that is incredibly powerful. You know, showing the perspiration, showing the training and stuff like that.
>
> (ibid.)

The visceral nature of what the producers wanted to portray was already encapsulated in the essence of another brand's televisual tropes. What they drew attention to within that was the mainstream positioning of high-performance athleticism. It was this essence and perspective that was really being borrowed, whilst of course, the creative originality remained their own.

As well as adopting the 'cool' style, a soundtrack was found that eventually underpinned all their programming and *The Last Leg* comedy satire show has continued to use it several years afterwards. It took considerable searching to find and once they had it, the marketing campaign was defined by the music. Nike had once borrowed The Beatles' *Revolution* to shape a commercial and Channel 4 borrowed Public Enemy's *Harder Than You Think* to define theirs.

Klein (2009) writes of the determination of some musicians to differentiate between commercial uses for their music, and that it is not always considered 'selling out'. In this instance Public Enemy actively chose to be involved, not with an existing brand of, for example, a cleaning product, but in the creation of a new brand of emerging 'Olympian' athletes. According to the band they did this because they identified closely with the Paralympic underdog predicament (Majendie, 2012). One of Klein's (2009) contributors acknowledges that some artists 'feel their music was created in so much emotion that they refuse ever to use it to promote a brand' (ibid., p. 111) even where the licence is sought to borrow from 'the essence of their music' (ibid.). There seems to be a fine line, therefore, between the emotional essence of the music and the sense of brand that essence can create. The underdog predicament of Public Enemy's identity, within their music, was understood by the television producers of the TV commercial, and the values and meanings borrowed to serve a purpose, to shape similar meanings in another context.

This use of a piece of hip-hop music as a soundtrack, for the *Meet the Superhumans* commercial, embedded a brand within a brand, resonating the intangible sense they were looking for, with a very tangible musical brand with its own complex associations. Hip-hop music emanates from a culture of the marginalised and dispossessed, with connotations of powerlessness for the predominantly black or Latino Americans within that ghetto culture (see Smitherman, 1997). Challenging safe middle-class norms of acceptability (ibid., p. 4) is exactly what Channel 4 wanted to do, in a similar way, to disrupt and change representations of the disabled athletes. Public Enemy, as one of the founding groups to emerge from within the hip-hop sub-culture (ibid.) have their own brand of rhetoric that is easily identifiable, and their defiant independent stance was epitomised in the song that was selected. The Head of Marketing told me:

> It completely blew us away, because that was the first time we'd heard that track and it was found by the Editor. And also, he found it because… he's a Public Enemy nut! He's a hip-hop nut! And he heard the song and just said, 'Lyrics' completely. Because they were about something else; they were about politics. Public Enemy are a real political band and the lyrics were about their struggle – Public Enemy's struggle and the sort of, you know – the sort of Civil Rights struggle in the US which is still going on but it was so applicable to disabled sport. [The lyrics] were all about overcoming problems and overcoming adversities and getting stronger and 'you're stronger than you think' and 'you've got strength', and it was just, wow this is perfect! This is absolutely perfect! Once we re-edited it to take out all the swear words, it was like, bang, this is it! This is our track for the Paralympics. I mean, we all knew instinctively, straight away. It wasn't conscious searching, searching, searching. The Editor found it; we heard it and we went 'Wow!'.
>
> (Head of Marketing, *Interview*, 2014)

It was conscious searching on the Editor's part, he told me, and he had spent a month looking for it, after the Film Director had come in and shown him the Jay-Z YouTube video of the track '99 problems', and said 'we want something like this' (Video Editor, *Interview*, 2014). This only meant 'a vibe' like this to the Editor, which has a kind of meaning attached to it, but when other producers heard the track it was understood more explicitly and differently, beyond just being 'a vibe'.

Interestingly, the lyrics *were* the significant element for the Head of Marketing, as well as a sense of a marginalised struggle:

> Yeah, you know it was just a powerful way – you've got two seconds to draw somebody in and make people think differently. But we did, using a kind of powerful hip-hop track. You know, by a group who were kind of famous for their defiant attitude. In a way […] with Public Enemy – when they started it was a very much kind of 'this is who we are, we

are black men in this time in America and we were going to stand up to racism', whatever. And they did it defiantly, and I think that attitude that you get from hip-hop music transcended into the Paralympians as kind of, 'this is who we are', not, 'if you don't like us we don't care' but there's an element of 'we are', you know – well yes they've been in a car accident or whatever but 'we've overcome that' – and it obviously stirred people and moved people.

(Head of Marketing, *Interview*, 2014)

The borrowed meanings and associations are very clear from the Head of Marketing as well as all the 4Creative team I interviewed. The key was that 'they instinctively knew' the meanings fitted. In this way the embedded values of the existing brand were exerting their power over the production team. Then that same defiance and fiercely independent attitude provided meanings with which the previously invisible Paralympians had not been linked.

According to Smitherman (1997) the hip-hop genre has a 'disturb the peace' vibe, which is very much what Channel 4 were trying to do for the Paralympians. Blended meanings are more pronounced here than with the corporate sponsors, whose brand associations simply added to the mix reassuringly and broadened the reach of audience. Disturbing the peace is also a kind of mission statement for Channel 4, as their parliamentary remit (see Chapter 4) requires them to challenge and broadcast perspectives that are not shown elsewhere, particularly for those being under-represented. With Public Enemy, therefore, the blend was organic, rather than additive, and the joint branding created new meanings beneficial to both. The band re-recorded their track for the television commercial, and then, after the Games, as a tribute to the athletes, re-edited their video for 'Harder Than You Think' to include the Paralympians even though most of them are white and none of them are from inner-city America. This collaboration demonstrates the irrevocable change in relationships that Klein (2009) has highlighted between advertisers, sponsors, and musicians. What they now share has morphed and both groups have benefited from the brand associations, expanding audiences and consolidating meanings for both groups.

Channel 4's audience have been prepared to expect an alternative take on life and an unusual perspective, as this is embedded into their on-brand programming (although not all of their current ratings-grabbing cheap format programmes are on brand, Lygo, then Head of Television, was quick to point out). Had this same content been transmitted or delivered by BBC1 the music might well have been understood as a burst of otherness, but when presented by Channel 4 it sat well within the brand's 'remit', 'feel', and 'tone of voice', connecting with the audience. The sense of underdogs emerging from their marginalised ghetto, as a sub-set of elite Olympians, was acceptable because of the audience priming, to expect the unexpected from

Channel 4. As more than one contributor proudly told me 'only Channel 4 could have done that!'. This may have felt to the producers like creative freedom but, according to Keller's (2009) definition, is actually branding. In practice it was probably both.

The Chief Marketing and Communications Officer said the ad 'hit the sweet spot' speaking of 'Channel 4ness'. Meanings were embedded within the brand as well as the programme content. The brands even have a tele-visual style. Back in 2010 two of the training slides read:

> Programmes like *The Boy Whose Skin Fell Off, The Strangest Village in Britain, Make Me Normal* and *The Undateables* show you can make disability rate...
> ...All great programmes each with a secret weapon: brilliant title or trails, innovative structure or storytelling, fresh treatment of disability, jaw-dropping heart-breaking moments.
>
> (C4TVC, 2011)

Branding within the programme inventory, then, clearly goes beyond snappy graphics and logos into narratives and rhetoric embedded within identifiable channel stylings, relating also to photography and editing. Editorial decisions at this level used to be made by creative film and television makers separately from other departments (Dornfeld, 1998, p. 178). They are now contributing to and part of a group product, as these corporate slides reveal.

Banet-Weiser (2012) explains that it is the socially imbued meanings that create the brand, in the sense that associations build over time and become part of how the brand is understood. Meanings attached to other brands were added together and associated with the Paralympic athletes and this works when 'the meaning of one thing is transferred to or made interchangeable with another quality whose value attaches itself to the product' (Dyer, 1982, p. 116). Whilst branding may hide the capitalist logic that guides it (Klein, 2009, p. 81), the power of branding to shape the possible range of decoding positions available to audiences is of great value even to those creative producers not seeking to directly profit from the brand association.

Building on the idea established by Williams (1983), that personal meaning must be linked to an object in order to sell it, Klein (2009) argues that viewers are happy to set aside what they know objectively in order to be entertained through the emotional experiences offered by advertisers (ibid., p. 82). She asserts that 'there is a joy in allowing oneself to be taken for the branding ride that discourages renunciation and prevents a lucid and commonsensical response for even the quickest of viewers' (ibid.). This ability of brands to temporarily 'discourage renunciation' of the advertising message means that, in the case of the London 2012 onscreen representations of disability, the ingrained audience reflex of revulsion (see Chapters 2 and 4) could be temporarily overcome in order to enjoy the persuasive normality associated with the other brands.

The interruption of typical responses during Klein's 'branded ride' (ibid.) suggests a suspension of disbelief is at play, at least for those advertisements which are artistic, entertaining, or pleasurable to watch. For the Paralympians to be normalised it was essential that the viewing public could identify with them and experience positive emotions. Branding was used as a quick route to creating these associations. As Klein (2009) points out, branding provides shortcuts to both authenticity and also social significance (p. 94). Banet-Weiser (2012) similarly suggests that we should no longer make a false distinction between consumer culture and authenticity, since the culture claims to be authentic, as well as defining the sense of it. In Channel 4's case, it is clear that, without the help of strong brand associations, reassuring the public with their own familiar meanings, depictions of authenticity and mainstream credibility could not have been achieved.

There was also an element of needing to *repair* their own brand. Brand relationships, in a variety of forms, affected how disability was portrayed and viewed and the overarching brand consideration, throughout the whole production cycle was to restore their own reputation in the process. In addition to all the other reasons I have explored in preceding chapters, the Business Director recollected:

> We were a year before Channel 4's 30th birthday, there was lots of talk about 'has Channel 4 lost its way?' And there was a lot of talk about 'well maybe the Paralympics is the right thing to put it back on track' and make people realise just what a fantastic organisation and what a fantastic force for good it is. We realised we should treat this with a bit more respect and reverence and time and attention and that's when things flipped really. You know, just the way we approach things internally.
>
> (Business Manager, *Interview*, 2015)

According to Aaker (1991), building a strong brand, from which to distribute your content, helps build a loyal audience. The brand identity, as discussed, also depends on past investments. When I spoke to Lygo, who had been Head of Television at the bid stage, he defended his choice of programme mix during his watch as Commissioning Chief. He also explained why he had axed *Big Brother* as part of getting that mix right. The channel was no longer offering programmes that were not being offered elsewhere, particularly as the reality show he had introduced as initially ground-breaking was now being copied in a variety of other guises. They needed to be distinctive, as part of their remit, and as part of their recognised public service channel identity. Instead format shows were taking over the schedules and the sense and identity of 'risk' was being lost. Although not at first, as the

Business Manager recalled above, the Paralympics was eventually taken seriously by the producers and used to build the Channel 4 brand back up, in time for its 30th birthday.

After that, their key element, 'Born Risky' was to become the branded Channel 4 company strapline. The phrase was also used to justify editorial choices during the profile-raising campaigns for the 2012 GB Paralympians. Decision-makers who made references to 'our remit', as I discussed in Chapter 3, also used the phrase as they might for an understood brand perception. Producers identified with the identity created by the remit and it became 'our brand of telly' as Lygo put it. An underlying understanding of the need for brand enhancement emerged quite early on during my production study. This sense of potential repair had clearly affected some of the producers and steered others as they were guided towards restoring particular edgy or risky representations to their output.

Walker, Head of Marketing, told me, just after they had decided on their strategy for Rio 2016, that they were going to remind people 'what they loved' about the London Paralympics. Feelings had been embedded in the brand to be re-triggered when required. Later, the Chief Marketing and Communications Officer, Dan Brooke, explained the brand enhancement saying that for Rio they wanted to extend the meanings associated with 'superhuman' to include musicians, artists, and everybody else. These mental associations affect behaviours towards the product (Keller, 2009; Aaker, 2001) and also the supplier; in this case a television channel, and the corporation who owns that. Thoughts, feelings, and consequent actions can produce growth for the brand, and their positive value adds to the brand equity (ibid.). This is something that the producers certainly felt the Paralympians now had and they realised that this was of value to the channel and corporation. Branding the Paralympians accorded them meanings that were designed to trigger favourable personal resonance. This resonance, encapsulated within the brand, was then reusable at a later date. In this way the superhumans signified a newly *created* brand of heroes, very closely associated with Channel 4.

The project, then, had started with a bid to utilise the 'golden brand' of Channel 4 to give signification to the 2012 Paralympic Games, and it ended with the newly defined 'superhuman' brand restoring memories and attachment to the channel for the benefit of their future inventory. At the closing of the London 2012 Paralympic Games, Lord Coe, former Olympic Gold Medallist and Chairman of LOCOG, said, 'We will never think of sport the same way and we will never think of disability the same way'. The advertising agency, 4Creative, have overdubbed this onto their own publicity material as the final words for their archived 'Meet the Superhuman' campaign portfolio on their website (4Creative, 2013). They won awards for their achievement to promote *ideas* as well as drive footfall to a product. Changes in audience/consumer perception were achieved by utilising known brands and *transferring their meanings* to the Paralympic athletes and the live sports coverage. In turn, using these brands to create a new brand created a whole new set of associated meanings. It is important to note, however, that within the unique mix of meanings that were made, some of that personality was derived from other products and well-known companies as I have shown above.

Conclusion

In this chapter I have revealed the deep penetration of marketing logics into the production processes and practices connected with the media coverage of the London 2012 Paralympic Games. I have shown that the marketing team at Channel 4 influenced representations of disability in order to fulfil their own brief and as part of the wider requirement to deliver the promises of the broadcasting rights bid. They were a powerful arm driving significant and influential messaging and their actions were intrinsic to how, and why, meanings were made about disability in the way that they were.

Whilst this newly developed 'superhuman' brand of disabled elite athletes did benefit from the media coverage, the *brand* of Channel 4, alongside the Paralympic brand, with its own mission and messaging, was also expected to reap a dividend. The net outcome for 'the Paralympics Channel' was a reinforcement and enhancement of its own brand reputation providing added value to future advertisers. 'Changing perceptions in society' also, therefore, included a hidden legacy of improved revenue opportunities for other brand inventory, to be associated and conveyed later. The uplift was to be achieved over time, both as promised for the Paralympics Movement but also for Channel 4 (C4TVC, 2009). It is here that the blur between the commercial and the creative is at its most enmeshed.

Authenticity was overlaid onto carefully constructed representations, and marketed to the widest possible audience, in a way that Klein (2009) suggests can potentially mask malevolent commercial objectives. In this case the objectives were not malevolent, nor was the project undertaken for financial gain, at least by the TV channel, but the marketing campaign was funded and driven by a need to enhance Channel 4's brand reputation (Project Leader, *Interview*, 2016), as much as to fulfil its diversity remit and represent the marginalised onscreen.

I have shown in this chapter that ideas and feelings were marketed as well as products. By adopting the advertising cool style that Nike also use, and using the essence of Public Enemy's legendary anti-authoritarian stance, Channel 4's edginess was safeguarded. Executives blended the known, Sainsbury's and BT, with the unknown, 'superhumans'. Producers applied unexpected military accident scenes to expected mainstream sports visuals and used these juxtapositions as their marketing campaign to promote new ideas on a scale they had never done before. Aspirational sporting performances and winning personality stylings are not new, but mixing them up with powerful national and international brands, to the advantage of an ignored and marginalised group, was ground-breaking. I have argued in this chapter that the role of the marketing strategy in the London 2012 media coverage was highly significant. Meanings about disability were shaped and influenced, not only by the creativity of the Marketing Department, but also by the strategic use of other familiar brands with their own associated meanings and messages.

How and why certain meanings about disability were made were influenced by the promotional needs of the channel, and brand reputational elements were woven into all aspects of the production process. Having separated these elements out in this chapter for analytical purposes, I now replace them into the mix of other influences to conclude my arguments for who, how, why, and what shaped onscreen representations of disability at the 2012 Paralympic Games. The core arguments of my findings are now revisited in the next chapter.

Bibliography

4Creative. 2013. *Work: meet the superhumans.* [online]. [Accessed 12 July 2016]. Available from: www.4creative.co.uk

Aaker, D.A. 1991. *Managing brand equity: capitalizing on the value of a brand name.* New York: Free Press.

Aaker, D.A. 2001. *Strategic market management.* 6th ed. New York: Wiley.

Abd Karim, N.K.B. 2015. *The production culture of religious television: the case of the Islam Channel.* PhD thesis. University of Leeds.

Banet-Weiser, S. 2012. *Authentic TM: the politics of ambivalence in a brand culture.* New York; London: New York University Press.

Banet-Weiser, S. and Sturken, M. 2010. *The politics of commerce: Shepard Fairey and the new cultural entrepreneurship.* Cambridge University Press.

Banks, M.J. 2009. Gender below-the-line: defining feminist production studies. In: V. Mayer et al. eds. *Production studies: cultural studies of media industries.* London: Routledge, pp. 87–98.

Barnes, C. 1992. Images of disability on television. *Disability, Handicap and Society,* 7(4), pp. 385–387.

Born, G. 2004. *Uncertain vision: Birt, Dyke and the reinvention of the BBC.* London: Secker and Warburg.

Brittain, I. 2010. *The Paralympic Games explained.* London: Routledge.

Brittain, I. 2012. British media portrayals of Paralympic and disability sport. In: *Heroes or zeros: the media portrayal of Paralympic sport.* Champaign, IL: Common Ground, pp. 105–113.

Brown, M. ed. 1990. *Television and women's culture: the politics of the popular.* Vol. 7. London: SAGE.

C4TVC. 2009. *Proposal for UK Broadcast Rights.* [Document] London: Channel 4 Television Corporation.

C4TVC. 2011. *MENTAL4 the Paralympics.* [PowerPoint]. Written and presented by Alison Walsh. London: Channel 4 Television Corporation.

C4TVC. 2012. *Annual Report 2011*. [Report]. London: Channel 4 Television Corporation.

Corner, J. 2004. Mediated persona and political culture. In: *Media and the restyling of politics*, pp. 67–84.

Davis, A. 2013. *Promotional cultures: the rise and spread of advertising, public relations, marketing and branding*. Chichester: Wiley.

Davis, L.J. 1995. The construction of normalcy. In: L.J. Davis ed. *The disability studies reader*. 4th ed. New York: Routledge, pp. 3–16.

Dayan, D. and Katz, E. 1994. *Media events: the live broadcasting of history*. Cambridge, MA; London: Harvard University Press.

Dornfeld, B. 1998. *Producing public television, producing public culture*. Princeton, NJ; Chichester: Princeton University Press.

Dyer, R. 1982. Don't look now. *Screen*, 23(3–4), pp. 61–73.

Dyer, R. 2002. *The matter of images: essays on representation*. London: Routledge.

Elias, N. 1978. *The civilizing process: the history of manners*. London: Blackwell.

Fiske, J. 1989. Moments of television: neither the text nor the audience. In: *Remote control: television, audiences, and cultural power*, pp. 56–78.

Garland-Thomson, R. 1997. *Extraordinary bodies: figuring physical disability in American culture and literature*. New York; Chichester: Columbia University Press.

Garland-Thomson, R. 2009. *Staring: how we look*. Oxford University Press.

Garnham, N. 1990. *Capitalism and communication: global culture and the economics of information*. London: SAGE.

Gilbert, K. and Schantz, O. 2008. *The Paralympic Games: empowerment or side show?* Maidenhead: Meyer and Meyer.

Gilbert, K. and Schantz, O. 2012. An implosion of discontent. *Heroes or zeros*. Champaign, IL: Common Ground, pp. 225–236.

Gitlin, T. 2005. *Inside prime time*. 3rd ed. Taylor & Francis.

Great British Bake Off. 2017. BBC1. Series Eight. Love Productions.

Grindstaff, L. 2002. *The money shot: trash, class, and the making of TV talk shows*. Chicago, IL: University of Chicago Press.

Hall, S. 1980. Cultural studies: two paradigms. *Media, Culture and Society*, 2(1), pp. 57–72.

Hall, S. 2012. *Representation: cultural representations and signifying practices*. 2nd ed. London: SAGE in association with The Open University.

Hearn, J. 2012. *Theorizing power*. London: Palgrave Macmillan.

Hesmondhalgh, D. 2013. *The cultural industries*. 3rd ed. London: SAGE.

Hesmondhalgh, D. and Baker, S. 2011. *Creative labour: media work in three cultural industries*. London: Routledge.

Hodges, C. et al. 2014. *Tracking changes in everyday experiences of disability and disability sport within the context of the 2012 London Paralympics*. [online] Available at: https://microsites.bournemouth.ac.uk/cmc/files/2014/10/BU-2012-London-Paralympics.pdf [last accessed 15 February 2020].

Howe, P.D. 2008. From inside the newsroom: Paralympic media and the 'production' of elite disability. *International Review for the Sociology of Sport*, 43(2), pp. 135–150.

Howe, P.D. 2011. Cyborg and supercrip: the Paralympics technology and the (dis) empowerment of disabled athletes. *Sociology*, 45(5), pp. 868–882.

Howe, P.D. and Jones, C. 2006. Classification of disabled athletes: (dis)empowering the Paralympic practice community. *Sociology of Sport Journal*, 23(1), pp. 29–46.

IPC. 1991. *Paralympics history of the movement*. [online]. [Accessed 15 July 2015]. Available from: www.paralympic.org/the-ipc

IPC. 2018. www.paralympics.org

Kapferer, J.-N. 2008. *The new strategic brand management: creating and sustaining brand equity long term*. 4th ed., New ed. London: Kogan Page.

Kapferer, J.-N. 2012. *The new strategic brand management: advanced insights and strategic thinking*. 5th ed. London: Kogan Page.

Keller, K.L. 2009. Building strong brands in a modern marketing communications environment. *Journal of Marketing Communications*, 15(2–3), pp. 139–155.

Kellner, D. 2003. *Media spectacle*. London: Routledge.

Klein, B. 2009. *As heard on TV: popular music in advertising*. Burlington: Ashgate.

Lieb, K. 2016. Pop stars perform 'gay' for the male gaze: the production of faux-mosexuality in female popular music performances and its representational implications. In: *Production studies, the sequel!: cultural studies of global media industries*. London: Taylor & Francis.

Majendie, M. 2012. *Paralympics diary: Public Enemy's D-light*. [online]. [Accessed 18 July 2016]. Available from: www.standard.co.uk/olympics/paralympics/paralympics-diary-public-enemy-s-d-light-8113205.html

Mann, D. 2009. It's not TV, it's brand management TV. In: V. Mayer et al. eds. *Production studies: cultural studies of media industries*. New York; London: Routledge, pp. 99–141.

Moor, L. 2007. *The rise of brands*. Oxford: Berg.

Newlands, M. 2012. Debunking disability: media discourse and the Paralympic Games. In: O.J. Schantz and K. Gilbert eds. *Heroes or zeros? The media's perceptions of Paralympic sport*. Champaign, IL: Common Ground, pp. 209–224.

Roche, M. 2000. *Mega-events and modernity: Olympics and expos in the growth of global culture*. London: Routledge.

Roche, M. 2006. Mega-events and modernity revisited: globalization and the case of the Olympics. *The Sociological Review*, 54(2_suppl), pp. 27–40.

Smitherman, G. 1997. 'The chains remain the same': communicative practices in the hip hop nation. *Journal of Black Studies*, 28(1), pp. 3–25.

Wardle, C., Boyce, T., and Barron, J. 2009. *Media coverage and audience reception of people with disfigurement or visible loss of function*. The Healing Foundation, Online, Available www.cardiff.ac.uk/jomec/resources/09mediacoverageofdisfigurement.pdf (accessed 16/12/2019).

Whannel, G. 1992. *Fields in vision: television sport and cultural transformation*. London: Routledge.

Whannel, G. 2008. *Culture, politics and sport: blowing the whistle, revisited*. London: Routledge.

Williams, R. 1983. *Culture and society, 1780–1950*. Columbia University Press.

Zoellner, A. 2009. Professional ideology and program conventions: documentary development in independent British television production. *Mass Communication and Society*, 12(4), pp. 503–536.

Chapter 7

Conclusion

At a time when public service broadcasters all over the world are coming under increasing pressure to justify their funding models, Channel 4's struggle to positively impact society by changing meanings about disability, through taking risks with the workforce as well as the onscreen content, is one whose details continue to matter.

The year 2012 had been a typically bad one for disability representations across the British media, with 'benefits cheats' making the news headlines, and 'embarrassing bodies' being paraded as onscreen entertainment. 'Subhuman' discourses were continuing as usual with negative imagery as the key constituent of disability stereotypes. Then suddenly, on 6 August, Channel 4 thanked the Olympic Games 'for the warm-up' and the British public were then offered the chance to 'Meet the Superhumans' as a precursor to the Paralympic Games. Apparently out of the blue, the UK's Channel 4 brought a disabled marginalised group into the mainstream, marketing Paralympic athletes as if they were non-disabled Olympians. The sporting event was then given 'live' all-day coverage, and treated as a mega-event in the mainstream Channel 4 schedule. This book has investigated that extraordinary piece of television history at the point of production, where meanings are encoded, exploring the particular production dilemmas around representation that are raised and illuminated by the intersection of the three bodies of sport, disability, and representation literature.

Notwithstanding the inevitable uplift in attention that a 'Home Games' would achieve (along with a compatible time zone for viewing), a transformational shift in attitudes was claimed by the organisers. Media representations were dramatically different, accompanied by a slick Nike-style ad campaign framing the athletes as 'cool'. Commissioned audience research conducted by academics before and immediately following the event (Hodges et al., 2014), and market research at the time (IPSOS, 2012), indicated that perceptions about disability were indeed changed (see also Jackson et al., 2015; Spence, 2018).

This book has explored the meaning-making process asking who decided to change society, and why? As Coleman (2008) points out, it is very much within the power of the media to shape the public mood, but Channel 4 sought to do much more than that. So, what made them take that challenge on, and how and why, at the point of production, were representations of a previously marginalised segment of the disability community transformed in this particular way? My research has established some of the influencing factors, and explored the context in which these new disability representations were produced, as a contribution to the study of both representation and production.

My findings matter because they show that internal and external influences on production do affect onscreen representations, in at least the variety of ways contributed by my participants. This study shows that there is still a valuable purpose in having a public service broadcaster, protected by parliamentary remit, in order to allow positive risk-taking with representations of non-commercially profitable minority groups. It also agrees with other recent work by showing the integration of marketing and branding into meaning-making. In this final chapter I first present the outcomes of my research in a brief summary of findings and core arguments. Then, returning to the key questions with which I began, I draw together the empirical facts, established by my contributors, before clarifying what this knowledge means and why it is important across inter-disciplinary fields. My discussion leads on to questions raised for further research, before I briefly outline the legacy that my investigation into the media coverage of the London 2012 Paralympic Games reveals, for representation, production, and disability on television.

Summary of core findings

There are three key points from this study that can help us understand future representations of disability and difference more generally. These are that regulatory structures protected and enabled the taking of production risks; that the inclusion of staff with disabilities positively affected disability representations; and that it was the coherent vision led by marketing, utilising the full force of brands and branding, that successfully promoted new meanings about disability, repositioning undesirable difference as acceptable within the mainstream.

Throughout the empirical chapters I have argued that, having adopted the riskiest of approaches (Chapter 3), and chosen to give the athletes representational parity with other elite athletes and normal human beings (Chapter 4), the producers adapted existing successful programme formats within particular genres (Chapter 5) to promote mainstream acceptance. My interviewees also clarified how they borrowed meanings associated with other powerful brands to market the Paralympians as reassuringly normal and project them into the mainstream culture (Chapter 6).

In the introduction I argued that, according to scholars across the disciplines of culture and political economy (see Klein, 2009; Zoellner, 2009; Wasko, 2011; Hesmondhalgh, 2013; Murdock and Golding, 2016), there is still more to be learned from the complex entanglement that occurs at the intersection of representation and production. This part of the 'circuit of culture' (Du Gay et al., 1997) remains an important one to be scrutinised and is the obvious point from which to understand what happened with the Paralympics media coverage.

Chapter 2 unpicks the dilemma of the Paralympic paradox. It examined media theories about representation, disability, and sport, and established that representations are constructed to mean different things in the three separate research areas. It emerges that there would inevitably be production dilemmas for how to represent disability sport onscreen, as the 'safe distance' (Hall, 1997) that the 'spectacle of the other' (ibid.) is designed to create for viewers, normally, is far from safe when portraying onscreen disability. This is because becoming disabled is a predicament that could suddenly happen to any of us (Shakespeare, 2013) and consequently carries with it connotations of repulsion (Barnes, 1992). The paraded 'spectacle' of disability, therefore, to a greater degree than other diversities, such as race and gender, is not an immediately obvious choice for promoting sport which needs to be marketable to a wide audience. The dynamics, as well as the meanings, are also different in a sporting context. Elite athletes, as spectacular others, are used to inspire and connect viewers to the teams and their countries being represented, rather than identify 'us' as separate from 'them' which happens when you stereotype 'others' more generally.

To investigate how producers handled this conundrum and the conflicting dynamics it would inevitably have caused, I outlined why semi-structured interviews would work best with an ethnographic spirit, together with internal documentation relating to meaning-making, based on methodologies adopted by previous production researchers exploring how realities are constructed (e.g. Schlesinger, 1987; Born, 2004; Mann, 2009; Mayer et al., 2009). Whilst expecting themes to emerge derived from these and other production studies, room was left as well for the unexpected within my investigation.

What was unexpected was that the structures investigated in Chapter 3, according to my contributors, actually enabled the producers to take risks, both with the make-up of the workforce and with portrayals of disability onscreen. As a clear example of where structures and agency collide or collude, the parliamentary remit, the organisational structure, and even the funding mechanism were shown to have affected how disability appeared onscreen. Whilst the power to define who 'others' are and what we should think about them reveals itself throughout all my chapters, I sought to disentangle the regulatory and organisational structures from the actions of the producers in this first empirical chapter. A thematic analysis of my semi-structured interviews revealed that, along with the funding mechanism for the television corporation, these external structures impinged upon and shaped depictions of disability with direct and 'concrete consequences' (see Golding and Murdoch, 2000).

Producers were enabled to take creative risks with the Paralympics media coverage in an 'edgy' and unconventional way, which they justified because of the regulatory structures that protected them. They were also free to create 'risky' representations without the intervention of shareholder vetoes, thanks to the structure of the organisation that preserved their autonomy and editorial power. The Head of Television, in his personal interview with me, valorised the autonomy that he personally had to authorise the bid for the Paralympics based on the funding mechanism that gave him freedom to do so. Channel 4 were in a unique position to compete for the project and also to subsidise the coverage with sponsorship deals.

It emerged through my study, which I discuss specifically in Chapter 4, that there were two competing strategies for the focus of the media coverage and these were held in tension by Channel 4, on one hand, and the various stakeholders on the other, in relation to LOCOG's goal of achieving a closer 'parity with the Olympics'. Stakeholder requests for portrayals and creative techniques to intentionally *minimise* disability and difference were rejected completely by Channel 4. Instead the editorial decision-makers insisted they 'show the stumps' *so that*, with physical differences duly acknowledged, the audience would then see past that and focus on the sport.

Whilst multimodal, content, and discourse analysis scholars will be able to textually analyse the media coverage of the 2012 Games for years to come, and have already begun to do so, my fourth chapter includes valuable first-hand recollections, by the meaning-makers, of their own involvement, passed on to me shortly after the production of their historic project. The producers explained how they disrupted existing disability stereotypes intentionally and consequently imbued the Paralympic athletes simultaneously with both normal human identities and elite sporting status. What the material gleaned from my contributors shows is that by highlighting, in the extreme, the elite attributes (e.g. international gold-medal winning performances, extraordinarily sensitive horsemanship, etc.), whilst 'showing the stumps' in unapologetic close-up, the interest in the sportsmen and women as elite athletes was not broken by the pointed referencing of their disabilities.

Reframing difference in this way, by absorbing the abnormal qualities into the mainstream tropes, was a consistent technique applied to all the programme formats. In Chapter 5 I evaluated the coverage output types and established that the intrinsic creativity of the production teams was used strategically to improve the meanings associated with disability. By tweaking and adapting well-known programme formats, whilst keeping them recognisably familiar, disability was introduced to a mainstream audience on their terms. First-person reality-style inserts, for example, were filmed for the breakfast magazine show connecting real people, who happened to have an impairment, with a wider audience. The disabled athletes were brought out of their sub-culture into the 'real world' of shopping and mixing with celebrities, and the public were given opportunities to respond to them in a new way, on camera. Next in the schedule, mainstream event coverage included extra information woven into the 'normal' sports commentaries providing a different voice, but with the tone that is expected for international athletics competitions consciously retained. By not compromising the tropes and treatments offered by mainstream television, even though necessarily adapting them, the producers I interviewed made sure the marginalised and ignored disabled athletes were given a platform that made them both visible and acceptable to a broader audience.

My argument is that, rather than adopting a weaker style to make some disability programming for the schedule margins, Channel 4 adapted mega-event framing to promote the Paralympians as the elite athletes they found them to be. This was a specific way that the athletes were brought into the mainstream, by retaining the familiar and known televisual framings and focus, and assimilating these 'others' into normal programmes. The programme genres for the coverage were not treated, either by format or content, like the Special Olympics, for the pitiable tragic, but used to reposition the Paralympics as a bona fide Olympics with athletes who are extraordinary in even more ways than able-bodied Olympians are.

Possibly the main repositioning came from the Marketing Department who were able to shape meanings about disability through their campaigns and their ideas about content. My contributors explained how the use of familiar brands and brand associations were used to *reassure the public* that the new mainstream positioning for a marginalised group was normal. New meanings about the group, with the power of known brands behind them, delivered a greater than normal social significance for the previously invisible group. My research, explored in this study, suggests that maybe only a public service broadcaster can provide this level of significance, but it seems certain that any network would not be able to do so anymore, without the help of internal marketing and a level of sponsor branding to go with it.

It is important to acknowledge here too how the tone of voice for the representations discussed in the earlier chapters was led and directed in collaboration with the Marketing Department. I have shown how brand identities were utilised for their own emotional associations with the public, and how meanings were shaped using brand resonances, associations, and understandings of those brands. The dynamics of these elements are understood well within advertising, but less so within programme production.

It is not just the genres and formats, or programme slot schedules that help to create the frames for representations within the media output (see Silverstone, 1985). Perceptions of the channel directly affect perceptions of the depicted content, as Born (2004) has argued, and for a commercially funded public service broadcaster this can be a two-way relationship. It would seem that the content, in the case of London 2012, and Rio 2016, was used to validate the channel just as Channel 4 were able to 'get away with' using hip-hop as an anti-authoritarian voice for the athletes. That hip-hop trope was then adopted and used for other sports media messaging, including the FIFA 2019 Women's World Cup media coverage, and '*Harder Than You Think*' became the working title for Tokyo 2020's Paralympic Story film destined for global distribution that year (although the 2020 Games themselves were postponed by the Covid-19 pandemic to 2021). I have included in Chapter 6 how several of my contributors commented on the singularity of Channel 4's brand and remit, and the permission that gave them to produce the unconventional representations that have since been reused by others.

The Project Leader articulated clearly to me that alongside the unorthodox portrayals very familiar brands were necessary to help resonate safe feelings for the viewers. If the 'safe distance' of making a spectacle of 'others' (see Chapter 2) was to be disrupted, then household brands were needed to reinforce mainstream cultural acceptance. It wasn't enough to just change televisual representations (see Chapters 4 and 5), the producers knew they needed to use the meanings associated with commodified brands. I have shown throughout my chapters that the entangled mesh of creative and commercial interests has a powerful collective influence on representations that others have shown (Silverstone, 2005; Mayer et al., 2009) can still shape society using television as its primary touch point.

Returning to and answering the key questions

I now return to the questions motivating this study:

- *Who decided to reframe meanings about disability?*
- *Why and how did they do it, and what influenced them?*

These questions matter because it remains important to understand how and why editorial power is used to shape meanings about 'others', and by whom. The decision-makers for the ground-breaking 2012 media coverage were cultural producers with a social-shaping influence. Because they chose to change the way Paralympians were represented to a mass audience, they therefore provided a unique opportunity to focus on the production of specific representations. This was in order to clarify what actually happens within the production process that shapes meanings. Although this research has been an exploration of disability media portrayals it has focused on representation for an important reason; it is here that complex entanglements are made visible (Kidd, 2015, p. 2) and in particular issues of power, ownership, authenticity, and meaning are revealed (ibid.). I wanted to establish the extent to which crucial decisions about representations were communicated throughout the roles, whether hierarchically or within creative pockets of power. The final query was whether any of the producers were actually disabled themselves, or whether they had been affected by disability in some other way, just in case there was a correlation of some kind.

In answer to the *who* decided and *why* questions, Channel 4 did not simply 'choose' to produce the London 2012 Paralympic Games. They had either presumed it would be covered by the BBC, as in previous years, or not considered it at all. A telephone call was made to the Commercial Lawyer, by a member of the International Paralympic Committee (IPC) to persuade him to put in a bid for the broadcasting rights. The IPC wanted a higher profile for their Games (ideally parity with Olympics, but without the financial backing) and Channel 4 could see there was the potential for audience 'growth' in it. The idea then reached the man with the most power, the Head of Television, and being the holder of their £700 million budget, it was he who made the decision to take the coverage on. His reasoning did not include anything to do with disability. He told me that it was because he had a gap in the summer schedule to fill, left by his decision to axe *Big Brother*. The live sports event would solve his problem and that it happened to be the Paralympics was less important, personally for him.

Out of office hours, a group of men organised by the lawyer ordered pizza and devised a plan. Their interest in producing the Paralympic Games coverage was not disability related either; they were excited about covering a live sporting event in London, as these did not often come up. My research demonstrates it was what happened next that produced the transformation in disability representations. The team that these executive men pulled together to make it happen *included disabled people* on purpose. Initially, they needed their long-standing Disability Executive, Alison Walsh, who manages a disability of her own, to 'write the disability section' of the bid. This would be natural for any production, and often occurs in the commissioning process, but she was later, in addition, given *executive editorial powers* over the commissioning editors and all the coverage.

It became noticeable, during my research, that internally the organisation was affected by an intentionally high level of editorial participation by those with first-hand experience of disability. Onscreen the gap between 'them' and 'us' was reduced by the presence of disabled presenters in the studio and the presenters were given equal status and power to their non-disabled counterparts. These representatives were not pundits, as they had been with the BBC coverage, but had equal status as TV anchors and reporters. I was able to interview production staff who had been hired by both companies and that comparison was made by my participants themselves about their own experience. It was also clear, as an outside observer, that the teams were no longer voyeurs of disabled sport, because there was disability within the studio as well as on incoming camera feeds. The new inclusivity within the production culture was collectively experienced, and this meant that the entire event was projected as more mainstream and less out on an awkward limb. *The Last Leg*, even with a joke in its title, blurred the distinction even more. It was the interchangeability between able and disabled and an equal emphasis within the presenting team, as well as with the mix of guests, that made the 'difference' more difficult to discern.

Another significant person with a disability, who was described as 'key' by executives, was a previous Paralympian, Ade Adepitan. He is well-known and uses a wheelchair. He had been employed by the BBC as a pundit for what they termed 'expert analysis' for their previous coverage of Beijing 2008 (BBC, 2008). With Channel 4 he was called in at a higher level of consultation (still a tokenism rung on Arnstein's [1969] ladder of participatory power) which then developed into a partnership, where his opinions appear to have gained equal status rather than simply advisory status. This senior consultation role at Channel 4 was different to the BBC's use of him, he said. The role was not just to deliver onscreen sports analysis, but also how to set it all up from the very beginning. Adepitan went from pundit to presenter onscreen, but also helped drive the production from behind the scenes as well. An example of this had been when the *Meet the Superhumans* marketing was still being conceptualised; his endorsement of the hip-hop vibe and the cool portrayals was circulated by email to the whole team from the Chief Marketing and Communications Officer, who was also on the Board of Directors. 'This has to happen for anything to change', he had said, and it did, on both counts.

Of those who were not disabled it was the Project Leader, who, whilst being asked about another topic, told me how she had been *influenced by* disability not related to her. This question about disability was one I had chosen not to ask anybody directly, so that genuine influence would emerge, if it existed. Her 'incident' affected her so much that she then, apparently, wanted disability portrayed in an *even more* visible way during their television coverage. An act of bigotry, against a parent with one arm at a school event, incensed her into discussing the need to actively display disability more prominently, during a phone call to the Network Creative Director (who also directed the *Meet the Superhumans* trailer). Their conversation is one they both referred to, in relation to challenging and inspiring new meanings across the entire production. There were other serendipitous moments affecting the production of representations too that I have also included throughout the chapters of this book, including a focus group in Leeds in 2009 and a series of staff away days that took place before the media production began. In answer to my initial question, many of the producers were affected and influenced by exposure to disability without actually possessing a disability personally.

Exactly *how* meanings about disability were reframed has been discussed in summaries in the previous section. The data answering these *who*, *what*, *when*, *where*, and *why* questions confirms, though, that the producers had not produced a media 'template' or blueprint for disability, which other television stations might be able to adopt, as mooted in the public discourse.

In fact, I have found that the producers were a group of individuals with a multitude of agendas from commercial to personal, for themselves and for others, who collaborated, tussled, resisted, and compromised, to produce an output that is unlikely to have occurred in this way outside of Channel 4. Sir Jeremy Isaacs, as founding Chairman of the UK's niche PSB, said to me that the London 2012 Paralympics coverage, in his opinion, epitomised the kind of coverage the channel had been set up for.

Additionally, spotting opportunity, the Commercial Lawyer recognised that it could hit 'the sweet spot' of the remit, and deliver audience growth, in one fell swoop. Without the commercial sponsorship funding the coverage, it could never have attained the high quality required of it by the parliamentary remit nor could the audience reach have been achieved without the massive push from the Marketing Department. The 'perfect storm', referred to by the TV presenter, who also presented the previous coverage for the BBC and fronted Channel 4's coverage in 2012 and 2016, was not necessarily a repeatable template for the future but a moment in time, assisted by excited interactions on social media. What that moment left behind which is permanent, however, both for production and representations of disability, is summarised at the end of this conclusion.

What this means for the production of representations

To consider the bigger question of improving representations of disability and difference more generally, within future media production, my research has demonstrated that coverage was shaped by three key factors. As my chapter summaries have shown, these were firstly structures, enabling risk at the organisational macro level and shaping meanings at the micro programme format level. Secondly, and directly linked with this, representation within the workforce of the 'others' was a key factor and empowered greater disclosure onscreen of physical anomalies in close-up. Thirdly marketing, with its campaigns, strategies, and programme advertising, was intrinsic to developing momentum and engagement for the successfully inclusive live digital coverage. These combined factors also have implications for theories of the production of representations and future research.

Firstly, I have shown that the representations of disability were constructed and shaped by individuals who had permission to take risks. Evidence from my interviews suggests that there were a number of elements that encouraged and enabled them to do so. In this case at least, on the macro level, government regulations protected these public service broadcasters from purely commercial agendas, from stakeholder opinions, and, most significantly, from stakeholder attempts to veto what they considered unpalatable content. The regulations also recommended that they take risks by employing untried and tested producers within the workforce. Of course, programmes have been made by teams with disabilities in the past, either for community access television or, often, late-night diversity slots, but mainly to serve niche audiences with niche content.

Therefore, having disabled 'others' on the inside of this *mainstream* sporting production, within the workforce and at the executive meetings, meant that normalisation was occurring within the organisational and more subtle structures as well as amongst the creative agents. This research reveals that from February 2010, after the broadcasting rights were won, that kind of integration was immediately set in motion at Channel 4. As a benign Trojan horse effect, it meant that producers working on the inside of the differently formatted shows and sports coverage were able to blend meanings about difference into normal televisual treatments, thus slightly reframing the programme content.

Elevating the Paralympic Games in 2012 to a televised, live, mega-event spectacle also enabled new framings for the negatively perceived marginalised group. The producers safely embedded Paralympic bodies in the known sporting context, as Team GB athletes there to represent *us*. They also saturated the schedules with coverage of the event so that we identified with them as sporting heroes, and also human beings, in spite of their physical differences.

Normally, extreme characteristics are chosen to depict the person or group who are *not like* us. This is easy to see in the sitcoms and other television comedies where we laugh at groups of people who have been depicted in a caricatured way (Fiske and Hartley, 2003). What is different with a sports production is that elite athleticism is depicted as extreme for a different inspirational reason, and not as a parody. The athletes at Olympic level have extreme training regimes to be the very best in the world in their fields and extraordinary feats are part of their trope. In other words, representations of them are spectacularised because the sporting event is already a spectacle.

Discussions with *The Last Leg* team clarified that introducing humour about the everyday and mundane was another way of exploring personal differences and outlooks. Between the London and Rio Paralympics, a senior Channel 4 executive told me that, in addition to the value of utilising live sports coverage, their future strategy would be to 'sprinkle the magic of *The Last Leg*' over all the coverage. He certainly understood that they had gained a new audience across more than one programme genre. This was not the mainstream four-yearly Olympic audience but a late-night disability-tolerating audience. By bringing stigmatised actors and their individual differences onscreen into a topical satire programme, the macro spectacle became personalised. The safe distance between 'us' and the 'other' was reduced and made safe by asking 'is it ok?' directly *to* those 'others' rather than *about* those others. The question, according to my contributors, closed the gap between the viewer and the presenters, as well as the viewer and the guests, and by using Twitter interactively, became part of the programme itself. What this means is that, in the context of the new hybrid format show, Hall's (1997) 'spectacle of the other' can now potentially be undone, through deliberate connection with the audience, and is already, at least, being disrupted.

For the topical satire show those 'others' were around on set too. They selected comedians, one disabled and one not, and wove a group dynamic with them alongside a sports journalist with a visible 'stump'. In this setting stereotypes were at the very least mixed up and collectively dumped, unexpectedly, onto the evening sofa of the satire programme. My contributors revealed that the format happened by accident and was improvised on the first day of shooting. It would seem, from their recollections, that the humour, openness, and explanation was deliberate and did indeed play a huge part in the change to representations across the formats. The Disability Executive, with her own disability, personally identified the Australian comedian with one leg and persuaded the team to hire him to bring humour for what was originally intended to be the sports highlights show. This elevated level of executive and editorial participation for diverse producers was a noticeable structure that was evident within the organisation.

Secondly, out of all the influencing factors described and evaluated within this case-study, the most significant was the change in attitudes within Channel 4, brought about by having disabled producers and executives *amongst* the decision-makers. What involvement of the 'others' on the inside of the production process achieved, in 2012, for disability representations was immeasurably more important than perhaps those executives who first decided to include them may have realised. Objectification and stereotyping are commonly understood to be accentuated by distance from those 'others' whom 'we' are not like. It is clear from this case-study that having close contact in a work environment *changed the culture* within the organisation and reduced the opportunities for cultivating negative perspectives. Other scholars have also found this elsewhere (see Luka, 2016). The stigma management process, according to Goffman (1963), is triggered by individuals negotiating disclosure or enacting difference in close proximity to those who think of themselves as 'normal'. When worked out in a creative labour context, this dynamic can directly affect onscreen content, since the 'normal' producers are seemingly changed by having those 'others' around.

Since Barnes (1992) made the connection between prevalent disablist imagery and lack of integration into the workforce, there has not been a television production study to confirm or deny any correlation. My research now does this, at least in the context of this one-time event. The production was not only integrated beyond any previous levels, to include diverse actors, the event coverage itself provided a dramatic change to representations. 'Othering', in this case, was dismantled consciously within the content, and also, perhaps inadvertently, *within the individuals* producing that content. The evidence from my research strongly suggests, therefore, that having 'others' on the inside of the production makes the onscreen representations of 'them' closer in meaning to more normal representations about 'us', and not just because both can present their perspectives. Removing the 'safe distance' during the production process also softens the stigma between the two groups by natural exposure. One of the *Last Leg* scriptwriters, who helped steer the programmes initially, mentioned to me that he 'didn't know how to shake hands with new staff at the start of production' but that, for him, 'there wasn't any disability at the wrap party'. Normalisation by osmosis can surely, therefore, only help diverse representations, especially if one's creative career includes, as it did in this case, writing jokes for others about yet another group of others.

I contend, therefore, in agreement with Born (2004), that both 'we' and 'they' are needed onscreen and offscreen in above-the-line and below-the-line production and executive roles to positively affect televisual representations. Born regarded under-representation onscreen and the lack of promotion for minorities within production teams as 'linked failures' (Born, 2004, p. 10). Even before Channel 4 committed to their Diversity Charter, which came about, they state, as a direct consequence of the Paralympics coverage (C4TVC, 2013), my research demonstrates what I would call 'linked successes' rather than linked failures, between visibility onscreen and inclusion of diverse others within the workforce in 2012. Whereas the 'social model' of disability (Oliver, 1983) has seemingly now run its course, within British disability scholarship (see Shakespeare, 2013), its highlighting of disabling social barriers within the labour context should remain still highly relevant to communication research in any country.

Thirdly, I have shown that portrayals of disability were improved across each of the programme formats but so were perceptions of the Channel 4 brand. The risky representations, paradoxically, were used to *reduce* risk for purchasing advertisers by strengthening the reliability of the brand for future financial revenues. This relationship between creativity and commerce was seemingly indirect in places, during Channel 4's season of Paralympic meaning-making and the planning for it. However, the entire project had an underlying driver, discussed in the original phone call between the Commercial Lawyer, Martin Baker, and LOCOG; there was more potential audience growth in this project than there would have been for the Olympics. Whilst a financial loss was a risk for the event itself, the enhancement to the brand was the prize to be won, including, as implied in the bid proposal, associated benefits to longer-term inventory. These benefits, in turn, were expected to reap dividends over time.

In spite of the commercial pressures, my contributors felt sincerely that they would raise the profile of disability more positively and other research suggests they achieved that (see IPSOS, 2012; Walsh, 2015; IPC, 2019), although critical disability scholars may not agree (such as McGillivray et al., 2019).

I have shown how, amongst other factors, the role of marketing in this process was central, entering the frame at the inception of the bid for the Paralympics media licence, and remaining until after the medal ceremonies were over. The repositioning of marketing power goes beyond creative advertising to having a voice across all associated organisations. In this case this voice was used to make the unusual familiar, in order to reach wider audiences across a plethora of platforms. Perhaps it is a social-shaping role that now only marketing can achieve. Commercial voices do seem to be an inevitable component for future media production, and it would appear more so now than was observed by, for example, Born (2004), Hesmondhalgh (2013), and Mann (2009). Certainly, this seems true when marketing sports coverage, which provided positive cultural leverage for the disabled athletes in this context.

None of this would have much impact in the fragmented, multi-platform world of modern televisual consumption, unless, as was true in the case of Channel 4 broadcasting the Paralympics, the full force of branding and marketing is also borrowed to promote the new meanings in a way that audiences can accept. My study supports findings that this kind of blanket marketing approach is potentially a prerequisite for changing representations, meanings, and paradigms. Channel 4 is the only UK PSB with that sort of flexibility, other than ITV, for whom the topic would not be viable. Disability is too niche a topic to attract the advertising revenues ITV would need to make the Paralympic Games profitable enough to purchase.

Clearly the power of brand relationships, whether brought on board or simply borrowed, can be useful as a shortcut when framing realities with embedded meanings. Other scholars have established that branding carries associated values and attitudes with it, through its own methods of trope and identity reinforcement (Davis, 2005; Klein, 2009; Banet-Weiser, 2012) and these familiar associations were very much relied upon in this case. Representations were challenged, utilising existing brand relationships to reassure the audience, whilst forcing the creative envelope to dismantle the previous understandings of existing artistic and psychological boundaries. My analysis reveals that the inherent branding structures functioned in similar ways to the programme genres and stereotypes discussed in previous chapters, affecting actors within the production process, as well as reassuring the audiences who ultimately decoded the onscreen content more positively.

Potential future research

Building on the results of my study it would be of value to clarify ongoing motivations and purposes of producers with further research, in order to understand any other influences on meaning-making. This case-study has explored the influencing factors impinging on decision-makers in a particular setting, and mapped the producers' roles, their creativity, and their power. As further changes to regulation, policies, organisations, and programme funding affect production and individual creativity in other settings, it matters that these influences should also be examined. Public Service Media is frequently under threat worldwide, and there is a risk of certain diversities either disappearing off the screens or being misrepresented as they have been in the past. This study has separated institutional influences and individual influences from the surrounding commercial environment, to map how each of these affect each other. More work needs to be done in this field to understand the complex production mechanisms and, also, the unexpected pockets of creative power.

Therefore, it is vital that ongoing production research asks similar questions to the ones in this study, related to other groups of diverse 'others' to investigate changes, if any, happening on the inside of other media productions. My research clearly demonstrates that editorial decision-makers are affected by those who are around them. Representation, both within the workforce and onscreen, could be researched using a similar methodology to mine, to explore linked meanings that are made, for example about women in sport, mental health, or disability in other media genres. My contributors have clarified that there are grades of power affecting meaning-making, in both hierarchical layers and nuanced pockets of creativity. Hall's (1997) threshold concept of the 'safe distance' that is created by making a 'spectacle of the other' relies on the others *not* being part of the decision-making process. If they are, as they were for the London 2012 Paralympics, then this is where representations and stereotypes are likely to be changed. My documentary evidence clearly shows that it is the decision-makers in the production stages who create or disrupt the safe distance of otherness that defines what normal is. Further investigation is therefore required to consider the mediated power being used, across other programme types. This is because the producers can shape not only the televisual cultural product but also the society into which it is distributed (see Hodges et al., 2014). Paterson et al. (2016) have questioned how well we understand the institutions which create our media and I hope I have shown in this book that, methodologically, a detailed production study can generate knowledge about who has power and how and why they use it to shape meanings, with some success.

A single account is, of course, not sufficient to generalise a direct correlation between onscreen representation and 'diverse' access into mainstream production. The empirical evidence set out in this book does seem to suggest that the link exists, as Born (2004) also observed that it might. Other production research is therefore needed to corroborate this correlation and might then be of value to policy makers as well as academics. Whilst a single case-study on this scale cannot be conclusive, or generalise from its findings, it adds to the body of literature that suggests representation is still an important field of research. The complex mechanisms of power examined by critical political economists of communication and cultural theorists alike are made visible in a detailed media production study, such as this one. Regulation, collaboration, risk, parity, and branded marketing are all elements affecting what appeared onscreen as the London 2012 Paralympic Games coverage. These influences need to remain under scrutiny.

In terms of future production research, diversity and inclusion appear to be higher on the agenda than before. Following a controversial Disability Initiative in 2015, Lucy Martin became the first BBCTV weather presenter to appear onscreen with one arm and a 'stump' in full view, normalised within the mainstream setting as she delivers the forecast during the peak-time schedule. There are now also full storylines for disabled actors in BBC dramas, for example, for Clarissa in *Silent Witness* (2018) who had a two-part personal story, developed out of her erstwhile plot device role. All the other characters treated her warmly as the central figure and she was given a back-story that was even discussed on *The One Show* (2018). The actress has a rare disease (AMC), has been in a wheelchair since she was seven, and was previously depicted as extraordinary. In December 2019 the BBC Elevate initiative was launched to include more disabled talent within TV production, including another character in that same show, and also onscreen in other programmes that have nothing to do with disability. What is expected is therefore changing, even if rare posi-tive instances have occurred before. Knowing how and why these inclusive representations of disability are now coming about would also enrich the existing body of research.

It may or may not be consequential that the Channel 4 Disability Exec-utive, Alison Walsh, moved on to the BBC from Channel 4, to be their Pan-BBC Disability Lead, after the major sporting event. This study has shown she was a driving force, with the London 2012 Paralympics cov-erage, for getting disabled talent onscreen *as lead presenters rather than assisting pundits*, and also for 'showing the stumps' 'when viewers least expect it'. Some of the recurrence of the medical model and supercrip nar-ratives observed by disability scholars during Rio (see McGillivray et al., 2019), and even a touch of the old ableism tone, may just have needed a nudge from the person who kept them at bay through the TV coverage for 2012. Of course, social media, operating outside the gatekeeping role of the sports broadcaster, also played a part in this apparent regression. How-ever, a research opportunity remains, to evaluate the role of diversity advi-sors, in relation to their editorial and executive powers, especially perhaps within state-controlled television services and media organisations beholden to shareholders. Representation and diversity are already examined within public service broadcasters in other countries (e.g. Abd Karim, 2015) and more production studies embedded within a range of global media systems could provide further valuable contributions for media sociology as well as adding a richness to current communication theory.

Legacies for diversity in production and disability on TV

In the light of this research, my evidence suggests that a significant and lasting Paralympic legacy provided by the media coverage is specifically the newly framed meanings associated with more graphic media representations of physical difference. Producers now have a greater creative range of acceptable media representations to choose from. According to Channel 4's commissioned research, because of the London 2012 portrayals, society's response to disability has been more inclusive since. But how disability is shown on TV has changed even more, at least for the 2012 host nation. There is a continuing and increasing visibility onscreen for disabled characters in a non-repulsive way, and not just on Channel 4. Cerri Burnell suffered vitriolic abuse from protective parents for not hiding her 'stump' arm when presenting children's television for CBeebies in 2009, but asserted that she would have been accepted more readily had she first appeared on TV 'after the Paralympics' (Gilmour, 2015). Within their valuable thematic analysis of existing empirical Paralympic Legacy studies, I note that Misener et al. (2013) do not include media representation legacies, either onscreen or off, within their analytical framework. This is potentially an important omission even for sports and disability researchers.

The role of the media representations in changing attitudes towards disability has already been established for the 12 days of the event coverage. For two weeks, as I found out from personal experience, deformity was allowed to have a sense of humour. The 2012 Paralympic Games media coverage with its claimed 'seismic shift' effect, also heralded a turning point in the types of representations that audiences have come to expect. It is surely a legacy of the media coverage, rather than the Games themselves, that there is now a gradually increasing visibility in the UK mainstream TV schedules for normalised disability. This means that those with anatomical variances, within our communities, can now see themselves reflected onscreen, in a way that they finally might want to recognise and identify with. As public service broadcasters under threat of being privatised, Channel 4 were able to fulfil their remit on this occasion, and for a range of commercial and creative reasons they also created other changes for everyone, including their own employees and production partners.

During production, Channel 4 disclosed and illuminated difference whilst at that same time de-stigmatising it. Seeing the opportunity to redefine the brand and enhance their reputation, they multiplied their productive efforts to *elevate* the athletes and *innovate* with their programme styles. My contributors made it clear that the channel wanted to show the BBC that it was *they* who were the real diversity champions, and that the diminutive Channel 4 could equally well host a national mega-event. In one sense the Channel 4 producers might be considered a reflection of the 'superhumans' themselves, in that they were previously underestimated and perhaps misidentified as the 'other' public service channel. They were certainly a challenger brand to the BBC, as my participants considered the Paralympic Games to be to the Olympics. By meeting the team who had put in their own superhuman effort, backed by the largest marketing budget in their history, I have been able to show in this study multiple reasons why they gave the Paralympians a boost. But it was *more* than a boost to the athletes' profiles. This media coverage changed the trajectory for media representations of disability as the decision-makers repositioned physically impaired athletes within the elite mainstream for a mainstream public.

Now much more broadly, across both fact and fiction, it is no longer inevitable that disabled actors on television have to play the anomalous plot device, or be repulsive or invisible. They have a chance for a normal onscreen presence, when and if producers, as they did for the Paralympians, choose to give them centre stage. The Paralympics coverage created space beyond the sporting genre for a wider range of disability portrayals, including aspirational and positive representations of difference. By celebrating diversity, but not for its own sake, the producers redefined inclusiveness representing 'others' as part of our mainstream culture. This book has revealed something of why that change happened, from first-hand accounts of those who produced that historic coverage.

As regards to representations for elite athletes in parasport, media planning is already underway for a Paralympic film called 'The Road to Paris 2024' (Nugent, Executive Producer, *Interview*) and another for Los Angeles 2028, where even the pre-production offices have disabled access next to the most accessible London transport stop, to make sure the workplace is fully inclusive. These media productions will contain more developed messaging about ability but also resourcefulness, as something that Paralympians draw on, but that is common to us all (ibid.). Building on the ground that was broken by the London 2012 depictions (ibid.), these new meanings are substantially evolved beyond the 'repulsive' and 'tragic' stereotypes that once prevailed (Goggin and Newell, 2003) but will need to be nuanced carefully not to be seen as 'inspiration porn' (see Young, 2012) which is understandably a matter of concern to many established disability scholars.

In the British marketplace, Channel 4 realised that you can better serve under-represented audiences if you bring in new producers from those audiences and give them a chance to produce and influence shows. For Rio 2016 they increased the diversity in their workforce from 50 per cent to 75 per cent in an effort to change onscreen meanings about parasports even more. Whereas 2012 was positioned for ableist digital consumers to see the difference first, get over it, then enjoy the sport, the way was then paved for Tokyo 2020 to focus purely on ability in whatever form, which was the vision of one of that event's documentary film makers (Nugent, Executive Producer, *Interview*). The LA 2028 committee have already prioritised the Paralympics years ahead of their event (Dannenberg-Sprier, IPC Head of Brand Engagement, *Interview*) but it will remain to be seen whether or not the US commercially and philanthropically funded broadcasters are able to serve their audiences in the way that public service media in other countries still have the agency to do.

Finally, in early 2020, the UK's Department of Digital, Culture, Media & Sport, acting on behalf of the British Government, announced that it was adding the summer and winter Paralympic Games to its 'crown jewels' list of protected sports events. This was the first addition to their list in 20 years, for significant events that must remain on free-to-air television 'for everyone to enjoy' (BBC, 2020). It was felt that the Paralympic Games, wherever it is being held in the world, is now fully within the UK public consciousness and belongs as part of the mainstream national culture. I hope the details in this book have shown that, to some degree, that transformational shift from side-show to mainstream cultural product has come about through the creative agency of independent media producers who were not bound by commercial constraints and chose collectively to take risks, shaping new meanings out of old stereotypes.

Bibliography

Abd Karim, N.K.B. 2015. *The production culture of religious television: the case of the Islam Channel*. PhD thesis. University of Leeds.

Arnstein, S.R. 1969. Ladder of citizen participation. *Journal of the American Institute of Planners*, 35(4), p. 216.

Banet-Weiser, S. 2012. *Authentic TM: the politics of ambivalence in a brand culture*. New York; London: New York University Press.

Barnes, C. 1992. *Disabling imagery and the media: an exploration of the principles for media representations of disabled people: the first in a series of reports*. Halifax: Ryburn Publishing.

BBC. 2008. *The 2008 Beijing Olympics and Paralympics on the BBC*. [online]. [Accessed 12 July 2016]. Available from: www.bbc.co.uk/pressoffice

BBC. 2020. *Paralympics to remain on free-to-air television*. [online]. [Accessed 24 January 2020]. Available from: www.bbc.co.uk/sport/disability-sport/51238375

Born, G. 2004. *Uncertain vision: Birt, Dyke and the reinvention of the BBC*. London: Secker and Warburg.

C4TVC. 2013. *Diversity Charter*. [Leaflet]. London: Channel 4 Television Corporation.

Coleman, S. 2008. The depiction of politicians and politics in British soaps. *Television and New Media*, 9(3), pp. 197–219.

Davis, N.A. 2005. Invisible disability. *Ethics*, 116(1), pp. 153–213.

Du Gay, P., Jones, S., and Hall, S. 1997. *Doing cultural studies: the story of the Sony Walkman*. London: SAGE in association with The Open University.

Fiske, J. and Hartley, J. 2003. *Reading television*. New York; London: Routledge.

Gilmour, L. 2015. *I wasn't surprised people complained about me*. [online]. [Accessed 12 July 2016]. Available from: www.mirror.co.uk/tv

Goffman, E. 1963. *Stigma: notes on the management of spoiled identity.* Harmondsworth: Penguin.

Goggin, G. and Newell, C. 2003. *Digital disability: the social contruction of disability in new media.* Lanham, MD; Oxford: Rowman & Littlefield.

Golding, P. and Murdock, G. 2000. Culture, political economy and communications. *Mass Media and Society*, 3, pp. 82–87.

Hall, S. 1997. *Representation: cultural representations and signifying practices.* London: SAGE in association with The Open University.

Hodges, C.E.M., Jackson, D., and Scullion, R. 2014. Voices from the armchair: the meanings afforded to the Paralympics by UK television audiences. In: *Reframing disability: media, (dis)empowerment, and voice in the 2012 Paralympics.* Oxford: Routledge, pp. 172–187.

Hesmondhalgh, D. 2013. *The cultural industries.* 3rd ed. London: SAGE.

IPC. 2019. *Change starts with sport: brand platform* [Corporate Document].

IPSOS. 2012. *Superhuman Paralympians change view on disabled people.* [online]. [Accessed 12 February 2015]. Available from: www.ipsos.com

Kesby, R. 2016. *Is public service broadcasting in terminal decline?* BBC World Service, 27 July.

Kidd, B. 2013. The Olympic Movement and the sports–media complex. *Sport in Society*, 16(4), 439–448.

Kidd, J. 2015. *Representation.* London: Routledge.

Klein, B. 2009. *As heard on TV: popular music in advertising.* Burlington: Ashgate.

Luka, M.E. 2016. CBC Artspots and the activation of creative citizenship. In: *Production studies, the sequel!: cultural studies of global media industries.* Taylor & Francis.

Mann, D. 2009. It's not TV, it's brand management TV. In: V. Mayer et al. eds. *Production studies: cultural studies of media industries.* New York; London: Routledge, pp. 99–141.

Mayer, V., Banks, M.J., and Caldwell, J.T. 2009. *Production studies: cultural studies of media industries.* New York; London: Routledge.

McGillivray, D., O'Donnell, H., McPherson, G., and Misener, L. 2019. Repurposing the (super)crip: media representations of disability at the Rio 2016 Paralympic Games. *Communication & Sport.* Online.

Misener, L., Darcy, S., Legg, D., and Gilbert, K. 2013. Beyond Olympic legacy: understanding Paralympic legacy through a thematic analysis. *Journal of Sport Management*, 27(4), pp. 329–341.

Murdock, G. and Golding, P. 2016. Political economy and media production: a reply to Dwyer. *Media, Culture and Society*, 38(5), pp. 763–769.

Oliver, M. 1983. *Social work with disabled people.* London: Macmillan, for the British Association of Social Workers.

Paterson, C., Lee, D., Saha, A., and Zoellner, A. eds. 2016. *Advancing media production research: shifting sites, methods, and politics.* Springer.

Schlesinger, P. 1987. *Putting 'reality' together: BBC News.* London: Methuen.

Shakespeare, T. 2013. *Disability rights and wrongs revisited.* Taylor & Francis Online.

Silent Witness. BBC1. 2-part series. Tx: 15–16 January 2018.

Silverstone, R. 1985. *Framing science; the making of a BBC documentary.* California: BFI.

Silverstone, R. 2005. *The sociology of mediation and communication*. SAGE.

Spence, C. 2018. *Transforming lives: London 2012 progress and challenges*. [online]. [Accessed 18 December 2019] Available at: www.paralympic.org/news/transforming-lives-london-2012-progress-and-challenges

The One Show. 2018. BBC1. 15 January, 19:00–19:30.

Walsh, A. 2015. Out of the shadows, into the light? The broadcasting legacy of the 2012 Paralympics for Channel 4. In: D. Jackson, C. Hodges, M. Molesworth, and R. Scullion eds. *Reframing disability? Media, (dis)empowerment, and voice in the London Paralympics*. Oxford: Routledge. pp. 26–36.

Wasko, J. 2011. The death of Hollywood: exaggeration or reality? In: *The handbook of political economy of communications*. London: Wiley, pp. 305–330.

Young, S. 2012. *We're not here for your inspiration – The Drum (Australian Broadcasting Corporation)*. [Accessed 29 May 2016] Available at: abc.net.au

Zoellner, A. 2009. Professional ideology and program conventions: documentary development in independent British television production. *Mass Communication and Society*, 12(4), pp. 503–536.

Index

Page numbers in *italic* refer to figures.